ENGLISH POLITICS
IN THE EARLY EIGHTEENTH CENTURY

BY

ROBERT WALCOTT

OXFORD
AT THE CLARENDON PRESS
1956

Oxford University Press, Amen House, London E.C. 4

GLASGOW NEW YORK TORONTO MELBOURNE WELLINGTON
BOMBAY CALCUTTA MADRAS KARACHI CAPE TOWN IBADAN

Geoffrey Cumberlege, Publisher to the University

PRINTED IN GREAT BRITAIN

ENGLISH POLITICS
IN THE EARLY
EIGHTEENTH CENTURY

PREFACE

THIS book is the outgrowth of a doctoral dissertation begun some twenty years ago at Harvard University under the direction of the late Professor Wilbur Cortez Abbott. He first suggested the topic and—more important—the method: an examination of parliamentary parties during Anne's reign by means of a detailed study of individual Members of Parliament. Fellowships from Harvard University during the years 1934–6 enabled me to work in the manuscript sources in England and to meet Professor Namier and others who were doing work on the history of Parliament.

The method used in this study is necessarily laborious, since it involves working out the personnel and relationships of a group of more than 1,000 individuals who sat in the Commons during the last parliament of William III and the first three of Anne. Such an investigation can never be complete nor more than provisionally accurate. The material I have accumulated over the past sixteen years since the submission of the dissertation has sharpened and in some cases altered the picture sketched in my essay on English party politics which appeared in the *festschrift* for Professor Abbott, published in 1941.

The materials on which this study is founded defy any comprehensive listing. They include not only the usual manuscript and printed sources for the history of the period, but also the whole range of biography and local history. The latter yielded many significant details about individual Members, but no attempt has been made to include the sources of such material in the bibliography. Documentation of the biographical data on individual Members given in this study—and particularly in the appendixes—would impossibly encumber the text and the already lengthy appendixes and has necessarily been omitted. References for this information are given in my notes on Members, which the History of Parliament has on microfilm.

The sources which proved most fruitful for my purposes were in general the obvious printed ones: the Journals of both Houses, the reports of the Historical Manuscripts Commission, the correspondence of Godolphin and the Marlboroughs printed by Coxe, the letters of James Vernon, and the like. Apart from the Hatton–Finch Papers in the British Museum there was no unpublished collection of anything like the value of the Harley Papers printed by the H.M.C. If the following work relies largely on printed rather than manuscript sources, it is not because the latter were overlooked. No doubt the extraordinary dearth of parliamentary diaries and of the private correspondence of leading politicians other than Marlborough, Godolphin, Nottingham, and Harley will ultimately be overcome by the efforts of those, like Sir Lewis Namier, who have already turned up caches of hitherto unknown material. At the present time, however, the gaps are still there.

In the course of preparing this work I have incurred numerous obligations, which I take pleasure in acknowledging. The staff of the Harvard College Library, of the British Museum, the Bodleian, and Dr. Williams's Library were unfailingly patient and helpful. To Harvard University, and to my teachers and former colleagues there, I am grateful for much and long continued assistance. I should mention especially Professor Owen and Professor Handlin of the Department of History, who gave me encouragement and made the helpful suggestion that I should sharpen this study by abandoning a lengthy narrative approach in favour of a shorter analytical treatment.

In conclusion, I am particularly indebted to President Howard Lowry of the College of Wooster for his generous encouragement to me in the course of bringing this study to the point of publication and for his pains in reading the original extended version; and to Sir Lewis Namier, who read and criticized all but the last chapter. My debt to him is obvious in the work that follows.

R. W.

CONTENTS

NOTE ON DATES

DURING Queen Anne's reign two calendars were in use. The Julian or Old Style used in England was—by the eighteenth century—eleven days behind the Georgian or New Style used in most Continental countries. On the Continent the year began on 1 January. Sometimes that reckoning was used in England; but for most purposes the year began on Lady Day, 25 March. Thus Queen Anne came to the throne on 19 March 1702 according to the New Style; but on 8 March 1701 according to the English reckoning.

In order to avoid the inconvenience of giving dates in the form 8/19 March 1701/2, all dates in this work are given in the Old Style, but with the year reckoned as beginning on 1 January. A few documents cited in the footnotes, particularly letters written by the Duke of Marlborough while on the Continent, are dated by the writer in the New Style. Wherever the New Style is used in a document, that fact is indicated by adding the abbreviation '(N.S.)'.

NOTE ON FAMILY AND PLACE NAMES

THE names of persons who appear in the *Dictionary of National Biography* or in the new edition of *The Complete Peerage* are spelt as in those two works; lesser figures according to the more usual practice in the *Official Return of Members of Parliament*.

Names of all parliamentary constituencies are spelt as in the *Official Return*.

CHAPTER I
Introduction

THE age of Queen Anne is so rich in dramatic incident and striking personalities that it will continue in all probability to interest writers and historians as it has in the past. From the contemporary pamphlets of Swift and Defoe through the memoirs and historical accounts of the eighteenth century down to Thackeray's *Henry Esmond* the Augustan Age has figured in a remarkable series of writings.

In the last thirty years the number of works dealing with this period has significantly increased, stimulated partly by the publication of rich sources of new material in the reports of the Royal Historical Manuscripts Commission. The nineteen-twenties saw published an American monograph on the party history of the first eight years of Anne's reign, which was followed four years later by an English account of the first Tory party—almost a third of it devoted to the reign of Anne. There followed in the thirties the volume on the later Stuarts in the Oxford History of England, a number of new biographies—of which the most striking was Winston Churchill's multi-volume life of his ancestor the Duke of Marlborough—and the Master of Trinity's three volumes on England under Queen Anne.[1] In all of these works party politics play a prominent role, for the age was one of heated political controversy and strong party loyalties. It is with this aspect of the period that this study is concerned.

[1] W. T. Morgan, *English Political Parties and Leaders in the Reign of Queen Anne, 1702–1710* (New Haven, 1920); Keith Feiling, *History of the Tory Party, 1640–1714* (Oxford, 1924); G. N. Clark, *The Later Stuarts* (Oxford History of England, 1934); Winston Churchill, *Marlborough: His Life and Times* (English edition, 4 vols., London, 1933–8); and G. M. Trevelyan, *England under Queen Anne* (3 vols., separately subtitled *Blenheim*; *Ramillies and the Union with Scotland*; and *The Peace and the Protestant Succession*; London, 1930, 1932, 1934).

Still another treatment of the party politics of Anne's reign would hardly be justified if it were not based either on new material or a significantly new approach. The general approach taken in the following chapters is not new in itself—to a considerable extent it is borrowed from Professor Namier and others who have reinterpreted the party history of George III's reign—but it is new as regards Anne's reign.

Our interpretation of every period of English history is constantly being questioned and revised, a leading English historian reminds us, but 'perhaps the eighteenth century has lately come in for more attention. . . . This is less true of the first half of the century than of the second, where Professor Namier has led and inspired a formidable attack on the accepted traditions; but the first half cannot remain unaffected by the criticism which is greatly changing our view of the second.'[1] Our object in this essay is to discover by a detailed analysis of the party politics of the period whether the 'accepted traditions' do in fact hold for the early eighteenth century and, if not, how they should be revised.

The accepted traditions about political parties and their constitutional function are so common even in the latest histories that one hardly need multiply examples. In a well-known one-volume history of England, often used as a text, one reads that the work of the Revolution of 1688 'was inevitably to transfer the executive power from the control of the Crown to that of a party'.[2] Trevelyan in his one-volume treatment of the Stuart period tells us that after 1688 the 'rule of England by the contests of the two parties now began in earnest';[3] while the author of another interpretation of the same period writes that 'Anne's reign owes its importance largely to the fact that it was the age

[1] Professor Pares, reviewing Basil Williams's volume on *The Whig Supremacy, 1714–1760* (Oxford History of England), in the *English Historical Review*, lv (January, 1940), 136.

[2] Esme Wingfield-Stratford, *History of British Civilization* (2nd ed., New York, 1930), p. 675.

[3] G. M. Trevelyan, *England under the Stuarts* (14th ed., New York, 1928), p. 448.

of apprenticeship for English parties'. 'Her reign is remembered for the first appearance of complete party government', and 'the failure of the coalitions in 1705 and 1711 proved that party government was inevitable.'[1]

This is the orthodox view; now for recent heresy. First, from a fairly recent study of politics in the later years of George III: 'Practically all the evidence points to the conclusion that neither the framers of the Revolution Settlement nor the first three rulers after 1689—William, Mary, and Anne—anticipated the constitutional developments of the next three quarters of a century.' 'Neither the two-party system nor the cabinet solidarity and joint responsibility of the nineteenth century was dreamed of in 1689.'[2] The parent of this heresy, Professor Namier, confines his generalizations to the second half of the eighteenth century. Between the politics of that period and those of the present day, he tells us, 'there is more resemblance in outer forms and denominations than in underlying realities, so that misconception is very easy. There were no proper party organizations about 1760, though party names and cant were current; the names and the cant have since supplied the materials for an imaginary superstructure.' He concludes that 'the political life of the period could be fully described without ever using a party denomination'.[3]

Namier's conclusions are based on meticulous study of the political correspondence of that period and are now generally accepted—at least for the 1760's and 70's. Professor Barnes has shown that they hold for the later years of George III's reign; but no one has made a comparable analysis for the early years of the century. Can the political life of that period be fully described without ever using a party denomination? Are the

[1] I. Deane Jones, *The English Revolution: an Introduction to English History, 1603–1714* (London, 1931), pp. 205, 207.

[2] D. G. Barnes, *George III and William Pitt, 1783–1806: a New Interpretation Based upon a Study of Their Unpublished Correspondence* (Stanford University Press, 1939), p. 1.

[3] L. B. Namier, *The Structure of Politics at the Accession of George III* (2 vols., London, 1929), I. vii (preface).

underlying realities of its politics disguised beneath an imaginary party superstructure?

Any generalizations about the actual workings of the English constitution in the early eighteenth century must be based on accurate information about a number of interrelated questions. Into how many parties was the legislature actually divided? How were these parties organized, and who led them? If a careful analysis reveals not two parties but numerous party groups, if it shows that the ministries of this period were inevitably coalitions of several party groups and that there are no examples of a single party in office faced by a single opposition party, then surely the traditional interpretation of how the constitution worked in this period needs revising. If the legislature was divided into a number of party groups, and if the largest and best organized of these groups was made up of officials and dependants of the Court, then the position of the sovereign and his chosen advisers must have been rather different from that generally assumed.

With a bloc of regular government supporters in the Commons the executive would be far less amenable to pressure from the party leaders. Moreover, if the non-government Members were divided at all evenly into Whig and Tory segments, the chief ministers might well hold the balance between them. According to several authorities Marlborough and Godolphin were in precisely such a position during the first six years of Anne's reign.[1] However, should analysis show that the Whig and Tory segments were themselves divided into divergent groups each under individual leadership, the traditional picture would prove badly out of focus.

Any disunity within either the Whig or Tory camp, any personal or political differences between individual party leaders would further strengthen the executive. Instead of being forced to choose between a set of Whig masters or of Tory ones, the

[1] This is Trevelyan's latest view, in his *Blenheim*, p. 478. W. T. Morgan held the same view. See his *English Political Parties and Leaders in the Reign of Anne* (hereafter cited as Morgan's *Political Parties*), pp. 227–30.

executive could select allies from a wide variety of party groups. With a substantial nucleus of government Members comparatively few additional votes would be required for a working majority in the Commons. When it came to bargaining for these votes, the executive would be in a stronger position than the party leaders. It alone had places to give; the party leaders, until given office, had only the votes of themselves and their immediate followers with which to barter. Should analysis show that no individual leader could be sure of more than a score of reliable followers, and that no combination of leaders could hold together their combined following for long in the face of disagreements among themselves and defections to the Court, the generalizations so often made about the early eighteenth-century constitution would no longer be tenable.

If neither the Whigs nor the Tories were effectively organized as national parties, there could hardly have been a 'two-party system' in the usual sense. Without two well-organized parties there could have been little progress towards a cabinet system as generally understood. Instead of the majority party in the lower chamber of the legislature controlling the executive, the executive could conceivably control instead the legislature—through its bloc of government Members reinforced by additional votes lent by individual party chiefs in return for a share of office and a subordinate voice in the determination of policy.

Which of the two—the traditional picture of early eighteenth-century government with two parties contesting for power; or the alternative view sketched above—comes closer to describing how politics actually worked in Queen Anne's reign ought to be decided on the basis of such evidence as is available and pertinent. This should include detailed data on the electoral system, on the composition of the House of Commons, on party organization, and on individual party members. The last point is important. The more we know about individuals, the better we can understand the actual workings of politics; and in this connexion it should be pointed out that the material presented on individuals in this essay represents the distillation of every scrap of biographical data on some 1,200 Members of Parliament that could be collected over a period of some fifteen years.

In the chapters that follow material of this sort is presented. We begin with an analysis of the electoral system as it operated in the first years of the eighteenth century. This should enable us to understand the important phenomenon of electoral 'interest'. There follows an analysis of William III's last parliament—the first to be chosen in the eighteenth century. This particular House of Commons is analysed first in terms of the Members' occupations and social status, and secondly in political terms. In the case of each Member there is an indication, based on some evidence, of how he got into parliament—through his own efforts, by government influence, or on the 'interest' of some titled or untitled patron.

Turning next to the personal connexions of Members we identify a number of distinct groups—family, personal, professional—the most important of which are described in some detail. Up to this point in our analysis it is possible to avoid pinning a party label on the various groups, and to this extent we have described political conditions without using party denominations. That becomes more difficult when we turn from the dissection of a single parliament to a study of the functioning of the political groups we have spread out on the operating table. This latter task is undertaken in Part Two.

We begin our study of the physiology of party by working out the case history of each of the major groups from the time it first appeared as an organized body in parliament down to the death of William III. We then follow these groups through a general election—that of 1702—which is analysed with some care as a case study of the way in which party politics actually worked in a specific political situation. From this case study we develop a working hypothesis about party politics, which is then illustrated by a brief discussion of the course followed by the party groups during the first five years of Anne's reign. This in turn leads into a second case study—of the parliamentary session of 1707–8. This session is analysed in some detail, in the belief that such analysis provides further evidence with which to test the general hypothesis. The general findings are summarized in a brief concluding chapter.

PART ONE
THE STRUCTURE OF PARTIES

CHAPTER II

The Electoral System in 1701

THERE is no adequate description of the electoral system as it operated in the early years of the eighteenth century. Macaulay does not describe it, either in his famous third chapter on the state of England in 1685 or elsewhere in his *History*; nor does Lecky, in his *History of England in the Eighteenth Century*. Trevelyan, in his recent *England Under Queen Anne*, devotes five pages to electioneering, but the electoral system itself he takes for granted. For an adequate description one must turn to the Porritts's work, to Halévy's admirable summary of the system as it was in 1815, or to Namier's detailed work on the electoral structure as it stood in the 1760's.[1] Unfortunately, of these three accounts the first two deal with the system after it had been modified by more than a century of development since 1700; while Namier's description, excellent as it is, can hardly be accepted as a reliable blueprint for the electoral machinery of fifty years before. In order to learn how Members of the House of Commons were chosen in Queen Anne's reign, we must investigate the electoral system anew.

[1] See G. M. Trevelyan's *Blenheim*, pp. 210–13; Edward and Annie G. Porritt, *The Unreformed House of Commons; Parliamentary Representation before 1832* (Cambridge University Press, 1903), chaps. 2, 3, 5, and 6; Elie Halévy, *History of the English People in 1815*, translated by Watkin and Barker (New York, 1924), pp. 109–30; and L. B. Namier, *The Structure of Politics*, i. 79–191 and *England in the Age of the American Revolution*, pp. 206–62.

Prior to the Union with Scotland in 1707 the House of Commons numbered 513 Members: 489 from England, 24 from Wales. Little need be said about the constituencies of Wales. In the twelve single-Member Welsh counties the franchise was vested in those possessed of a freehold worth forty shillings a year. The twelve single-Member borough constituencies also had large and fairly uniform electorates, with one exception.[1] The voters numbered from 300 to a thousand, and in general were independent and not easily bribed. Outsiders with guineas or letters of recommendation from some magnate were coolly received by the voters of the Principality, who unmistakably preferred those of Welsh birth. The votes which the outsider could not buy were at the disposal, however, of the principal local families—a phenomenon perhaps explained by the semi-feudal conditions of a somewhat backward agricultural society. At all events the representation of Wales was monopolized by a handful of county families.[2]

Of the English representatives eighty were knights of the shire, two for each of the forty English counties. In the shire constituencies the franchise extended to all the forty-shilling freeholders—that system having in fact been extended from England to Wales—and as in Wales knights of the shire did not come from the yeoman class nor from the small landowners, but were drawn almost exclusively from the upper ranks of the landed gentry. In a sense this was fitting, for the great landed proprietors were the natural leaders of a society in which estates, irrespective of their owners, commanded a surprising measure of allegiance; nor were the outlook and interests of the estate-owner widely divergent from those of his tenants.

This natural ascendancy the leading county families improved in a number of ways. Theoretically the freeholder could make an independent choice, but in practice this freedom was

[1] i.e. Beaumaris in Anglesey, where twenty-four corporation-members elected the Member for the borough.

[2] This is borne out by the lists and descriptions of Welsh M.P.s in W. R. Williams, *The Parliamentary History of the Principality of Wales, 1541–1895* (Brecknock (privately printed), 1895), *passim*.

limited to choosing between candidates previously fixed upon at informal meetings of the local landowners. Moreover, the freeholder was often a tenant for some other land and amenable to pressure from the landlord. Add to this, open polling, treating, and free transport to the often distant polls, and it becomes obvious how easily elections could be managed by the leading local families. The local grandees, of course, often fell out among themselves, especially in counties where the independent country squires were at loggerheads with the peer—usually some great noble with Court and London connexions—who tended to dominate the county. Later in the century such disagreements were usually compromised, and the 'peace of the county' maintained by letting one seat go unopposed to one, and the second to the other. In Queen Anne's reign, however, such an arrangement was unusual; and disagreements were fought out at the polls. As a result ruinously expensive election contests were common in more than half the counties.

In the remaining counties opinion was more nearly unanimous. The country squires named unopposed candidates for one or both seats in eighteen shires,[1] while in nine counties candidates named by the leading noble houses were generally recognized as the most fitting representatives.[2] Time after time Lancashire returned a Stanley of the Earl of Derby's family; and Cumberland, a Lowther of the clan that acknowledged Lord Lonsdale as its chief. Such noble houses might furnish knights of the shire for generations, but tact was essential. Lord Lonsdale was thought to have gone too far when he suggested on his death-bed that the county return his uncle in a coming election—'in my opinion a very improper legacy to his county',

[1] Viz. Berks. (both seats), Devon (2), Dorset (2), Durham (2), Essex (1), Hereford (2), Herts. (1), Kent (2), Lancs. (1), Northants (2), Oxon (2), Somerset (2), Staffs. (2), Suffolk (2), Warwick (2), Wilts. (2), Worcester (1), and Yorks. (1).

[2] Viz. Duke of Bedford in Beds. (both seats); and Lords Wharton (Bucks., 1), Lonsdale (Cumberland, 1), Derby (Lancs., 1), Manchester (Hunts., 1), Lindsey (Lincs., 1), Somerset (Northumb., 1), Newcastle (Notts., 1), and Wharton again (Westmorland, 1).

a gentleman complained, 'for I never heard that Knights of the Shire were disposed of by will'.[1]

With the counties we may properly class the university constituencies of Oxford and Cambridge; for they, too, had a uniform franchise and returned members identified with a distinct social group—not the landed gentry in this case, but the Church. All the graduates of Oxford and Cambridge University had a right to vote for their university Members, but in practice the clergy tended to dominate the choice of representative. This was partly because clergymen made up a larger proportion of the graduates than later on; but the influence of the Church in university elections was due more to geography. The graduates on the spot—the university dons and country parsons from nearby parishes—were all clergymen; while the non-clerical graduates were scattered all over England. Contests were frequent, but on almost every occasion the clerical vote gave the decision to candidates whose narrow Anglicanism corresponded to that of the lower clergy. However, the university and county Members so representative of the Church and the landed interest comprised less than a fifth of the membership of the House. The great majority of representatives sat for the 200-odd English boroughs. It is to these borough electorates that one must look for the most important and striking characteristics of the eighteenth-century electoral system.

The most distinctive feature of the borough franchise was its diversity. Each of the 203 parliamentary boroughs differed from every other in the size of its electorate or the exact nature of the franchise. Each was to some extent *sui generis*, yet each falls within one of three general categories, depending on whether the franchise was based on residence or the payment of local taxes, on the ownership of 'burgages' or freeholds to which the franchise was attached, or on membership in some corporate body. This classification, used by the Porritts and

[1] James Graham of Levens to a freeholder, 9 Sept. 1700 (*Bagot MSS.* (Historical Manuscripts Commission (hereafter referred to as *H.M.C.*), 10th Report, Appendix iv, p. 335.)

later by Halévy, is a logical one, since each type of electoral qualification gave rise to a distinct variety of electoral 'interest' and required particular electioneering methods; but it is incomplete, for it does not take into account the size of the electorate —always an important factor. In addition to describing the three main types of borough franchise, it will be necessary to distinguish between the large and the small boroughs in each class, if we are to describe the electoral structure accurately.

Examples of the ridiculous and inequitable anomalies of the unreformed electoral system have been cited so often that it is easy to overlook the fifty-five boroughs in which the franchise was at least as broad as that introduced by the first Reform Bill. In seventeen constituencies the right to vote belonged to all the inhabitants not receiving alms, or capable of boiling their own pot (whence the picturesque term 'potwaller' or 'potwalloper');[1] while at one borough the franchise was vested in all the inhabitants without exception, so that a regiment of soldiers or a troop of beggars present on election day were legally entitled to vote.[2] Less democratic but nearly as extensive was the franchise in the thirty-nine boroughs where all the inhabitants paying 'scot and lot' (i.e. local taxes) had the right to vote.[3] In other words the franchise in more than a fourth of the English boroughs was wide enough to satisfy the standards established by the first Reform Bill.

[1] Viz. Aylesbury, Bedford, Bridport, Callington, Cambridge, Hastings, Hertford, Hindon, Honiton, Ilchester, Minehead, Northampton, St. Germans, St. Ives, Taunton, Tregoney, and Wendover. The data are drawn from the latest determination of the House of Commons.

[2] This was Preston. See *Journal of the House of Commons* (referred to hereafter as *C.J.*), viii. 36.

[3] Viz. Abingdon, Agmondesham (hereafter referred to as Amersham), Arundel, Bridgwater, Chichester, Cirencester, Dorchester, Dover, Eye, Gatton, Great Marlow (hereafter referred to as Marlow), Guildford, King's Lynn (hereafter referred to as Lynn), Leicester, Leominster, Michael, Milborne Port, Morpeth, Newark-on-Trent (hereafter referred to as Newark), Newport (Cornwall), New Shoreham (hereafter referred to as Shoreham), New Windsor (hereafter referred to as Windsor), Nottingham, Penryn, Peterborough, Reading, Rye, Seaford, Shaftesbury, Southwark, Steyning, Stockbridge, Tamworth, Wallingford, Wareham, Warwick, Weobley, Westminster, Wootton Bassett.

Constituencies with such a franchise cannot be termed 'popular' or 'independent', however, unless the number of electors is also taken into account. In this connexion we must guard against equating the size of the electorate with the actual population of a borough, remembering that in many cases large groups of the population were barred from the franchise because of living outside the limits of the 'parliamentary borough'—an area within ancient boundaries which usually excluded the newer parts of town. This explains to some extent why thirty of the inhabitant and scot-and-lot boroughs had electorates of less than 200. Constituencies of this size are obviously undemocratic. One cannot call the scot-and-lot borough of Gatton a 'popular constituency', considering that its twenty voters lived close beside the two capital mansions and returned the lords of the manors of Upper and Lower Gatton time after time.[1] Similar conditions obtained in most of the smaller boroughs of this type—Amersham, Minehead, and Callington were the 'pocket boroughs' of local landlords, the Drakes, the Luttrells, the Rolles, and Corytons.[2]

The smaller scot-and-lot boroughs were often dominated by a patron, but the twenty-odd medium-sized and large constituencies of this type were perhaps the most independent and least venal of all the boroughs. We must except, however, the metropolitan boroughs of Southwark and Westminster, largest of all English constituencies, with four and nine thousand voters, respectively. Elections at these places were notoriously venal and turbulent. Wealthy beer-barons with hireling armies of draymen battled for the representation of Southwark; while the mass of Westminster electors were marshalled out, with considerable efficiency, to vote for candidates set up by the Court.[3]

[1] *History and Antiquities of the County of Surrey*, by Owen Manning, continued by William Bray (London, 1804–14), ii. 227 ff.

[2] For Amersham see G. Lipscomb's *History and Antiquities of the County of Buckingham* (1847), iii. 154–5, 161–2. For Minehead see H. C. Maxwell Lyte's *Dunster and its Lords* (privately printed, 1882), pp. 99–100. For Callington see C. S. Gilbert's *Historical and Topographical Survey of the County of Cornwall* (London, 1817), ii. 467–72.

[3] See T. Carew, *An Historical Account of the Rights of Election* . . .

The franchise in the inhabitant and scot-and-lot boroughs was based logically on residence and payment of taxes; but there was a large class of boroughs in which the electoral qualifications were manifestly absurd. In medieval times the right or obligation to vote was an incident of feudal burgage tenure, and the franchise was inseparably connected with a particular holding. In the early eighteenth century the parliamentary vote was still attached to certain 'ancient tenements' or 'burgages' in no less than forty-three boroughs.[1] These were the 'pocket boroughs' *par excellence*. A burgage was a piece of property—an old house, a ruined barn, a garden or cellar-hole—which could be bought outright; and where the franchise was vested in the proprietors of burgages, ownership of a majority meant absolute control. Later in the century concentration of burgage holdings in a few hands had gone so far that most boroughs of this type were controlled by some wealthy family or individual. In 1700, however, this process still had a long way to go. The elder Pitt's grandfather bought a bloc of Old Sarum burgages in 1691; but the Pitts had to face opposition from two other proprietors for fifteen years before they were able, for the sum of £500, to buy up the last burgage necessary for a majority.[2]

The burgage boroughs, located chiefly in Yorkshire and in

(London, 1755), Part II, p. 145. This useful work is a compilation of all reports of the Committee of Elections of the House of Commons, taken from the Commons Journals and arranged under the particular constituency.

[1] Viz. Aldborough (Yorks.), Appleby, Ashburton, Beeralston, Bletchingly, Boroughbridge, Bossiney, Bramber, Calne, Castle Rising, Chippenham, Clitheroe, Cockermouth, Corfe Castle, Cricklade, Downton, East Grinstead (hereafter referred to as Grinstead), Great Bedwin (hereafter referred to as Bedwin), Haslemere, Heytesbury, Horsham, Knaresborough, Lichfield, Ludgershall, Malton, Midhurst, Milborne Port (this borough, which had about fifty scot-and-lot voters and is accordingly listed on p. 12, n. 3, above, also had nine burgage tenures), Newton (Lancs.), Newtown (I. of Wight), Northallerton, Okehampton, Old Sarum, Petersfield, Pontefract, Reigate, Richmond, Ripon, Saltash, Tavistock, Thirsk, Westbury, Weymouth-Melcombe Regis, and Whitchurch.

[2] See correspondence between Gov. Pitt and his son, in *H.M.C. Fortescue MSS.* i. 12–17, 22–24.

Wiltshire, varied in size from Richmond with its 271 burgages to Old Sarum with its dozen; but the number of burgages was of little significance. It cost as much, in money and effort, to buy up Old Sarum as it did to win control of a borough with ten times as many burgages. More important than the difference in number of burgages was the very real distinction between boroughs where the franchise was vested in the owner, and those in which it was vested in the actual occupier, of the 'ancient tenement'. The second type of franchise introduced complications and made it more difficult for the proprietor to gain and keep control. For every election he must draw up so-called 'snatch papers'—fictitious deeds to his burgages; and these he would hand to his dependants, his 'faggot voters', so that they could legally occupy his burgage tenements, or 'vote houses', and thus exercise the privilege of the vote. After the election the deeds were returned, and the proprietor resumed ownership.[1] Similar legal skullduggery was used to multiply voteworthy freeholds in the boroughs where the franchise was attached to freeholds, and 'splitting' was feasible. At the double constituency of Weymouth and Melcombe Regis, for example, 250 new freeholds were carved from existing ones on the eve of a general election.[2] Ultimately these methods were perfected, and enough burgages united in the hands of a single proprietor to ensure control; but in 1700 only half the burgage boroughs were so controlled, and even where the independent burgage-holders had long since sold out, there was always the possibility of a successful invasion by some wealthy outsider.

There was even more danger of losing control in the third type of constituency, the corporation boroughs. In forty boroughs the franchise was restricted to the corporation, the governing-body of the town. This oligarchy might be limited to a definite number, or it might include an indefinite number of

[1] For a detailed account of this machinery see William Albery's *Parliamentary History of the Ancient Borough of Horsham, 1295–1885* (London, 1927), pp. 39–70.

[2] *C.J.* xvii. 654, 663 (Report of the Committee of Elections on the controverted election for Weymouth-Melcombe Regis, 1713).

members chosen by co-option. In the nineteen boroughs where the corporation was fixed in number, the electorate was very small, ranging from thirteen at Buckingham and Malmesbury to fifty-six at Salisbury.[1] Small in numbers, these corporative electors were by no means easy to manage. 'I need not tell you what coy mistresses boroughs are', Lord Hervey told his brother-in-law,[2] summing up his experience with the Bury corporation of thirty-seven, which he himself wooed with such success that it seldom flirted and was almost never unfaithful.[3]

Few patrons of corporation boroughs had experiences as satisfactory as this. More pressure could be brought to bear on thirteen voters than on thirteen hundred, but the thirteen knew well the value of their votes. Were the elections for sale, as at one Norfolk borough, 'fifty guineas for a vote is their price'.[4] At all these boroughs elections called forth the most lavish promises and the most varied and elaborate methods of influence,[5] if not such extravagant bribes; but, even so, few corporations stayed long in anyone's pocket. At Malmesbury Lord Wharton was overthrown on one occasion, 'after he had treated

[1] The names of these boroughs and the numbers in the corporation are as follows: Andover 24, Banbury 26, Bath 33, Bewdley 14, Bodmin 37, Brackley 33, Buckingham 13, Bury St. Edmunds (hereafter referred to as Bury) 37, Camelford 25, Harwich 32, Lostwithiel 24, Malden 26, Malmesbury 13, Marlborough 21, Newport (I. of Wight) 24, Salisbury 56, Scarborough 38, Thetford 32, Tiverton 26, and Truro 25.

[2] *The Letter Books of John Hervey, First Earl of Bristol* (Wells, 1894), i. 273. This Lord Hervey should not be confused with his son, the memoir-writing Lord Hervey, termed 'Lord Fanny' by Pope.

[3] Hervey himself, his son, father-in-law, brother-in-law, his doctor, and his friend the Recorder monopolized the representation of Bury from 1701 to 1714. See *Letter Books*, vol. i, *passim*.

[4] Humphrey Prideaux to John Ellis, Sept. 1708 (*Letters from Humphrey Prideaux, Sometime Dean of Norwich, to John Ellis, Under Secretary of State, 1674–1722* (ed. E. M. Thompson, Publications of the Camden Society, New Series, xv. London, 1875), p. 200). Prideaux was writing about the Thetford corporation of thirty-two.

[5] For a vivid and realistic description of electioneering in a corporation borough, see Stanley J. Weyman's *Chippinge Borough*. Malmesbury is the original of 'Chippinge', and while the novel is laid in the 1830's, the election tricks go back at least to the days of Queen Anne.

and threatened the town for ten days together'. Such an efficient manager did not give up easily, but he had to retire temporarily, after 'a farewell Benediction that, as they had been an ungrateful and perfidious Corporation to him, so he would endeavour to extirpate them as such, and would never more be seen within their villainous town'.[1]

Management was perhaps easier in the twenty-one boroughs where the corporation included an indefinite number of 'free burgesses' selected by the corporation itself.[2] Once a family or group had managed to work its way into the governing-body of one of these boroughs, it could effectively win and maintain control by limiting subsequent additions to the corporation to its own relatives and dependants. At the small Hampshire borough of Lymington, for example, these tactics were used by the Duke of Bolton and a local family named Burrard in order to establish their joint control of the corporation. From the start of their partnership in 1686 until 1701 these two families allowed none but their own friends and relations to be added to the corporation.[3] Since there was no residence requirement, most of these 'gentleman outburgesses' were outsiders; but they took their turn in the mayor's chair and helped build up the interest of their patrons. Such a well-built interest could hardly be overturned, and for forty years the two families had their own way at Lymington. The Duke of Bolton named one Member; the Burrards the other; and the arrangement was eventually upset only because one patron declared war upon the other.[4] Similar conditions prevailed at Portsmouth, but

[1] James Craggs to Marlborough, 22 July 1707 (Add. MSS. 9100 (Coxe Transcripts), f. 93).

[2] Camelford, Christchurch, Devizes, Droitwich, Dunwich, Hedon, Helston, Hythe, Launceston, Liskeard, East Looe and West Looe, Lymington, Much Wenlock (hereafter referred to as Wenlock), Orford, Portsmouth, Totnes, Wigan, Wilton, Winchester, and Yarmouth (I. of Wight).

[3] Paul Burrard to Lord William Powlett (brother of the 2nd Duke of Bolton), 27 June 1722. The letter is printed in Sidney Burrard's *Annals of Walhampton* (London, 1874), p. 31. Burrard writes, 'all the old Burgesses now alive (except one), from the year 1686 to 1701, were made by us. . .'.

[4] For the representative history of Lymington see Burrard's *Walhampton*,

at this dockyard town the nomination of the honorary non-resident members of the corporation lay with the government. The roll of 'out-burgesses' bristles with the names of courtiers, Admiralty big-wigs, and dockyard officials,[1] indicating that the government managed Portsmouth exactly as the Duke of Bolton managed his borough not twenty miles away.

It is difficult to draw the line between the larger corporation boroughs like Portsmouth and Lymington and some of the 'freeman' boroughs where a similar type of corporative franchise prevailed. In sixty constituencies the franchise was vested, not in the corporation alone, but in all the 'freemen'—members, originally, of the trade-guilds or companies of the borough.[2] In some of these boroughs men still acquired their 'freedom' according to ancient guild custom: the eldest sons of freemen, by inheritance; others, by seven years' apprenticeship to a freeman. Sometimes, as in London, Newcastle-on-Tyne, and Carlisle, the companies still controlled the admission of freemen; but more often this function had passed to the borough corporations. Since the rules governing the admission of freemen were seldom fixed, the franchise was to some extent under the corporation's control.

and Charles St. Barbe's *Records of the Corporation of the Borough of Lymington, in the County of Southampton* (London (privately printed), 1849), pp. 10–12, 18–19, 22–23.

[1] R. East, *Extracts from the Portsmouth Borough Records* (new edition, Portsmouth, 1891), pp. 369–77.

[2] Aldborough (Yorks.) (a burgage-right here, also), Barnstaple, Berwick-on-Tweed (hereafter referred to as Berwick), Beverley, Bishop's Castle, Boston, Bridgnorth, Bristol, Cambridge, Canterbury, Carlisle, Chester, Chipping Wycombe (hereafter referred to as Wycombe), Clifton Dartmouth Hardness (hereafter referred to as Dartmouth), Colchester, Coventry, Derby, Durham, East Retford (hereafter referred to as Retford), Evesham, Exeter, Gloucester, Grantham, Great Grimsby (hereafter referred to as Grimsby), Great Yarmouth (hereafter referred to as Yarmouth (Norfolk)), Hereford, Higham Ferrers, Huntingdon, Ipswich, Kingston-on-Hull (hereafter referred to as Hull), Lancaster, Lichfield (a burgage-right here, also), Lincoln, Liverpool, London, Ludlow, Lyme, Maidstone, Monmouth, Newcastle-on-Tyne, Newcastle-under-Lyme (hereafter referred to as Newcastle (Staffs.)), New Romney, New Woodstock (hereafter referred to as Woodstock), Norwich, Oxford, Plymouth, Plympton, Poole, Queenborough, Rochester, Sandwich, Shrews-

This control could usually be exercised with some pretence of legality. In order to vote a freeman must be formally admitted to his freedom and have his name enrolled on the borough records. These were formalities, but they required corporation action; and in many boroughs the governing-bodies abused this power, granted them by charter, and refused admittance or enrolment to duly qualified freemen. Much more prevalent abuses arose from the right, enjoyed by many corporations, to make honorary and non-resident freemen. Few governing-bodies which enjoyed this right could resist using it to model the electorate to their liking. Take, for example, the borough of Plympton in Devonshire. Here the corporation was controlled by Judge Treby, a lawyer of national prominence and Plympton's most illustrious resident. This borough was known as 'Lord Chief Justice Treby's town',[1] and the governing-body rejected and admitted freemen at the judge's bidding. According to testimony given before a parliamentary committee, 'several foreigners were made free to serve Mr. Treby'; and when he was asked 'why he made so many strangers free', he retorted that 'he would make more if they were not enough'.[2]

Sometimes, of course, the corporation was divided, with one faction and then the other in control. In that case each side invariably tried to swamp the other with new honorary freemen recruited from their own friends. In Queen Anne's time, for example, this occurred at Ipswich. The faction in power early in the reign enfranchised some fifty supporters from among the local gentry. Once in power the other side retaliated. In 1711 'they proceeded to vote the freedom of the corporation to no less than fifty-two gentlemen of the county, and some of London, among whom are seven baronets'.[3] By the end of the

bury, Southampton, Stafford, Stamford, Sudbury, Tewkesbury, Winchelsea, Worcester, and York.

[1] Defoe to Harley (1705); see *H.M.C. Portland MSS.* (Harley Papers), iv, 270.

[2] Carew, op. cit., Part II, p. 51. See also J. B. Rowe's *History of the Borough of Plympton Erle* (Exeter, 1906), pp. 188–96.

[3] Carew, Part I, pp. 303–4. See also *The History and Description of the Town and Borough of Ipswich* (by G. R. Clarke) (London, 1830), pp. 71–83.

reign they had made more than a hundred honorary freemen, and they added twenty-four more in the beginning of the next reign.

The making of honorary freemen was a favourite device with politically minded corporations; but in many constituencies honorary freemen were not allowed to vote. This prevented the governing-body from manufacturing electors, but it did not outlaw the non-resident freemen, who formed a reservoir of valid and easily purchasable votes. In the absence of a residence requirement it was customary for duly qualified freemen to retain the franchise for life, no matter when they had left the borough or how far off they lived. In time their sons became freemen, and they, too, could vote in a borough which they might never have seen. Living in and around London for the most part, these freemen from provincial boroughs could always be persuaded to return and cast their vote for any gentleman who made it worth their while. At a Sudbury election, for example, non-resident freemen were paid a pound a head for travelling the fifty-six miles between their homes in London and the polls, or half a guinea if they came from Colchester, eighteen miles away.[1]

Actually, elections could be won by the votes of non-resident and honorary freemen in the smaller constituencies only. We have described electioneering methods in the freeman and corporation boroughs as though they were everywhere effective; but in practice their effectiveness depended largely on the size of the electorate. In the nineteen corporation boroughs where the governing-bodies were fixed in number the electorate was always small; and all but four of them were under individual or government control.[2] The electorate in the twenty corpora-

[1] Carew, op. cit., Part II, p. 175 (citing evidence before the Committee of Elections). See also Carew, Part I, p. 371, *sub* 'Maidstone'. In this Kentish borough non-resident freemen were liberally paid to come from Rochester (9 miles off), Canterbury (28), and Westminster and London (35 miles away).

[2] The four exceptions were Bath, Salisbury, Scarborough, and perhaps Tiverton, where Lord Sunderland had a great deal of influence, but not enough for complete control.

tion boroughs with governing-bodies of indefinite size was as small as the politicians could keep it: around fifty in eight boroughs, 100 or less in another nine. In only three cases did it approach 200; but these relatively large constituencies were hardly more exempt from outside control.[1] Only two of these boroughs could be called 'independent', and both of them were notoriously corrupt.[2]

Narrow constituencies formed a much smaller proportion of the freeman boroughs. Of the sixty boroughs of this type only ten had electorates of one hundred or less; but nearly all of these were pocket boroughs dominated by patrons, or rotten boroughs ready to sell out to the highest bidder. The three smallest were controlled by the government; another four were in the pockets of London merchants or neighbouring county families; and two of the remaining three had unenviable records of elections controverted and voided because of bribery.[3] Grimsby, for example, was frankly corrupt, seeing that its 'freemen did enter into treaties with several gentlemen in London, for sale of the choice of burgess [i.e. M.P.] to such as would give most money'.[4]

In these small constituencies financial considerations played a major role. Voting at parliamentary elections was a regular means of livelihood and bribery was welcomed. The thirty-one medium-sized freeman boroughs with electorates between 100

[1] The three largest were Launceston (*c.* 140), Portsmouth (*c.* 200), and Wigan (also *c.* 200). Portsmouth has been already discussed. Launceston was controlled by the Hydes, Earls of Rochester; Wigan, by the Bradshaighs of Haigh.

[2] Viz. Camelford and Devizes. For the first see *C.J.* xvi. 274 ff.; for the second, *H.M.C. Portland MSS.*, iv. 175–6, 244–5.

[3] See Carew, op. cit., Part I, *sub* 'Great Grimsby' and 'Bishop's Castle', for the last two. The three boroughs controlled by the government were New Romney, Winchelsea, and Queenborough. Dartmouth was controlled by the Hernes, a family of London merchants; Aldeburgh (Suffolk), by a Blackwall shipbuilder named Sir Henry Johnson; Beverley, by two families, the Hothams and the Wartons; and the single-Member constituency of Higham Ferrers, by the family of Watson-Wentworth, later Marquesses of Rockingham.

[4] Carew, Part I, *sub* 'Great Grimsby'.

and 1,000 were much less venal; but here, too, influence played its part. Three of them were dominated by the government; six were pocket-boroughs of neighbouring landowners; and the same class of local magnates exercised the predominant, if not the sole, influence in at least a dozen more.[1] The remaining nine were fairly independent, as were all nineteen of the freeman boroughs with electorates of over a thousand.[2] Conditions were not entirely above-board in these constituencies, of course, for the freemen were generally a rude, uneducated, and often mercenary lot. Elections were disorderly and turbulent; bribery and treating played their part; but the electors showed considerable independence. In the larger cities they usually chose fellow-citizens prominent in business and municipal life; while in the provincial towns they often followed the lead of the shopkeepers and complimented the local magnate with one seat, thereby safeguarding and perhaps increasing profitable accounts that might otherwise be taken elsewhere.

In these boroughs, as elsewhere, it is difficult to draw the line between undue influence and the natural deference paid in that age to the nobility and gentry. It seems fairly obvious, however, that undue influence was often exercised in the 'narrow constituencies'—a generalization that is important in view of the

[1] The three boroughs under government influence were Plymouth, Rochester, and Southampton.

The six boroughs controlled so firmly that they amounted to pocket boroughs were: Monmouth, controlled by the Morgans of Tredegar; Newcastle (Staffs.), by the Leveson-Gowers; Plympton, by Judge Treby (as above, p. 19, n. 1); Stamford, by the Earl of Exeter and by the Berties of Uffington; Woodstock, by the Duke of Marlborough; and Wycombe, by Lord Wharton.

The twelve boroughs where there were strong interests approaching control were: Boston, Lord Lindsey; Cambridge, the Cottons of Madingley; Carlisle, the Earl of Carlisle; Derby, the Duke of Devonshire; Evesham, the families of Rudge and Parker; Grantham, the Duke of Rutland; Huntingdon, the Earl of Sandwich; Ludlow, the related families of Lyttleton and Powys; Retford, the Duke of Newcastle; Sandwich, the Oxenden family; Stafford, the Foleys; and Tewkesbury, the family of Dowdeswell.

[2] These larger freeman boroughs were: Bridgnorth, Bristol, Canterbury, Chester, Colchester, Coventry, Durham, Exeter, Gloucester, Hereford, Lancaster, Lincoln, Liverpool, London, Newcastle-on-Tyne, Norwich, Oxford, Worcester, and York.

fact that more than 40 per cent. of the boroughs had less than 100 voters, that nearly two-thirds had less than 500, that only one-eighth had 1,000 or more electors, and that only three—less than 1½ per cent.—of the boroughs had electorates of more than 4,000.

An electoral system with such a large proportion of small constituencies offered a fine field for the attentions of realistic members of the government and the upper class, once it became apparent that the respect accorded them in the smaller boroughs could be converted into effective control.

CHAPTER III

The Composition of the House of Commons in 1701

OUR analysis of the electoral system and the varied electioneering methods to which it gave rise clearly shows how important a part the nobility and gentry played in choosing Members of Parliament. The sum total of their efforts in the constituencies must certainly have affected the composition of the House of Commons, but to what extent? How many of the Members who supposedly served the townspeople of the boroughs and the yeomen and freeholders of the counties actually represented the peerage or the landed gentry? The last parliament of William III, the first to be elected in the eighteenth century, can serve us as a sample. By classifying the 513 Members of this House of Commons according to their occupation and, secondly, according to their social position we can get some indication of the economic and social make-up of the popular branch of the legislature.

Using occupation as the criterion it becomes apparent at once that a large majority of this House of Commons must be described as 'of no occupation', or landowners possessed of estates by inheritance, with no business other than supervising the management of their property. To give more precise figures is difficult, and we must fall back on maximum and minimum totals. If we include in our total every M.P. who owned at least a manor or sizeable fraction of one and devoted at least part of his time to managing this property and to the country pursuits typical of the squirearchy, we reach a maximum figure of 350. All these gentlemen were 'squires' in the eyes of their tenants and villagers; but if we define squire more narrowly, as one *primarily* or *exclusively* a landed proprietor, eighty of our 350 'squires' will have to be ruled out.

Although landed proprietors these eighty gentlemen were also engaged in occupations which lay outside the sphere of the ordinary country gentleman. Ten of the 350 'squires' in the Commons were serving as officers in the army or navy in 1700, or received commissions soon after; and they should be classed as representatives of the fighting services, although they were landed gentry originally and differed from their fellow officers in having no long career of military service behind them. Another fifty, though landed gentry by origin, had been holding Court and official positions for many years and consequently spent most of their time at Court or in their offices in London. They, too, have been included among the squires; but they should properly be classified as members of the Court and official group. Finally there were a number of Members whose pursuits distinguished them from the usual gentry. Some, like Sir John Lowther and Sir Humphrey Mackworth, were chiefly interested in the mineral resources of their property; or, like the Lowthers of Whitehaven and the family of Trefusis, developed local seaports; but they remained essentially members of the landed interest for all their industrial and commercial activities. In the nineteenth century Disraeli referred to these 'men of metal' as forming part of the landed interest no less than the 'large-acred squires'.[1] Others, with extensive financial interests in the chartered trading companies or the proprietary colonies, had closer ties with the trading community than with the squirearchy. Landowners engaged in economic activities of this nature and those who held commissions in the army or navy or positions at Court can hardly be termed true representatives of the landed interest; but even if we exclude these border-line cases, the landed gentry in parliament would still number at least 270. At the least they made up 55 per cent., at the most, 70 per cent., of the House of Commons, outnumbering all other occupational groups combined by approximately two to one.

Of the remaining Members roughly one-third represented

[1] I am indebted to Sir Lewis Namier for this reference.

the commercial interest. Sixty-one Members of the 1701 parliament were in trade. Forty-three were merchants: fifteen of them in the East Indian trade, eleven in the West Indian and American, five engaged in commerce in the Mediterranean and Turkey, and one in the Baltic; plus eleven merchants from outports such as Bristol, Exeter, Hull, Lynn, and Newcastle. A dozen were bankers: seven of them directors of the Bank of England, the rest independent financiers. Another five were in the liquor trade: four, brewers from London, Southwark, and Kent; the fifth, a distiller from Berwick-on-Tweed. Finally there were six representatives of various miscellaneous trades and manufactures: a shipbuilder, an ironmonger, a saltmaker, a stationer, an apothecary, and a manufacturer of copper coins for the Treasury. Two-thirds of these businessmen were citizens and residents of London.[1]

The City of London returned four Members of Parliament; the entire metropolitan area only ten; yet there were forty representatives of the London bourgeoisie in the House. Where did they all find seats? London and Southwark returned men in trade and were represented in the 1701 parliament by four Bank directors and two brewers; but the other metropolitan constituencies were cool to men of this class, Middlesex returning two landed proprietors to this same parliament and Westminster two politicians recommended by the Court. In other words, all but six of the London businessmen had to secure their elections at constituencies in the provinces. This was no simple matter, for London merchants lacked the family prestige, the ancestral acres, and the assured social position to compete on equal terms with the gentry, who looked on most of the smaller boroughs as their private preserves. Citizens of London could, however, convert their commercial profits into landed wealth; and as landed proprietors, by purchase, if not by inheritance, they could aspire to found new 'county families'

[1] It is impossible in this space to document this analysis of the commercial interest. The individual businessmen are listed and classified in Appendix I, Part I.

and establish an 'interest' of their own in some local borough. The ranks of the gentry were gradually being recruited from below in this fashion, and eight or ten of the merchants in the 1701 parliament were already becoming local magnates. Sir Henry Johnson, the great Blackwall shipbuilder, sat for Aldeburgh (Suffolk), which he had purchased; Sir Robert Clayton, London banker and the wealthiest commoner of England, owned the manor and borough of Bletchingly; and half a dozen others in William's last parliament owed their seats to the estates and political influence which they had purchased in some pocket borough.[1]

Outright purchase of a small constituency was one avenue to the House, but it was not the only one. Eleven representatives of the commercial interest in William's last parliament, though residents of London, came originally from some distant parliamentary borough. Known to some voters, and remembered by more, these successful native sons gained the favour of all by frequent visits and generous donations, and ended up as their representatives in parliament. Among those who entered the House by this route we might mention the well-known London bookseller, Thomas Guy, who represented his native borough of Tamworth for fifteen years, and the brothers Robert and William Heysham, West Indies merchants, who were returned to nine successive parliaments by the voters of Lancaster, a town which they had long since left for London.[1]

Approximately half the London capitalists in the Commons owed their seats either to local influence of this sort or to property purchased in some pocket borough. The others represented constituencies to which they were utter strangers, usually seaports or 'rotten boroughs'. Wealth was all they needed here, and they dissipated fortunes made in trade on expensive election contests, often with one another, in such corrupt constituencies as promised success. Sometimes they were invited to stand for some decaying seaport, which expected them to bring business to the town. A certain Mr. Taylor of London

[1] See Appendix I, Part I.

was invited to stand for Sandwich, 'because Ramsgate, a member of this Port, had been made a flourishing town by Mr. Taylor's means; and they were in hopes, if this borough chose him a Member of Parliament, he would transfer his kindness to them, and engage some families to come and live there; it wanting inhabitants'.[1] Other boroughs, such as Grimsby, which has already been mentioned, approached wealthy Londoners with less praiseworthy motives, frankly prepared to sell out to the highest bidder. More than a dozen seaports and inland towns, scenting ultimate commercial benefits for the town or immediate cash for the voters, welcomed the candidacy of London capitalists and returned fourteen of them to the 1701 parliament. In all, representatives of the commercial interest, sitting for rotten boroughs, pocket boroughs, or large urban constituencies, made up 12 per cent. of the House, or one Member out of eight.

The profession of arms claimed almost as large a share of the membership of the House. Nearly fifty officers of the army and navy sat in the Commons: seventeen colonels of regiments (including four major-generals and three brigadier-generals), seven lieutenant-colonels, four majors, six captains, five lieutenants and cornets of horse in the army; and five admirals and four captains in the navy.[2] These officers did not quite equal the merchant Members in numbers, but they did quite eclipse them in rank—that is, the army officers did; the navy men were mostly of less distinguished background, and a higher proportion of them owed their seats to government influence rather than family connexion.

Among the army officers there were two eldest sons who were heirs apparent to English peerages, two younger sons, two younger brothers, and five other close relatives of English peers; two Irish lords and one Scottish one; two baronets and four baronets' sons. (Of the navy men, one was heir to an English

[1] Carew, op. cit., Part II, p. 114, quoting evidence given at a Sandwich election inquiry.

[2] See Appendix I, Part II.

peerage, one was younger brother, and one was younger son to an English peer.) Almost all the rest of the army officers were scions of old county families. Men with connexions like these had an easier road into the Commons than did the merchants. Twenty of them owed their seats to the estates or influence which their families possessed in some constituency; sixteen were nominees of some titled relative or patron with borough influence. Eight of the army officers sat for boroughs where the government had some interest (chiefly the garrison towns and Isle of Wight boroughs); while five of the nine naval officers sat for Admiralty boroughs.[1]

The legal profession, less aristocratic than the army, but more respectable than trade, was represented in parliament by sixty-two Members: fifty-eight barristers in the 1701 House of Commons, together with two admiralty and two chancery lawyers. Few of these gentlemen of the long robe were aristocrats. There were three younger sons of English earls; but none of the rest was connected with the peerage; unless we count two brothers-in-law of Lord Somers, a self-made lawyer of obscure birth who was made a baron only in 1697. Three were baronets or heirs to baronetcies, and another thirty were also representative of the landed gentry; but no less than twenty came from undistinguished middle-class families with no right to arms.

To all these members of the Bar a seat in parliament was a professional advantage. Legal offices usually went to Members of Parliament, and more than a third of the lawyers in the House held places of profit under the Crown. Conversely, the chief legal position in a parliamentary borough, that of Recorder, in many cases carried with it sufficient electoral influence to win the incumbent a seat in parliament. Fourteen of the barristers in the 1701 parliament were Recorders of boroughs, and all but two of them represented the boroughs where they held office. Their fellow-barristers came into the House by more familiar routes. A dozen, members of county families with long-estab-

[1] See Appendix I, Part II.

lished electoral interests, represented family boroughs. Another fifteen were henchmen, in many cases legal representatives, of some magnate who returned them to parliament. Seven or eight, holding important official positions, were returned through government influence; while half a dozen of the self-made lawyers relied, as did some merchant Members, on cash and promises to get themselves returned for some little constituency to which they were utter strangers.[1]

There remains one important occupational group,[2] the civil servants and professional politicians. One hundred and thirteen Members of William III's last parliament held offices of profit under the Crown.[3] Fifty-five of the places held by Members of Parliament were minor positions, mostly part-time sinecures in the Royal Household and the like. Posts of this nature—Gentleman of the Privy Chamber, Clerk of the Board of Green Cloth, and so on—went mostly to well-connected courtiers. Seventeen were legal positions held by gentlemen of the Bar, and eight were military and naval posts—governorships of garrisons and dockyard posts—held by regular officers of the fighting services. The thirty-one remaining offices were considerably more important. Departmentally they were distributed as follows: eight in the Admiralty and Navy Office, five in the Treasury (including Customs and Excise), three in the War Office and Ordnance, three in what would now be called the Foreign Office, two each in the Post Office and in Ireland, one in the Mint, and six others—including the position of Solicitor-General and Speaker of the House of Commons.[4]

[1] See Appendix I, Part III.

[2] The presence in this parliament of one professor and physicist (Sir Isaac Newton, M.P. Cambridge Univ.), one architect (Sir Christopher Wren, M.P. Weymouth), and one physician (Dr. John Hutton, M.P. Richmond) is unusual; considering the individuals, extraordinary.

[3] For a list of office-holders in the 1701 parliament see Appendix II, Part IV. The total is about average. Compare the contemporary *List of Gentlemen that Are in Offices Employments, &c.* (Cambridge, 1705). There is a copy in the Bodleian. This lists with surprising accuracy—when checked against official lists—the places held by 120 Members of the 1705 parliament.

[4] See Appendix II, Part IV.

Nowadays a sharp distinction would be drawn between twenty-three of the offices just listed, which would be filled by civil servants barred from the House of Commons, and the policy-making positions filled by active politicians. There was less distinction in the early eighteenth century, when both civil servants and cabinet members sat in the Commons; but even at that date the full-time administrators, like the hard-working Secretary of the Navy, were clearly differentiated from the leading politicians who held the important ministerial posts: Lord of the Treasury, Chancellor of the Exchequer, Secretary of State, Secretary at War, Lord of the Admiralty, Attorney- or Solicitor-General, and Speaker—at that time virtually a ministerial position. Of all the more than 100 'government Members' in William's last parliament only the twenty-three full-time administrators could be described as 'professional' government officials. The rest depended to a much less extent on income from government sources. Another twenty of the placemen in the Commons made politics their real career and derived the larger share of their income from the Crown; but the majority of the placemen—whether high or low—could afford to lose their positions or pensions. Of the total group nearly forty owed their seats in the Commons to government electoral influence.

Civil servants and professional politicians, lawyers, army and navy officers, and businessmen, these were the significant occupational groups within the House of Commons. As early as 1700 over 200, or more than 40 per cent., of the representatives in parliament were business or professional men. For politicians engaged in managing parliament knowledge of a Member's occupation was important. For a lawyer, a merchant, an officer, or a placeman there existed special avenues into the House and special inducements relating to his business or profession which could be used to advantage by the political manager. Knowledge of a Member's social status interested him less; but it is of some importance to the historian interested in the relations between the House of Commons and the peerage.

In the early eighteenth century the lower branch of the legislature, although powerful in money matters, had not yet become the dominant Chamber. In its proceedings it was apparently influenced, and to some degree controlled, by the Lords, who took great pains to find seats in the Commons for their relatives and dependants. To one unfamiliar with English usages the eighteenth-century House of Commons would seem very 'Uncommon'. William's last parliament, for example, included among the Commons one marquis, three earls, five viscounts, and thirteen Members styled 'Lord'. None of these was of course a peer of England. Four were peers of Scotland, seven were Irish peers, and the rest held courtesy titles.[1]

The twenty-two titles, together with the seventy-three baronetcies held by members of the House of Commons in 1701, tell us something of the social composition of that body; but little about the influence of the House of Lords. More significant is another figure—ninety-seven: the number of Members nearly related to men sitting in the Upper House. This figure breaks down as follows: thirteen eldest sons, one younger brother and heir presumptive, one younger son, nineteen younger brothers, thirteen uncles, eight nephews, seventeen first cousins, and twenty-five assorted kinsmen and in-laws less closely connected but included because the relationship seems to have had political

[1] The Scottish peers, with their constituencies, were: the Earl of Dysart (Suffolk), Viscount Irwin (Yorkshire), Viscount Newhaven (Amersham), and Lord Fairfax (Yorkshire).

The Irish peers were: the Earl of Orrery (Grinstead), the Earl of Ranelagh (West Looe), Viscount Fitzharding (Windsor), Viscount Bulkeley (Anglesey); and Lords Coningsby (Leominster), Cutts (Cambridgeshire), and Sherrard (Leicestershire).

Courtesy lords—of whom there happened to be only English ones—in William's last parliament will be found listed in Appendix I, Part V. The eldest sons of dukes and earls were by courtesy given their father's secondary title. Thus the eldest son of the Duke of Devonshire is identified in the *Official Return* as 'William Cavendish, commonly called Lord Marquis of Hartington'. Similarly, the eldest son of the Earl of Rutland was styled 'Lord Roos', until his father received a dukedom, when the son became known as the Marquis of Granby. Younger sons of dukes, but dukes only, were also styled 'Lord', in their case as a prefix to their Christian and family name: thus 'Lord James Russell', for a son of the Duke of Bedford, and so on.

significance.[1] One may object that almost any two aristocratic families of the eighteenth century will be found to be related; but in the case of this group of nearly a hundred individuals, there is evidence of only seven who belonged to a political group opposed to that of their titled relative; while another fifteen possibly owed little or nothing to their connexion with a peer.

With nearly a hundred Members attached to them by family ties it is easy to see what an important part the peers could play in directing the activities of the Lower House; but their influence is only partly indicated by the number of their relatives in the Commons. As many Members more were attached to them by equally strong ties: of friendship, gratitude for favours received, and the hope of more to come. A discussion of these clients of titled politicians falls, however, outside the scope of this chapter, which deals with the occupational and social make-up of the House of Commons. The political organization of parliament is another matter—one which doubtless would interest an eighteenth-century politician far more than an analysis of occupational and social groups. He would want to know, not whether a Member was well-born or in trade, but whether he was connected with Lord A—— or Lord B——; not whether he was a landowner or a barrister, but whether or not he would vote with the Court.

[1] See Appendix I, Part V.

CHAPTER IV

Party Groups in the Last Parliament of William III (1701–2)

An analysis of the House of Commons into political and party groups is far more important, and at the same time far more difficult than an analysis in terms of social and occupational groups. At first sight this may not seem true; for surely it should be comparatively simple to divide the Members into the two principal categories, those who voted Whig and those who voted Tory. Unfortunately the problem is not so simple. The most satisfactory information we have regarding the votes of Members of Parliament is contained in published division-lists; and these unofficial 'blacklists', published for party purposes, are not so frequent, so complete, nor so reliable as one could wish, largely because publication of a Member's vote was a breach of privilege. In all, I have been able to discover only twelve division-lists for the reigns of William and Anne, but fortunately they are concerned with nine of the most controversial issues of the period.[1] On each of these issues there was theoretically a 'Whig' and a 'Tory' position, and Members should have voted consistently on one side or the other time after time. Unfortunately the lists do not square with this theory. The 'Tory' side in any one division inevitably includes many who at other times voted 'Whig', and vice versa.

These inconsistencies not only make the task of classification into Whig and Tory extremely difficult, they demand an explanation; and of possible explanations two seem most likely. If we assume that parliament was split between those owing allegiance to Whig principles and Whig leaders and those

[1] See my article on 'Division Lists of the House of Commons, 1689–1715', printed in the *Bulletin of the Institute of Historical Research*, vol. xiv, number 40 (June 1936), pp. 25–36.

following Tory principles and leaders, inconsistencies in the division-lists will be laid to the independence, the wavering, or the desertion of individual Whig and Tory Members. On the other hand, if we assume that the Whig or Tory majority in any one division was made up of several groups united only on that particular issue or for that session, we may argue that the inconsistencies simply reflect the movement of individual groups from one coalition to another.

The choice between these two explanations will depend, of course, on one's interpretation of the party system; but since one object of this investigation is to test the validity of the two-party concept, a discussion of that subject would be premature at this point. Whether parliament was divided into two major parties and only two is a question which we must postpone, but whichever way we answer it, we can hardly close our eyes to the existence of numerous small political groups which were either component parts of larger parties or maintained separate identity.

This condition, attested by all the evidence at our disposal, is a perfectly natural one. Membership in the same class or profession and more particularly the relationship between neighbours, between the members of a family connexion, between the dependants of a magnate, and between politicians who having been associated in office elected afterwards to hold together—these furnished effective bases for cohesive groups. By correlating scattered data on the antecedents, economic interests, family and personal relationships, and political affiliations of individual Members of Parliament we should be able to identify many personal and family groups. In the succeeding pages we shall describe those which seem most important, indicating in each case the electoral strength and the number of Members returned to the 1701 parliament, together with some description of the leaders and their lieutenants; but we shall try to avoid any discussion of the politics of each group. If these knots of from five to thirty Members are the fundamental units of political organization within the House, as seems likely, our first task must be to recognize them. Once we have learned the A, B, C's of our political alphabet we can try to see how they combined to spell 'Whig', or 'Tory', 'Court', or 'Country', 'Junto' or 'High Flier'.

The only political group in the Commons organized on a professional rather than a personal or family basis was made up of administration Members, officials returned through the influence of the government. At some twenty-five constituencies the proximity of military, naval, or administrative establishments, together with the extensive patronage involved enabled the government to set up official candidates with every expectation of success. This was true of the dockyard and garrison towns. Queenborough, a 'miserable, dirty, decay'd, poor, pitiful fishing town',[1] was only five miles from Sheerness, and its seventy voters were content to be directed by the officers of the great dockyard and garrison. These gentlemen had a firm hold on both seats for Queenborough, which was usually represented by the Governor and Lieutenant-Governor of Sheerness.[2]

Similar conditions prevailed at Portsmouth and Plymouth, where elections almost invariably resulted in the return of the governor of the garrison or his nominee to one seat and an Admiralty candidate to the other. At Rochester, which had no garrison, the Admiralty had no competition from the army. One seat was invariably held by a naval officer, and in every parliament but one during Anne's reign both seats were held by admirals. The proximity of the Chatham dockyards assuredly gave the Admiralty a 'great stroke in that election'.[3]

The Isle of Wight with no dockyards and a small garrison was less important to the army and navy, but its Governor enjoyed more electoral influence than any other. Of the three island boroughs Newport, scarce a mile from the Governor's

[1] Daniel Defoe's *Tour thro' the Whole Island of Great Britain* (London, 1927 edn.), i. 110.

[2] For detailed information on this and the following constituencies see Appendix II ('Representation of Government Boroughs').

[3] Lord Weymouth to Harley, 7 Oct. 1701 (*H.M.C. Portland MSS.* iv. 24).

residence, was inevitably dominated by the government. The Governor and Lieutenant-Governor usually served as Mayor and Deputy-Mayor of the corporation and lined up the votes of the remaining twenty-two electors behind the official candidates.[1] In the other two boroughs the wishes of local borough-managers had to be respected, but since these gentlemen held commissions in the army or navy they usually worked in harmony with the Governor. 'Upon the whole matter', concluded Governor Lord Cutts, 'the King may (if he please) be master always of six voices in parliament.'[2]

Civilian officials of the administrative departments managed elections for the Court in the other boroughs where the government had influence. The Admiralty, the Treasury, and the Lord Warden of the Cinque Ports divided this influence in the eight constituencies known as the 'Cinque Ports'. In the seventeenth century the Lord Warden customarily nominated one Member for each of the Cinque Ports, and although this practice was forbidden by statute in 1691, an active incumbent could still intervene in Cinque Port elections with some success. His efforts were seldom as effective, however, as those of the Treasury and Admiralty officials, who enjoyed more extensive patronage. The voters of these little constituencies returned three Admiralty and two Treasury nominees to the 1701 parliament, as against two Members set up by the Lord Warden.[3]

The government had offices and local patronage at a number of other boroughs, and there too departmental officials enjoyed special electoral influence. The offices of the Duchy of Lancaster were located at Preston in Lancashire, and the voters of that borough normally 'complimented the Chancellor' of the Duchy by accepting his nomination for one or both seats.[4] Government influence was equally strong at Windsor, with its great royal

[1] See Sir Richard Worsley's *History of the Isle of Wight* (London, 1781), p. 157 and note (containing a list of the Newport corporation in 1698).

[2] Lord Cutts's 'Reflections upon the Government of the Isle of Wight, with regard to the Civil Power' [1693?], in *H.M.C. Frankland-Russell-Astley MSS.*, p. 77.

[3] See Appendix II.

[4] *H.M.C. Portland MSS.* iv. 325; and see Appendix II.

establishment, and both Members for this borough were usually connected with the government or the Court. At the port of Harwich, a naval centre and headquarters for the Post-Office packets plying between England and the Continent, the government influence was shared by the Post-Office, the Treasury, and the Admiralty. All three departments sought to pack the corporation with employees and dependants, and their efforts met with considerable success. Early in Anne's reign the corporation included: one Navy Storekeeper, together with his uncle, who was Steward of the borough, and the latter's son; two other Admiralty employees; five captains of Post-Office packets; the local Post-Office agent and his brother-in-law; and two government contractors.[1] Together they comprised nearly half the membership of the corporation, whose thirty-two members alone voted in parliamentary elections; and the representation of Harwich reflected this efficient modelling of the electorate. A navy commissioner and a government banker sat for Harwich in the 1701 parliament.[2]

At the remaining boroughs which returned official candidates the government influence was less direct, though often effective. In half a dozen of the smaller seaports the patronage at the disposal of the Customs and Excise branches of the Treasury and that dispensed by the Admiralty enabled those departments to return employees or friends. To the 1701 parliament Arundel returned the Surveyor of the Navy; Shoreham, a navy commissioner and a contractor for the navy; Southampton, a West Indies governor and the chief clerk in the War Office; and the double-constituency of Weymouth–Melcombe Regis, another navy commissioner, the Surveyor of the Works, a major-general, and a pensioner.[2] Finally, the borough of Westminster returned official candidates on occasion. In 1701 it chose the Secretary of State for the Northern Department as

[1] See the report of the Committee on Elections, in *C.J.* xvi. 51; xvii. 541–2, 708–10. Both the sitting Members and the petitioners conceded that all these placemen were corporation members. The question was whether their votes were still valid once they ceased to reside at Harwich.

[2] See Appendix II.

one of its Members, and a well-known Court politician as the other.[1] All in all thirty-eight members of William's last parliament were returned from these 'government boroughs'—the majority owing both their offices and their seats to government influence.[2]

Sometimes outstripping the government in the business of electioneering was a group of prominent lords and commoners whose political influence must now be briefly assessed. Since these men are the *dramatis personae,* they have to be listed here; and although the catalogue of names, relationships, and parliamentary constituencies which follows makes dull reading indeed, it is a necessary prelude to much of the later discussion.

Greatest election manager of the period, and so acknowledged by his contemporaries, was Thomas, fifth Lord Wharton. Head of a family established in the north in the reign of Edward I, Wharton inherited large estates in half a dozen counties. In Cumberland and Westmorland the family interest, based on land wrested from the monasteries during the Reformation, was strengthened by the purchase of burgages at Cockermouth and Appleby. At both boroughs Wharton faced competition from titled rivals, but one seat at each constituency usually went to his nominees. Wharton was equally successful in returning his friends for Richmond and Northallerton in neighbouring Yorkshire, where he had similar interests based on burgage ownership and strategically located estates.

In the south Wharton's electoral influence was even more impressive. From his mother he had inherited considerable Buckinghamshire property; and the boroughs of Aylesbury, Wycombe, and Marlow, which bordered upon his estates, were under his control. To return candidates for the shire and the remaining Buckinghamshire boroughs was more difficult, but with the assistance of strategically placed henchmen even this was possible. At elections for the town of Buckingham 'my

[1] See Appendix II.

[2] See Appendix III: 'Party Groups in the 1701 Parliament', Part I.

Lord Wharton and several others of his Gang appear'd there and made interest',[1] and the thirteen electors usually returned his Lordship's friends. At Wendover the trick was turned with the help of a kinsman, Richard Hampden, who had a family interest in that borough, based on large estates near by; while in county elections the 'crew that herded with Lord Wharton'[2] helped him to return his nominees. Amersham, pocket borough of the Drakes, was the only constituency in the county which Wharton could not influence; but he made up this deficiency to some extent by picking up still another seat at the borough of Brackley close by in Northamptonshire.

Elections in Wiltshire tell much the same story; for Wharton owned considerable property in this county, and had important political friends in at least four Wiltshire boroughs. At Malmesbury he named both Members; and by concerting measures with his Wiltshire 'gang' he was able to influence elections at Chippenham, Cricklade, and Calne. Seldom powerful enough to name candidates for the county, Wharton was unflagging in his efforts to return men who were friendly, whether standing for Wiltshire or Yorkshire, for Cirencester or Devizes; and altogether he managed to secure the election of ten kinsmen plus fifteen other followers, including five Yorkshire Members, to the last parliament of William III.[3]

The success with which Wharton managed this aggregation of electoral interests was a tribute to his skill, no less than to the length of his purse and the excellence of his horses at election time. His electoral influence, great as it was, however,

[1] *Remarks and Collections of Thomas Hearne* (ed. for the Oxford Hist. Soc. by C. E. Doble, 1885–1918), i. 117.

[2] *Verney Letters of the Eighteenth Century from the MSS. at Claydon House*, ed. Lady Verney (London, 1930), i. 159 ff., 164. The *Verney Letters* throw a revealing light on Bucks. elections, as does also the anonymous *Memoirs of the Life of Thomas, Late Marquess of Wharton* (London, 1715).

[3] For Wharton's part in Wiltshire elections see the interesting correspondence between him and his henchmen printed by Lord Lansdowne in his article 'Wiltshire Politicians *circa* 1700' (in *Wiltshire Archaeological and Natural History Magazine*, xlvi. 60–81). For a list of his followers in the 1701 parliament see Appendix III, Part II.

was only a part of a larger aggregate; for Wharton had three close associates, the Lords Somers, Halifax, and Orford, each of whom possessed electoral influence in his own right, influence which stemmed from individual family estates and connexions but which was pooled for the common benefit of the group. The lords of the 'Junto', as the alliance was called by contemporaries, had formed a partnership early in William's reign. Later we shall have much to say of the role which the Junto played in national politics; but at this stage of the argument we are interested in these men solely in their capacity as borough managers.

In the sphere of electioneering John, first Lord Somers, was the least important. Son of a Worcestershire attorney, Somers used his great talents to win brilliant success at the Bar. Entering parliament he became a leading statesman, ultimately attaining the woolsack; but lacking noble connexions and great estates his electoral influence was slight. A grant by King William of the manor of Reigate in Surrey gave him control of a seat for that borough; but this was the extent of his electoral interest, unless we include Tewkesbury, which was controlled by a son-in-law of his first friend and patron, together with Worcester, where his influence as former Member and distinguished native son was considerable enough to secure the return of a friend and associate in the 1701 election. Himself a famous member of the Middle Temple, Somers named two lawyers of that Inn as his candidates for Reigate and Worcester; and counted among his henchmen other Middle Temple barristers—in particular his two brothers-in-law, Charles Cocks and Sir Joseph Jekyll. Including these two, whose election was secured only indirectly by their titled brother-in-law, Somers's following in the 1701 parliament numbered only six Members.[1]

In the business of electioneering Somers was outstripped by those members of the Junto who sprang from long-established, noble families with widespread hereditary electoral interests.

[1] For Somers's electoral influence see the anonymous *Memoirs of Lord Somers* (London, 1716), p. 41; and see Appendix III.

Charles Montagu, first Lord Halifax, was a cadet of such a family—one with three earldoms. True, he was the younger son of a younger son and had to carve out his own career in politics and public finance; but the political influence which he won by his brilliant conduct in the office of Chancellor of the Exchequer during William's reign was supplemented by the important electoral influence of the Montagus.

Halifax's elder brother, head of the cadet Montagus of Horton, controlled one seat at Northampton, five miles from his estate, and returned his younger brother to the 1701 parliament. The neighbouring county of Huntingdon was traditionally the preserve of Halifax's Montagu cousins, the Earls of Manchester and Sandwich. Lord Manchester, head of the Kimbolton Montagus and a stepson as well as first cousin of Halifax, usually returned one Member for the county; but from 1698 to 1705 this proved beyond his powers. The remaining three Huntingdonshire Members were usually named by the Montagus of Hinchinbroke, Earls of Sandwich; but here, too, there were difficulties. The Hinchinbroke interest, built up by Pepys's patron, the first Earl, was supposedly managed in this period by his grandson, the third Lord Sandwich, who like Manchester was doubly related to Halifax. This nobleman unfortunately, was *non compos mentis*, so that control of the family interest remained in dispute between his two closest relatives. Under the circumstances the second county seat also went by default, while the earl's mother and his uncle quarrelled over Huntingdon borough, just outside the gates of Hinchinbroke. In the 1701 parliament one seat was held by a cousin and nominee of Lady Sandwich; the other, by a younger son of the Honourable Sidney Wortley Montagu, the earl's uncle, who was likewise trustee and mortgagee of the family estates and was soon to win both Huntingdon seats for his branch of the family, which already held two seats in parliament not counting that for Huntingdon.[1]

[1] For the representative history of Huntingdonshire in this period see the account, based on papers at Hinchinbroke, in *The Victoria History of the*

To these four Montagu relatives of Halifax sitting in the 1701 parliament must be added a brother-in-law sitting for a Hampshire borough, a first cousin, Lord Irwin, knight of the shire for Yorkshire, and, finally, the celebrated Sir Isaac Newton, Member for Cambridge University in this same parliament, who, although not a kinsman, owed his seat largely to the good offices of his friend and patron Halifax.[1] All in all there were seven Members of William's last parliament attached to the Montagu interest.[2]

Lord Orford, fourth member of the Junto, might well be included among those attached to the Montagu interest, for he and Halifax were distantly related; but Orford, like Halifax, could count on a large and influential family interest in his own right. Born Edward Russell, of the ducal house of Bedford, Orford sprang from a great titled family, but like Halifax he was the younger son of a younger son and had to make his own way. Entering the navy he rose soon to high rank, and after his victory at La Hogue in 1692 was rewarded with first place at the Admiralty Board and a peerage. In the course of his career Orford built up an important following of naval officers and administrators, some with seats in parliament which they owed originally to Admiralty influence. Two of Orford's professional henchmen held seats in the 1701 parliament, although both they and their chief no longer held office.[2]

To these navy Members must be added one Member returned through Orford's own influence in Cambridgeshire. An important landowner in the county and Lord Steward of the borough of Cambridge, Orford managed to name one knight of the shire in 1701,[3] but this local influence was of far less importance than

County of Huntingdon, ii. 22–38. See also *Court and Society from Elizabeth to Anne*, edited from the papers at Kimbolton by the Duke of Manchester (London, 1864), ii. 85.

[1] For Newton see L. T. More, *Isaac Newton: a Biography* (London, 1934), chap. 12.

[2] See Appendix III, Part II.

[3] See 'The Representative History of the County, Town and University of Cambridge', unpublished thesis by D. Cooke deposited at the Institute for Historical Research, London.

the fact that the admiral was 'supported by so many relations and strong alliances'.[1] Chief among these, of course, was the senior branch of Orford's own family, the Bedford Russells, which usually managed to name all four Members for the county and town of Bedford, plus two more for the Devon borough of Tavistock, which was surrounded by the Duke of Bedford's estates. With the first Duke of Bedford, head of the family until his death in 1700, Orford was closely connected in the double capacity of nephew and son-in-law—the third Junto lord to be connected, through blood and marriage both, with the chieftain of the clan. With the old duke's grandson and successor, a lad barely out of his 'teens, the admiral was less intimate. The young duke was a great admirer of one of Orford's enemies, and Junto candidates would have fared badly in the Russell boroughs had the choice been left to him; but fortunately the old duke's surviving sons were content to follow the lead of their cousin and brother-in-law. Together they held both Tavistock seats and one for Bedfordshire in the 1701 parliament, and the three remaining Russell seats were held by Members similarly inclined.

Later the Devon seats were to be lost to the Junto until the young duke 'recovered from his infatuation and returned to the principles of his family'.[2] Meanwhile Orford benefited from the electoral influence of the young duke's brothers-in-law, who were also nephews of Orford, but better disposed. The Marquesses of Hartington and Granby, sons and heirs apparent of the Dukes of Devonshire and Rutland, respectively, were protégés of Orford and helped to place the electoral influence of both great families at his disposal, so that Cavendish candidates for Derby and Manners candidates for Grantham and Leicestershire were usually friends of Orford. Half a dozen Members, including the two marquesses and their friends and relations,

[1] *The Private Correspondence of Sarah, Duchess of Marlborough* (2nd edn., London, 1838), i. 205.

[2] *Private Correspond. of Lady Marlborough*, i. 206. For the representative history of Tavistock see J. J. Alexander's article on 'Tavistock as a Parliamentary Borough' in *Devonshire Association Reports*, xliii. 370–7.

were returned for these constituencies and helped swell the total of Orford's following in William's last parliament to fifteen in all.[1]

This total, respectable as it is, does not include the little group of M.P.s centred on Charles, Lord Spencer, last of Orford's 'many relations and strong alliances'. Youngest by far of the Junto lords and the last to be taken into the partnership, Spencer hardly ranks as one of the firm until later. Son and heir-apparent of Robert, second Earl of Sunderland, a notoriously shifty politician, Spencer was elected M.P. for Tiverton upon his coming of age in 1695 and held the seat until he inherited the title soon after the death of King William. In addition to his influence at Tiverton, which the young lord charmed with his personality and the gift of a 'large Fire Engine', Spencer had some slight influence in Northamptonshire and a more solid interest at Coventry in Warwickshire, cemented by a friendship with the wealthy and influential family of Hopkins, one of whom sat for Coventry in the 1701 parliament.[2] With the addition of Spencer himself, his colleague at Tiverton, and his friend Hopkins, the number of M.P.s in William's last parliament grouped around Orford reaches the surprising total of eighteen[1]—only seven less than the indefatigable Wharton could muster.

Each of the groups which we have just described—the numerous henchmen of Wharton and Orford as well as the smaller following of Somers and Halifax—was clearly made up simply of 'friends and relations' and formed one of those personal blocs which it seems to us were the fundamental units of party organization in this early period. Already, however, by treating these four groups together we have carried our

[1] See Appendix III, Part II.

[2] For Tiverton and the 'fire engine' see W. Harding's *History of Tiverton* (Tiverton, 1847), ii, Book 3, p. 224. For the Hopkins family see 'Memoirs of Edward Hopkins', selections from a MS. autobiography edited by M. D. Harris, in the *English Historical Review*, xxxiv. 495 et seq. See also T. W. Whitley, *The Parliamentary Representation of the City of Coventry* (Coventry, 1894), pp. 110–46.

classification one step farther and have started to combine some of the letters of our political alphabet, to use the same metaphor, into a larger entity which we have termed the 'Junto connexion'. Nevertheless, we are still confining the discussion to the limits set forth some pages above, inasmuch as the Junto leaders themselves formed just such a personal group as was there defined. The four older Junto chiefs were Members of the Lower House together until some years after the Revolution, three of them were related, and all four were old friends and had been associated together in office. The fact that their combined following totalled fifty-six Members in the 1701 parliament was due simply to the exceptional electoral influence of each individual Junto lord, which was no different qualitatively from that of many another titled borough manager.

Actually the Junto connexion was even larger, for we must take into account the nominees of another seldom-mentioned adherent of the Junto, the Duke of Bolton. Charles Powlett, second Duke of Bolton, owed his position as principal landowner of Hampshire to the many acres of monastic land bestowed by Henry VIII on his ancestor William Powlett, first Marquis of Winchester. Styled 'Marquis of Winchester' until the death of his father in 1699, Bolton served a political apprenticeship of eighteen years as Member for Hampshire, plus a year as a Lord Justice in Ireland. A close friend of the Junto lords he proved a valuable associate. In alliance with a local family he controlled the Hampshire borough of Lymington.[1] At Whitchurch, Petersfield, Andover, and Winchester in the same county, and at St. Ives in Cornwall, he recommended candidates with considerable success, returning in all nine Members to the last parliament of William III.[2]

We could easily include among the adherents of the Junto other peers who frequently co-operated at election time and occasionally found seats for friends and relatives of the Junto leaders; but these nobles were not, like Bolton, of the inner

[1] See p. 17 for the borough of Lymington.

[2] See App. III, Part II.

group of personal friends. To list their followers at this point as though they too belonged to the Junto connexion would be to go beyond the limits which we set for this stage of the discussion. We must return instead to the business of cataloguing the separate oligarchic groups led by territorial magnates like Bolton, but differing from Bolton's in that they formed no integral part of the Junto connexion.

Chief among these was the following of John Holles, first and last Duke of Newcastle of that creation. Inheritor of huge estates from the Holles and Cavendish families, Newcastle dominated Nottinghamshire elections, naming three Members to the 1701 parliament from that county.[1] In addition he had just purchased two pocket boroughs in Yorkshire; and while he had not yet consolidated his hold on Aldborough and Boroughbridge as early as 1701, one of the successful candidates for these two constituencies was a Newcastle man.[2] Apart from the help which he could furnish to candidates for Westminster, where he owned a great deal of property, these four Members were all that Newcastle himself could return; but this little group by no means represented the whole of the duke's parliamentary influence.

Perhaps the wealthiest peer of all England,[3] Newcastle was also the central and most influential figure in a network of important relationships embracing the families of Pierrepont, Watson, Fane, Pelham, and Townshend. The Earl of Kingston, head of the Pierreponts, and Lord Rockingham, head of the Watsons, were first cousins. Kingston, like Newcastle, was an important landowner in Nottinghamshire and helped the duke return candidates acceptable to them both.[4] Rockingham,

[1] See Appendix III. Cf. also Newcastle's correspondence, in *H.M.C. Portland MSS*. ii. 173–230, *passim*; Carew, op. cit., *sub* 'East Retford', 'Newark', and 'Nottingham'.

[2] See the election correspondence regarding these two boroughs, printed in *Records of a Yorkshire Manor*, ed. by Sir Thomas Lawson-Tancred (London, 1937), *passim*.

[3] *H.M.C. Portland MSS*. ii. 182. Newcastle's income was estimated at £40,000 a year. See Cornelius Brown, *History of Nottinghamshire* (London, 1891), p. 206.

[4] *H.M.C. Portland MSS*. ii. 182, 185–6, 195.

together with another of the duke's cousins, Thomas Fane, Earl of Westmorland, owned property in Kent and helped return a brother-in-law to William's last parliament.[1] In the matter of electoral influence, however, the most important of all the families allied with Newcastle were the Pelhams, headed by the duke's brother-in-law, and the Townshends, whose chief was a second cousin of Newcastle and an in-law of the Pelhams.

Sir Thomas Pelham, brother-inlaw of Newcastle and also of Townshend, was the fourth baronet of the family of Pelham of Laughton, an important landowner in Sussex, and the manager of electoral interests in the county and the local constituencies of Lewes, Seaford, Hastings, and Rye. In William's last parliament both Members for Lewes were Pelhams; and the two Members for Sussex and one of the Cinque Port barons were attached to the Pelham connexion.[1] Pelham's electoral interests in Sussex were matched by the influence which his son-in-law Townshend enjoyed in Norfolk. As Lord Lieutenant and the only Protestant peer of any consequence in that county, Charles, second Viscount Townshend, enjoyed a natural ascendancy which was reflected by the return in the 1701 election of his brother and a friend as knights of the shire.[1] In addition Townshend was closely connected with the one family that had a comparable influence in Norfolk politics—the Walpoles of Houghton.

Inheriting the title as a child, Townshend was brought up by the elder Robert Walpole, his guardian until he attained his majority. He and the younger Robert Walpole were together at Eton and King's College, Cambridge, and their early association developed into a close friendship which was strengthened some years later by Townshend's marriage to Walpole's sister. From the beginning their careers ran together. Townshend took his seat in the Lords in 1698, and soon after, his friend Walpole, become unexpectedly the head of his family, left college, abandoning all thought of the Church, for which as

[1] See Appendix III, Part III.

a younger son he had originally been destined, and joined Townshend as a novice in politics.

Entering the House of Commons was the first step and an easy one. At Castle Rising, a little borough owned originally by the Dukes of Norfolk, the Walpoles had purchased sufficient burgages to give them control of one seat. Walpole's father had represented this constituency from 1689 until his death twelve years later, and Walpole simply took his father's place in William's last parliament.[1] To two of the older Norfolk Members—those for Lynn—he was no stranger. This flourishing seaport was represented in this period by two members of the Turner family, which had long been prominent in the trade and politics of the borough. Sir John Turner had represented Lynn since 1679, and his nephew since 1695. Both were associated with the Walpoles, and Sir Charles Turner, the junior Member, was Robert Walpole's brother-in-law. They were soon to be colleagues as well, for in the 1702 election Walpole exchanged Castle Rising for Lynn, replacing the elder Turner, who retired. For the next forty years the brothers-in-law were returned in election after election, until the death of one and the removal of the other to the Lords at length broke up this long association.[2]

Together Walpole and Townshend accounted for six Members in William's last parliament, Pelham for five, Rockingham for one, and Newcastle for four, bringing the total for the Newcastle connexion to sixteen Members. Only four other family connexions, in addition to those already discussed, could boast of delegations in the Commons as large as, or larger than this; but before turning to them it would be well to dispose of five peers of high rank whose territorial influence enabled them to nominate Members of Parliament, but who lacked the extensive family alliances of a Newcastle and seldom mustered more than a handful of disciples in the Lower House. These were the

[1] See H. H. Bradfer-Lawrence's 'Castle Rising and the Walpoles', in *A Supplement to Blomefield's Norfolk* (ed. Clement Ingleby, London, 1929).

[2] See Bradfer-Lawrence's 'The Merchants of Lynn', also in *A Supplement to Blomefield's Norfolk.*

Duke of Somerset, and the Earls of Carlisle, Pembroke, Radnor, and Stamford.

Through his wife, heiress of the Earls of Northumberland, Charles Seymour, sixth Duke of Somerset, controlled the great estates of the Percies. These enabled him to return one or more Northern Members; while his own extensive holdings in Sussex and Wiltshire gave him considerable electoral interest in these two counties. We can identify as nominees of the duke two Members in William's last parliament, one for the Cumberland borough of Cockermouth, the other for the Wiltshire constituency of Marlborough.[1]

Somerset's electoral interest in the north was quite overshadowed by Lord Carlisle's. Charles Howard, third Earl of Carlisle and holder of the ancient baronies of Gilsland and Greystoke, controlled both seats at Morpeth, usually named one Member for Carlisle, and had considerable influence in elections for the counties of Cumberland and Northumberland. In William's last parliament both Morpeth Members and one of the Carlisle representatives can be identified as the Earl's nominees, and three of the four knights of the shire for Cumberland and Northumberland undoubtedly owed their election largely to Lord Carlisle's assistance.[1]

Carlisle's influence in the north was matched by Lord Radnor's influence in Cornwall. Charles Bodvile Robartes, second Earl of Radnor, inherited the estates of at least three wealthy West Country families, a fact which partly explains his electoral influence at Bodmin, Bossiney, Lostwithiel, and Tregoney—small Cornish boroughs which together returned five members of Lord Radnor's family to the 1701 parliament.[1]

The Earls of Pembroke and Stamford had no such extensive interests. Thomas Herbert, eighth Earl of Pembroke and fifth Earl of Montgomery, was Lord of the manor of Wilton and controlled elections at that little Wiltshire borough. Extensive estates in the Welsh Marches enabled him to influence elections

[1] See Appendix III, Part IV.

in Monmouthshire as well. Three Members of William's last parliament owed their seats to Pembroke; and half a dozen to Lord Stamford. Thomas Grey, second Earl of Stamford, was proprietor of the Devonshire borough of Beeralston and named both its Members. He was also Steward of Leicester, some five miles from his seat at Broadgate, and local and official influence combined enabled him to secure the return of his Deputy as Member for Leicester in the 1701 election.[1]

One could name a dozen more peers who had electoral influence in single constituencies; but there is no need to catalogue them here. Rather we should go on to describe the four great family connexions comparable in size to the Junto group, organized on the same family and personal basis, and headed by Marlborough and Godolphin, by Lord Nottingham, by Lord Rochester and Sir Edward Seymour, and by Robert Harley, respectively.

Although John Churchill did not achieve his fame until the reign of Anne, he had long been recognized as an accomplished courtier and politician. His father, Sir Winston Churchill, was a Court politician and placeman, a protégé of Lord Arlington, and a Member of the Cavalier parliament; and as such could place his children in positions about the king. His daughter Arabella was the first to come to Court, and in the sixties she became maid of honour to the Duchess of York, and in due course one of the duke's mistresses. Soon afterwards her brother John was made one of the duke's pages, and it was due to James's influence that he received his first commission in the Guards. From 1670 to 1675 Churchill saw active service, swiftly attaining the rank of colonel, success due partly to the patronage of Barbara Villiers, the king's mistress, in whose favours Churchill had a generous share. Military service ceased in 1675, and thereafter Churchill turned once more to the Court.

It was there that he found his wife, the beautiful and

[1] See Appendix III. As Chancellor of the Duchy of Lancaster Stamford named three Members for Duchy boroughs as well.

imperious Sarah Jennings, maid of honour to the Duchess of York. It was a love match, opposed from the first by Churchill's father, who had picked out a desirable heiress; but it proved a milestone in Churchill's career. For during the succeeding years, while Churchill was in constant attendance on the duke and engaged in carrying out his numerous commands, Sarah consolidated her extraordinary hold on the duke's younger daughter, the Princess Anne. When her future husband came from Denmark to woo the Princess, it was Colonel Churchill who escorted him. Soon all the Churchills were intimate members of Anne's family circle. Sarah became one of the Princess's Bedchamber Ladies; her brother-in-law became one of Prince George's Gentlemen, together with Charles Churchill, the last of the brothers; and royal favour no doubt assisted Charles and George Churchill's rapid rise in the army and navy, their respective professions. John Churchill had his rewards, as well. His services to James earned him a barony. His timely adherence to the Prince of Orange won him an earldom; but Anne was not satisfied and urged William to promise him the highest honour, the blue ribbon of the Garter.[1]

The favoured position which the Churchills enjoyed at the Princess Anne's Court was strengthened by a certain amount of electoral and parliamentary influence. George Churchill held a seat in William's parliaments for the Hertfordshire borough of St. Albans, where Lady Marlborough's family owned property and enjoyed a family influence. The Churchills owned Dorset estates, and the other brother Charles represented Weymouth in that county from 1698 until his death. Marlborough's secretary also held a seat in William's last parliament.[2] The Churchill connexion in parliament was not limited to these three Members, however, for it also included the followers and kinsmen of Marlborough's closest friend.

The intimacy between Marlborough and Sidney, first Baron

[1] See the letters of Anne to William, printed in Sir John Dalrymple's *Memoirs of Great Britain and Ireland* (London, 1790), iii. 255–6.

[2] See Appendix III, Part V.

Godolphin began when they were pages at Court together. Thereafter as trusted servants of Charles and James Stuart they were in constant association, and the growing friendship between them was cemented in 1698 by the marriage of Marlborough's eldest daughter to his friend's eldest son. In the private correspondence between the members of Anne's circle, the Princess was 'Mrs. Morley'; the Marlboroughs, 'Mr. and Mrs. Freeman'; and Godolphin, 'Mr. Montgomery'.

'Mr. Montgomery' was not only a close friend, he was an important ally as well; for he possessed considerable electoral influence. In addition to both seats for the Cornish borough of Helston, which was under his control and which returned two members of his family to the 1701 parliament, he could count on seats at Penryn, Tregoney, and Truro, Cornish boroughs controlled by his kinsmen, the Boscawens of Tregothnan. Three of the six Members returned for these boroughs in William's last parliament can be identified as relatives or nominees of Godolphin's nephew, Hugh Boscawen the younger, who had just succeeded to the family estates. The son of Godolphin's sister, and the husband of Marlborough's niece, Boscawen was doubly tied to the Churchill connexion, but in 1701 he was not yet of age to represent any of the family boroughs in person.

We should include finally in the Churchill's group, Godolphin's own cousin, Lord Fitzharding, who was a kinsman as well of Marlborough and like the Churchills held a post in the Princess's household, together with a seat for the Court borough of Windsor; and also Lady Godolphin's cousin, John Hervey of Ickworth, patron of the Suffolk borough of Bury, which he and his father-in-law represented in William's last parliament.[1] In all, then, the Marlborough–Godolphin connexion mustered twelve Members in the 1701 parliament.[2]

A family connexion far more extensive than that of Marlborough and Godolphin centred on Daniel Finch, second Earl of Nottingham, son of Charles II's chief law officer and subse-

[1] See above, p. 16. [2] See Appendix III, Part V.

quent Lord Chancellor. Although a prominent figure and the political leader of the group, Nottingham himself had comparatively little electoral influence outside the tiny county of Rutland, where his chief estate was located. Many of his relatives, however, possessed electoral influence or themselves held seats in parliament. His brother, Heneage Finch, had succeeded their father as Member for Oxford University and was elected for the sixth time in 1701. In 1700 Heneage had married his daughter to William Legge, second Lord Dartmouth, so that he counted a son-in-law as well as a brother in the Lords.

The Upper House, as a matter of fact, was the Chamber where lay Nottingham's chief strength; but he counted among his kinsmen so many friends and followers in both Houses that it will pay us to follow out the Finch family connexions systematically and in some detail. We may well begin with Nottingham's relatives on the Finch side. In addition to his brother Heneage, his immediate family included an only sister, Lady Elizabeth Finch, who married Sir Samuel Grimstone, son of the well-known Sir Harbottle Grimstone and M.P. for St. Albans for some twenty years. By Sir Samuel she had an only daughter, married in 1687 to William Savile, Lord Eland, son and heir-apparent of the great 'Trimmer', George, first Marquis of Halifax. Halifax died in 1695, his son in 1700, and Sir Samuel Grimstone in the same year; but the connexion between the Finches and the Saviles, which had other links as well, was of considerable importance during Lord Halifax's later years. As for Lady Grimstone, she died soon after marriage; but her brother Nottingham apparently remained on close terms with her nephews by marriage. These included Sir James Howe, who had electoral influence at Hindon in Wilts. and represented that borough for some years, though not in the 1701 parliament; Colonel Henry Lee, Member for Canterbury in 1701 and in five previous parliaments, thanks partly to the Finch connexion; and Sir George Rooke, naval officer and Member for Portsmouth since 1698.[1]

[1] See Appendix III, Part VI.

Nottingham's only remaining relative on the Finch side was his second cousin, Charles, third Earl of Winchilsea, head of the senior branch of the family. Seated at Eastwell in Kent, Winchilsea had some electoral influence in that county and was probably partly instrumental in the return of four Members for various constituencies in that region in the 1701 election. But Winchilsea's interest, like Nottingham's, was less important than the electoral influence at the disposal of his various relatives, in Winchilsea's case Lord Weymouth and Lord Bruce. Thomas Thynne, first Viscount Weymouth, was Winchilsea's uncle, as well as Halifax's own cousin (another link between the Finches and the 'Trimmer') and a close friend of Nottingham. Weymouth had large estates and a good interest in Wiltshire, and considerable influence at Weymouth (Dorset) and Tamworth (Staffs.); but we can identify only one Thynne nominee in William's last parliament, Weymouth's son Henry, who was returned, however, for two different constituencies. The other family connected with Winchilsea, the Bruces, inherited estates in Wiltshire from the Seymour family. Charles, Lord Bruce, son and heir-apparent of the exiled Jacobite, Thomas, second Earl of Ailesbury, did not come of age until 1703; but as acting head of the family and owner of Tottenham and Savernake Forest he was in a position to influence elections at Bedwin and Marlborough. Lord Bruce apparently made no effort to set up candidates in 1701; but in the following year he secured seats for two Bruce uncles. A second cousin of Winchilsea Bruce later became allied with the other Finches through his marriage, in 1706, with Lady Anne Savile, granddaughter of the 'Trimmer' and of Nottingham's sister, Lady Grimstone.

Nottingham's connexions through his mother and his two wives were more widespread and more important. Little need be said about Nottingham's first countess. Daughter and co-heir of Robert Rich, third Earl of Warwick, she bore her husband an only daughter, through whom Nottingham was connected by still another link with the Saviles; for three days before Halifax's death his only surviving son married this Lady Mary

Finch, who became the second Lady Eland in succession to her father's niece. Various other relatives of the first Lady Nottingham might also be mentioned: namely her two nephews, Henry St. John, of whom more below, and Sir Charles Barrington, Member for Essex since 1694 and a follower of Nottingham; together with her first cousin Warwick Lake, M.P. for Middlesex since 1698, and the latter's uncle, Edward Brereton, M.P. for Denbigh since 1689.

Lord Nottingham's connexions through his second countess were far more important. Only daughter (whose issue became sole heir) of the Viscount Hatton, the second Lady Nottingham had a surprising number of kinsmen in both Houses. Her father, Christopher, first Viscount Hatton, still attended parliament on occasion, though nearly eighty; as did his brother-in-law, Viscount Longueville. Her mother was a Tufton, sister of Thomas, sixth Earl of Thanet, a follower of his nephew Nottingham in the Lords and patron of the Westmorland borough of Appleby, which was persuaded to return Lord Thanet's uncle in the 1701 election, despite stiff opposition from Lord Wharton.[1]

Finally, Lady Nottingham was connected through her Montagu grandmother with no less than five peers, most of whom were friends and allies of her husband. Of her first cousin Lord Yarmouth we need say little, since he refused the oaths and was barred from the Lords; nor need we say much of her second cousin Lord North and Grey, who had a seat in the Upper House, but was too busily engaged in military campaigns to take more than a nominal interest in politics until late in Anne's reign. Lady Nottingham's other North cousins, however, cannot be passed over so lightly.

Her first cousin once removed, Francis North, first Baron Guilford, was long associated in office with Nottingham's father, whom he succeeded as Attorney-General and later as Lord Keeper. His eldest son Francis, second Lord Guilford, was second cousin of Lady Nottingham and one of those who voted

[1] See Appendix III, Part VI.

with Nottingham in the Lords. Patron of the Oxfordshire borough of Banbury, scarce two miles from the family seat at Wroxton, he secured the return of his brother Charles North to William's last two parliaments and all of Anne's but the last. In addition he had in-laws with political influence. His father-in-law Fulke Greville, fifth Lord Brooke, was another who voted with Nottingham in the Upper House; and like Guilford he was also a borough patron, for the Grevilles owned historic Warwick castle and controlled the borough, which was represented in the 1701 parliament by Francis and Algernon Greville, sons of Lord Brooke and brothers-in-law of Guilford.

Three more distant kinsmen of Lady Nottingham should also be mentioned, the Earls of Abingdon, Exeter, and Anglesey; for, while only third cousins of Nottingham's wife, all three were close friends and clearly belong to the Finch connexion. Montague Bertie, second Earl of Abingdon, headed the junior branch of that important family. His uncle Robert, third Earl of Lindsey, who headed the elder line, seated in Lincolnshire, was a near relation of Danby and one of his disciples. No friend of Nottingham he was identified, at least after the Revolution, with the Court. His half-brother James took a different line. Eldest son of the second Lord Lindsey by his second wife, granddaughter and heiress of the last Norreys Earl of Berkshire, he inherited from his mother important estates in Oxfordshire and Berkshire in addition to the Barony of Norreys of Rycote. As though this were not enough he married the heiress of the Wiltshire family of Danvers, who brought him the manor of Westbury and he was subsequently created Earl of Abingdon.

His son Montague, who succeeded him in 1699, had sat in the Commons for ten years as knight of the shire for both Berkshire and Oxfordshire. Throughout this period he voted with the Finches and must be counted as one of Nottingham's most important adherents, chiefly on account of his electoral influence. Patron of Westbury and one of the most important landowners in the counties which he represented in parliament, he managed to return no less than six members of his family to William's last parliament.[1]

His cousin Lord Exeter was likewise a kinsman and follower of Nottingham, but not nearly so influential. John Cecil, who succeeded as sixth Earl of Exeter in 1700, had sat for the previous five years as Member for Nottingham's home county of Rutland. Lord of the Honour and Castle of Stamford and High Steward of the borough he controlled one seat for that Lincolnshire constituency, which was represented in 1701 by his brother William Cecil; and doubtless contributed to the return of the second Member, Abingdon's uncle, Charles Bertie. Exeter's first cousin, John Annesley, sixth Earl of Anglesey, the last of these three kinsmen and friends of Nottingham, was less important. Succeeding to the title at the very end of William's reign, his political activities and those of his Annesley relatives were wholly confined to the period of William's successor.

We have finally to speak of Nottingham's relatives through his mother, daughter of a London merchant named Harvey and niece of the celebrated Dr. Harvey who discovered the circulation of the blood. Her brother, Sir Daniel Harvey, was Ambassador to the Porte and Member of Parliament during Charles II's reign; but his sons did not enter parliament until after 1702. The same is true of the Derings, another family allied with Nottingham through the Harveys. Sir Edward Dering, second baronet of Surrenden and head of a Kentish family long associated with the Finches, married Sarah Harvey, Nottingham's aunt. He was a Member of all of Charles II's parliaments, and his son sat in the Commons during part of that reign, as did his son-in-law Sir Robert Southwell, a diplomat of note and Clerk of the Privy Council; but no member of the family was returned during William's reign.

The case was different with the Bulkeleys, an influential Welsh family headed by Robert, second Viscount Bulkeley in the Irish peerage, who married Nottingham's other Harvey aunt. This family virtually monopolized the representation of

[1] See Appendix III, Part VI.

Anglesey and Carnarvon, two north-western shires of Wales. Carnarvonshire was represented by Lord Bulkeley during Charles II's later years and by his brother during most of the next thirty years. County Anglesey was even more of a family preserve, returning Lord Bulkeley to James II's parliament, his brother to the Convention, his son and successor to the next six parliaments, and his grandson, the fourth Viscount, to all of the succeeding eight parliaments save one. Beaumaris in Anglesey was under similar control. Having returned Nottingham's father in the 1660 election, it generally continued faithful to Bulkeley nominees, being represented in William's last parliament by Robert, younger son of the elder Lord Bulkeley and like his brother, the Member for Anglesey, own cousin of Nottingham. Patrons of three seats in parliament the Bulkeleys soon provided a second link between the Finches and the Berties, with the marriage in 1702 of Nottingham's cousin, the fourth Lord Bulkeley, to Lord Abingdon's eldest sister.

A final group allied with Nottingham and soon to be connected with him by marriage centred on Sir Roger Mostyn, third baronet of Mostyn in Flintshire, who became Nottingham's son-in-law in 1703. Besides Mostyn, who represented Flintshire in the 1701 parliament, it included Mostyn's brother Thomas, Member for Flint in the two previous parliaments; his first cousin Sir Thomas Hanmer, returned in the 1701 election not only for Flintshire but also for Thetford, where his wife the Dowager Duchess of Grafton had a strong interest; Hanmer's brother-in-law, Sir Henry Bunbury, Member for Chester from 1700 till his death; and Bunbury's colleague, Peter Shakerly, who was first returned for Chester in 1698. This group of Members from the neighbouring counties of Flint and Cheshire was on close terms with Nottingham even before the marriage of its leader to Lady Essex Finch and certainly ranks as still another part of the extensive Finch connexion.[1]

Obviously the Nottingham interest mustered surprising strength. In the Commons there were thirty-one Members

[1] See Appendix III, Part VI.

attached to the Finch connexion; while the House of Lords included no less than fourteen of his kinsmen, of whom two were Non-Jurors. Of the remaining twelve, all but a couple were on good terms with Nottingham; and we may safely count Lords Dartmouth, Winchilsea, Weymouth, Hatton, Thanet, Guilford, Brooke, Abingdon, Exeter, and Anglesey (to list them in the order in which they were discussed) among Lord Nottingham's friends and followers in the Upper House.

Large as it was the Finch connexion was overshadowed, at least in the Commons, by the network of alliances centring on the Hydes. A rather obscure Wiltshire family in the early seventeenth century the Hydes owed their rapid rise to the outstanding abilities of Edward Hyde, first Earl of Clarendon and greatest of Royalist statesmen. While Chancellor to Charles II Clarendon managed to arrange a marriage between his daughter and James, Duke of York. By 1701, less than thirty years after the death of this greatest of the Hydes, his grand-daughter, the Princess Anne, was about to ascend the throne which her sister Mary had already occupied; both his sons held earldoms; and their children were connected by a series of strategic marriages with the important families of Leveson-Gower, Granville, and Seymour—from which, in the male line, descend the present Duke of Sutherland, the Duke of Somerset, the Marquess of Hertford, and the Earl Granville.

Nearly allied to the royal family and to three of the great Restoration Houses the Hydes inevitably enjoyed great political power and electoral influence. The second Lord Clarendon, who succeeded as head of the family in 1674, had played an important role in the reigns of Charles II and James; but he refused to take the oaths to William III and retired from politics at the time of the Revolution. The leadership of the family thereupon passed to his younger brother Laurence, who had been raised to the peerage in 1681 as Earl of Rochester. It was Rochester who arranged for the publication of his father's *History of the Great Rebellion,* and the posthumous appearance of this celebrated work increased the prestige which he enjoyed as the uncle of two queens. Rochester possessed considerable electoral influence as well. Proprietor of the pocket borough of Christchurch in Hampshire and an important Wiltshire landowner he nominated both Members for Christchurch and usually secured the election of a kinsman as knight of the shire for Wilts.[1] His sister-in-law, Lady Sandwich, returned a cousin as Member for Huntingdon in the 1701 parliament;[2] and Sir John Pakington, who married Rochester's cousin, had sufficient influence in Worcestershire, where lay his chief estate, and at Evesham and the Buckinghamshire borough of Aylesbury, of which he was Lord, to secure his own return to William's last parliament (as Member for Worcestershire), together with his father-in-law (who married a Hyde) and another Rochesterite as Members for the other two constituencies. Rochester's son, Lord Hyde, sat for the Cornish borough of Launceston —together with another Hyde connexion—on the Granville interest; two other Hyde kinsmen sat for Bishop Trelawny's Cornish borough of West Looe; and another pair of Rochester's relatives represented Oxfordshire and Corfe Castle—bringing the total of Rochester's kinsmen in William's last parliament to an even dozen.[3]

Several of Rochester's friends and relations—as noted—owed their seats not to Rochester himself, but to his powerful allies, the Seymours and the Granvilles. The electoral influence of the latter family, less scattered and more extensive than Rochester's, was concentrated in Cornwall. John Granville, first Earl of Bath and head of a Cornish family famous for its royalism, was the trusted servant of Charles II and his brother James and managed Cornish elections in the Court interest with such success that he was nicknamed 'the Prince Elector'.[4] His death in 1701 having been followed within a fortnight by that of his eldest

[1] Robert Hyde, who often represented Wiltshire on Lord Rochester's interest, was not, however, returned to the 1701 parliament.

[2] See above, p. 42.

[3] See Appendix III, Part VII.

[4] *The Diary of John Evelyn* (ed. Austin Dobson, 3 vols., London, 1906), iii. 163–4.

son, so that 'there were three Earls of Bath above ground at the same time', the title passed to his only grandson, a child who died still under age and unmarried ten years later, the last of the Granville Earls of Bath. Meanwhile the leadership of the family passed to the first Earl's younger son, Colonel John Granville, heir-presumptive to the title.

His eldest sister (and eventual co-heir), having married Sir William Leveson-Gower, had issue: Sir John, later first Baron Gower; Catherine, wed to a Wyndham of Orchard Wyndham; and Jane Leveson-Gower, married in 1692 to Henry, 'Lord Hyde', Rochester's son and heir-apparent. This last alliance was of major political significance, for it linked the acting head of the Granvilles both to the chief of the Leveson-Gowers and to the prospective leader of the Hydes, thereby bringing into one system the electoral interests of these three important families. We have discussed the Hyde interest. That of the Gowers, Lady Hyde's family, was less extensive. Important landowners in Staffordshire they controlled the borough of Newcastle (Staffs.), which was represented in all of Charles II's parliaments and the first two parliaments of William's reign by Granville's brother-in-law Sir William Leveson-Gower, who was succeeded as Member for Newcastle by his son and heir Sir John, Member from the time of his father's death in 1692 until his removal to the Lords eleven years later.[1]

Lord Gower and his descendants continued to control Newcastle throughout the eighteenth century; but Sir John was outstripped as a borough manager by his uncle John Granville. In Cornwall and five of its boroughs the Granvilles had hereditary influence, and seven of the Cornish and Devon Members in William's last parliament can be identified as members of 'the Granville interest'—the most important being Granville himself, who sat for the county, and his nephew Lord Hyde, who represented Launceston, together with one of his wife's

[1] For the representative history of Newcastle see Colonel Wedgwood's volumes on 'The Parliamentary History of Staffordshire', in *Collections of the William Salt Archaeological Society*, 1917, and 1920–2.

connexions.[1] Counting the Hyde, Gower, and Granville nominees together we find that the three related clans mustered twenty-one votes in William's last parliament.[2]

This group, although a respectable one for the period, was smaller than the bloc of Members returned through the influence of the Seymours of Berry Pomeroy, last of the great families connected with the Hydes. Sir Edward Seymour, fourth baronet of Berry Pomeroy in Devon and Maiden Bradley in Wilts., was descended in the elder line from the Protector Somerset and rather looked down upon his kinsman the 'Proud Duke' of Somerset, as a descendant in the cadet line. A Member of Parliament since 1661 and at one time Speaker and a Lord of the Treasury, Seymour's close relations with the Hydes dated from the later years of Charles II's reign. The political association between the two families was soon to become a family affair with the marriage early in Queen Anne's reign of Rochester's daughter to Sir Edward Seymour's son.

Long before this wedding Rochester was finding seats for Seymour's kinsmen, a compliment which Sir Edward found no difficulty in returning. Manager of a formidable electoral interest which Defoe nicknamed 'Tsar Seymskie's Western Empire',[3] Sir Edward usually secured seats for himself and a friend at Exeter, where he was Recorder and a power in the corporation, leaving two seats to spare at his pocket borough of Totnes near by. To these two Devon constituencies must be added the town of Pymouth and four small Cornish constituencies controlled by his close relatives. His brother-in-law Sir Joseph Tredenham had St. Mawes in his pocket and represented that borough with one or another of his sons or relatives for more than thirty years without a break. Seymour's younger brother was Tredenham's colleague and nominee for no less than seven parliaments; while Sir Joseph's son-in-law owed his seat at Grampound to the same influence.

[1] See Appendix III, Part VII, for the M.P.s for Bossiney, Fowey, Honiton (Devon), Penryn, St. Ives, and Michael connected with Granville.

[2] See Appendix III, Part VII.

[3] *H.M.C. Portland MSS.* iv. 222.

Even more important a borough-owner was Sir Edward Seymour's cousin-germain, Sir Jonathan Trelawny, Lord Bishop of Exeter; for this worthy prelate usually managed to 'muster up a squadron'[1] of half a dozen Members, a brace for each of the adjoining boroughs of East and West Looe and another pair from Plymouth. In the 1701 parliament two Trelawnys, one Seymour, and one cousin of the Seymours, together with one cousin and one understrapper of Lord Rochester, owed their seats to the Bishop of Exeter.[2]

Turning to Somerset one discovers that there also Seymour had influential relatives with electoral interests so extensive that together they could sometimes return half the Somerset Members. Foremost among these kinsmen was Sir Edward's own brother, Henry Seymour 'alias Portman', to use the contemporary style. Both brothers were grandsons of Sir John Portman of Orchard Portman, the first baronet and head of one of the leading Somerset families. In 1690 the last of the Portmans died without issue, and the family became extinct; but its estates and electoral influence at Taunton and Wells devolved on Henry Seymour, who assumed the Portman name. As representative of the Portmans he was soon able to abandon the close boroughs of Totnes and St. Mawes for the larger and more respectable constituencies of Wells, Taunton, and eventually Somerset itself.

The representation of that county, traditionally divided since the Restoration between the friends and relatives of the Pouletts, Barons Poulett of Hinton St. George, and the kinsmen and dependants of the related families of Portman and Wyndham of Orchard Wyndham, soon included more of Sir Edward Seymour's relatives than did his native Devon, or adjoining Cornwall. In William's last parliament the Somerset Members included Seymour's brother, elected for both Taunton and

[1] The quotation is from a letter of Godolphin to Robert Harley, written in 1701 (*H.M.C. Portland MSS.* iv. 28).

[2] See Appendix III, Part VII. Rochester's two kinsmen, sitting for West Looe, have already been mentioned above, p. 61.

Wells; one nephew; two first cousins; three second cousins; and two gentlemen less closely related, but apparently attached likewise to the Seymour 'interest'.[1]

Dorset, the last of the south-western counties, was dominated (like Somerset) by a small group of county families; and with two of these Seymour was related. His second cousins, the Napiers of Middlemarsh Hall, had electoral influence at Dorchester, which returned two Napiers to William's last parliament, and at Corfe Castle, which returned a kinsman.[1] The Nicholas family were related in the same degree, the head of that family like the chief of the Napiers having married one of Seymour's Wyndham cousins. Sir Edward Nicholas, founder of the family and Secretary of State to Charles II, was a Surrey man; but his son purchased estates near Shaftesbury in Dorset and lived to see his son elected Member for Shaftesbury, which continued to return old Sir Edward's grandson and namesake to thirteen consecutive parliaments.[1]

We have finally to speak of one outlying electoral interest which ought to be mentioned at this point, although it is obviously no integral part of Seymour's 'Empire'. This was the interest managed by one of Seymour's closest associates, Sir Christopher Musgrave, fourth baronet of Edenhall in Westmorland. Since the days of Charles II's 'Pensioners' Parliament' Musgrave and Seymour had worked together, and in 1701 Sir Christopher was one of Seymour's nominees for Totnes. It was a bad year when a Musgrave had to take refuge in a Devon pocket borough. Head of a clan prominent in the northern counties and sometime Governor of Carlisle, Sir Christopher had previously represented Oxford University for three years, Westmorland for twice that length of time, and Carlisle for no less than thirty years; and he could usually count on two or three Cumberland and Westmorland seats for nominees of his own.[2]

[1] See Appendix III, Part VII.

[2] See R. S. Ferguson, *Cumberland and Westmorland M.P.s from the Restoration to the Reform Bill of 1867* (London, 1871), *passim*. See also Appendix III, Part VII.

Even with no reinforcements from his northern ally Sir Edward Seymour could count on twenty-five kinsmen and nominees in William's last parliament, not including his second son William, who came into that parliament under other auspices.[1] If we include further the nine Members attached to the Granville interest and the twelve elected through the influence of Lord Rochester and his near relations, we find that the total strength mustered by these three leaders was forty-seven votes in the Commons, fourteen short of the total rolled up by the Junto.[2] Such strength speaks for itself, and we need only add that in 1700 the Hyde–Granville–Seymour interest was managed as a single combination. That it was no loose 'Triple Alliance' is proved by the fact that in the 1701 election Seymour procured seats for two of Rochester's particular friends; that Rochester returned two of Seymour's kinsmen; and that Granville returned another of Seymour's relatives together with Rochester's son[2] —evidence which taken together indicates a high degree of co-operation between the three leaders.

There remains but one large family connexion to be considered, that which centred on Robert Harley and included as well Henry St. John, later Viscount Bolingbroke. Robert Harley, leader of this group, sprang from an untitled family seated at Brampton Bryan in Herefordshire. His maternal great-grandfather was Viscount Conway, and Harley later made much of his kinship with the ancient family of De Vere, Earls of Oxford, notwithstanding the fact that the connexion was absurdly remote.[3] Nevertheless, the Harleys were plain country gentry, distinguished from other county families, not because of aristocratic connexions, but rather for their Presbyterian sympathies

[1] Francis Seymour *alias* Conway was returned for Bramber on Lord Windsor's interest; William Seymour, for Cockermouth, on the recommendation of his distant kinsman, Somerset. See Appendix III, Part VII; and also Part IV, for William Seymour.

[2] See Appendix III, Part VII.

[3] Harley's great-grandmother's *sister* married Lord Vere of Tilbury, son of a younger son of the fifth De Vere Earl of Oxford. Consequently Harley had no trace of De Vere blood, although he adopted their title.

and their alliance with a newly arrived family founded only a few generations back by a Stourbridge ironmaster.

Their political importance the Harleys owed to their electoral influence in the Welsh Border counties. Four generations of the family had sat for Herefordshire; while a grant from William III of a lordship in Radnorshire and the site of Radnor Castle clinched their control of that county and borough. Much of their influence, however, was due to their connexion with the Foleys. This family, which owed its rise to an enormously successful iron manufacture, invested its wealth in land to such good effect that by 1688 the Foleys ranked with the leading territorial magnates of the Marches. In Staffordshire, Herefordshire, and Worcestershire they owned estates and enjoyed sufficient local influence to return candidates at five of the eleven boroughs in these counties and to influence elections for knights of the three shires. This was the family with which the Harleys became doubly allied when Robert and his brother married two Foley sisters.

Three Harleys, three Foleys, and a Foley in-law sat together in William's last parliament,[1] but these seven Members comprised only the nucleus of the Harley connexion. More than a dozen Members more were connected with Harley by ties of family and friendship; and of these associates the closest were surely Henry St. John and Simon Harcourt. Harcourt, a kinsman and former schoolfellow of Harley, was a lawyer and the Recorder of Abingdon, which lay close to his Berkshire and Oxfordshire property and chose him as its Member for the sixth consecutive time in 1701. A cousin of Harley Harcourt was related as well to two members of the Upper House. Lord Paget, a first cousin, headed a Staffordshire family which had intermarried with the Foleys and like them counted a member of the family among the representatives for that county in William's last parliament. Lord Poulett, a more distant cousin of Harcourt and a kinsman of Harley as well, enjoyed a similar influence in Somerset. Poulett successfully named one candidate

[1] See Appendix III, Part VIII.

for that county in the 1701 election and counted a kinsman and follower among the Yorkshire Members.[1]

Henry St. John, first returned to parliament in 1701, was the prospective head of a Wiltshire family which controlled the borough of Wootton Bassett. Attaching himself to Harley, St. John brought his 'Master', as he called him,[2] not only his own vote and interest at the family borough, but important recruits from among his friends and relatives as well. These included: Thomas Coke, Member for Derbyshire; Lord Chandos's son and heir, James Brydges, who shared the representation of Hereford with a Foley, to whom he was related; Brydges's first cousin, Sir Thomas Willoughby, M.P. for Notts. and another connexion of the Foleys; and finally St. John's second cousin, Colonel Edmund Webb, patron of the Wiltshire borough of Ludgershall, which he represented in 1701 together with his son, General John Richmond Webb, a familiar figure to readers of his descendant's novel, *Henry Esmond*.

Among Harley's friends and neighbours we should consider, finally, Thomas Mansell of Margam and Judge Robert Price. Mansell controlled both Glamorganshire constituencies, which he and a cousin and namesake represented in William's last parliament; while Price had considerable influence at Weobley and represented that Herefordshire constituency in 1701 as on four previous occasions. Including Price and the Mansells, the total Harleian connexion in the 1701 parliament came to twenty Members.

We are now in a position to summarize the results of our detailed examination of groups in the 1701 House of Commons. They fall into three broad classifications: the Court interest; the family connexions; and the unattached, independent, or unconnected country gentlemen. The 'government interest', strictly speaking, included only the thirty-eight Members holding

[1] See Appendix III, Part VIII.

[2] See St. John's letters to Harley in *H.M.C. Portland MSS.* iv. 176, 180, 223, et seq.

office and (all but seventeen) returned for government boroughs. On most occasions, however, they would be reinforced by about 100 Members less directly connected with the Court—sixty-eight 'Court Whigs' and thirty-three 'Court Tories', not including those returned by the group of aristocratic Court peers.

The second classification—Members belonging to the political family connexions—totalled 212. This figure breaks down as follows: (1) Junto connexion, 64; (2) Newcastle–Pelham–Townshend–Walpole connexion, 16; (3) the Court peers: Somerset, Carlisle, Radnor, Pembroke, and Stamford (not really a 'connexion'), 22; (4) the Marlborough–Godolphin connexion, 12; (5) the Nottingham–Finch connexion, 31; (6) the Hyde–Granville–Seymour connexion, 47; and (7) the Harley–Foley connexion, 20.

There were finally the unattached and independent Members, who totalled something under 150 Members, who can be roughly classified as: 'Country Whig', 34; 'Country Tory', 60; and independent 'High Church', 48. They and the unorganized Members with 'Court' leanings together outnumbered the Members grouped in the official government interest and in the seven family connexions; but they were far outstripped by these organized groups in importance. It was from the organized groups that most of the offices were filled; they provided most of the debaters in the House; and it was they who mustered their 'regulars' when the House divided.

Having identified these groups as they stood in the year 1701, we must now broaden the scope of our inquiry to try and learn how these groups were related one to another and to certain larger political aggregations such as a 'Country Party', a 'Court Party', a 'Tory Party', or a Whig one. In order to do this we must trace briefly the political course followed by each of the major family connexions in the years before 1701.

PART TWO

THE FUNCTIONING OF PARTIES

CHAPTER V

Introduction. The Party Groups in Action Prior to 1702[1]

In Part One we analysed the structure of parties, dissecting a single House of Commons in order to show the various party groups into which it was divided. We introduced this analysis with a description of the electoral system as it operated early in the eighteenth century; then turned to an analysis of the parliament elected in 1701, first in terms of occupation and social status, then in political terms. This showed that approximately half of the 513 Members of that parliament were gathered by personal ties of family, friendship, neighbourhood,

[1] In this chapter I have drawn on the following primary sources: *The Earl of Ailesbury's Memoirs* (2 vols., Roxburghe Club, 1890); Gilbert Burnet's *History of My Own Time* (Oxford edition, 1833, with notes by Swift, Dartmouth, and others; hereafter cited as Burnet's *History*); *The Clarendon Correspondence* (2 vols., ed. S. W. Singer, London, 1828); *Ellis Correspondence* (ed. G. A. Ellis, London, 1829); *Essex Papers* (Camden Soc. Publ., N.S., 47); Grey's *Debates* (London, 1763); *Hatton Correspondence* (Camden Soc. Publ., N.S., 21); *H.M.C. Finch, Ormonde*, and *Portland MSS.*; *Savile Correspondence* (Camden Soc. Publ., 52); *Diary of Henry Sidney* (ed. W. R. Blencowe, London, 1843); and *Letters Illustrative of the Reign of William III from James Vernon* (ed. G. P. R. James, 3 vols., London, 1841; hereafter cited as *Vernon Correspondence*). Among secondary works, besides the very useful *Tory Party* of Feiling, I have relied on H. C. Foxcroft's *Life of George Savile, Marquis of Halifax* (2 vols., London, 1898), especially important for Halifax's letters and the 'Spencer House Journals'.

or profession into seven major groups ranging in size from less than a dozen to over sixty. These groups, which might be called the fundamental cells of the party structure, were described in some detail, but without reference to their politics.

The existence of each group was postulated on evidence of close personal relationship between the members of a single connexion—not on common allegiance to a set of political principles or the pursuit of a common course of political action. We must assume, of course, that each group did share common political views and followed their natural leaders along a common line of political action—otherwise they would have no political significance—and we must now try to establish the political affiliations of each connexion. To do this we must enlarge our field of vision to include the past political activities of each group, which in some cases will take us back to the middle years of Charles II's reign.

The history of party in the thirty years before the accession of Anne is extremely complex—more so than most authorities on the period seem to realize, except for Feiling; and he tends to force the details of party history, which he knows thoroughly, into the two-party pattern, although with considerable difficulty. Feiling assumes that the reign of Charles II saw the creation of the two historic parties, and in this assumption he is joined by most historians. Given this point of departure, most of the literature on party history is concerned with origins, with attempts to determine at what date the two parties were born and what the relationship of these parties was to the political divisions which separated the English people in preceding and subsequent periods. Most historians now seem agreed that a Whig and a Tory party were both organized on a national basis in the late 1670's, that they were descended from the Roundhead and Cavalier parties of the Civil War respectively, and that they have persisted with little fundamental change of identity down almost to the present day.[1]

[1] This is the view of Feiling, Trevelyan, and virtually every other historian.

Regardless of the accuracy of this view (and we do not intend to challenge it at this stage) its general acceptance has so coloured party history that it has become almost impossible to discuss any political figure or group without assigning them a place in one or the other of the two historic parties. This, however, is exactly what we intend to do. By dealing with each of the political groups described in the last chapter as though it were an individual we shall try to discover its politics not in terms of Whig or Tory, but with respect to its position towards the king's government and the stand which it took in parliament and out on the more important issues of the day.

To small groups, such as we have analysed above, it is perfectly feasible to assign 'ages'. They will be relative, of course, and somewhat arbitrary (being a composite of the ages and political experience of the leaders and principal lieutenants of each group); but data on the seniority of party leaders and most of their followers as of 1700 are available and indicate marked differences in the 'ages' of the various groups—differences which are significant and which at the same time simplify our problem.

It appears at once that the various political connexions range in age from the Hyde and Seymour groups, with leaders in their late sixties and henchmen who had entered politics in the days of Charles II's 'Pensioners' Parliament', to the Townshend–Walpole connexion, whose leaders were not even born until some fourteen years after Rochester, Seymour, and Musgrave first entered the Commons. In between come the Marlborough–Godolphin group, most of them in their fifties; the Finch connexion, of whom Nottingham and his brother were in their fifties while most of their followers were younger; the Junto group, all of them except Wharton in their thirties or forties; and the Harley interest, of whom Harley, the eldest, was still in his thirties.

When arranged on the basis of age the party groups clearly fall into two classes: those which played an active role under Charles II and James II; and those which at the time of the

Glorious Revolution were comparative newcomers to politics. The Hyde–Seymour, Marlborough–Godolphin, and Finch connexions clearly belong in the first classification; while the others belong as clearly in the second. Only in the case of the three 'older' connexions need we go back much beyond the year 1688.

Turning to these older groups, let us examine briefly their position *vis-à-vis* the Court and on the important political issues of the sixties and seventies. To what extent were they united in a single 'Tory party'? To what degree did they follow the same policy in parliament?

According to the careful tallies by Lord Danby's aides, all three groups were included in Danby's 'Court party' of the seventies. On these lists of 'Court Members' were Seymour and his followers, various members of the Finch connexion, and all the Churchills, Godolphins, and their kinsmen then in the Commons.[1] The history of the three Exclusion Parliaments furnishes further confirmation, apparently, of joint action presumably by a united Court party. The minority opposing the first Exclusion Bill included Seymour, Rochester, Godolphin, and Nottingham—all four then Members of the Commons.[2]

United opposition to Exclusion and common action as members of Danby's majority of the mid-seventies have usually been considered sufficient evidence that the groups in question were part of a united Tory party; but there is also strong evidence indicating that the coalition was only temporary. There is no evidence, for example, of such a coalition before the mid-seventies. For one thing, the Hydes would not be included. Rochester and his brother, as Members of the Commons, were part of Chancellor Clarendon's following; they defended their father against the Cabal; and after his fall they went into opposition and for some time were forbidden the Court. At this

[1] These lists are printed in consolidated form by E. S. DeBeer, in *Bulletin of the Institute of Historical Research*, xi, no. 31 (June, 1933).

[2] There is a list of the minority in Cal. S.P. Dom., Carol. II, vol. ccccxvii, no. 232 (1), printed in Feiling's *Tory Party*, pp. 494–5.

time there was no Hyde–Seymour alliance, and Seymour's group followed an opposite course. Seymour was a henchman of Buckingham, one of the Cabal, and was one of Clarendon's bitterest opponents—as was Danby. Both took office under the Cabal; both deserted Buckingham when the Cabal fell apart; and when Danby became Treasurer, Seymour succeeded him as Treasurer of the Navy and was his chief lieutenant in the Commons. Not until Danby had consolidated his position in the seventies did the other 'older' groups—Godolphins, Finches, and Hydes—become part of Danby's Court coalition.

The 'Tory party' of the seventies was something new, then. Formed just before the Exclusion controversy, it began to disintegrate soon afterwards. Even Feiling recognizes this, for he distinguishes three separate 'factions' within the post-Exclusion Tory party: the 'Courtiers', with whom he places the Marlborough–Godolphin connexion; the 'Trimmers', meaning Halifax's following, including the Finches; and the 'Tories' proper, including the Hydes and Seymours. Of the seven groups[1] which voted against Exclusion only two apparently, were really 'Tory'![2]

As a matter of fact it is very difficult to find a united Tory party either during Charles II's last five years or under his brother James II. By 1681 co-operation between the 'Tory factions' had given way to bitter rivalry. Until Charles's death the Halifax–Finch party held the upper hand; but with the accession of James his kinsmen the Hydes came into power. With them were associated the Granvilles (soon to be allied by marriage); but the third element of the Rochester connexion of 1700—Seymour and his following—remained in opposition.[3] The Finch connexion also dissociated itself from the Court,

[1] Viz. Halifax's following, the Finches, Danby's following, the Hydes, the Seymour connexion, the Marlborough–Godolphin group, and a number of 'Country' moderates.

[2] Feiling, *Tory Party*, pp. 187–97.

[3] Seymour's opposition to the Court and the Hydes was largely personal: he held Rochester responsible for his own failure to reach high office. Moreover, the Hydes' friend, Lord Bath, had ridden roughshod over Seymour's interests in a number of Cornish boroughs in the 1685 election. Ibid., pp. 188–91, 206.

acting in harmony with Halifax. The great Trimmer and the younger Nottingham were very close at this time;[1] and when Halifax was 'kicked upstairs', Nottingham left the Admiralty, and the other members of the Finch connexion soon joined him in opposition.

The middle years of James II's reign are a curious commentary on Tory party unity: Seymour in opposition, while his subsequent allies, the Hydes, clung to office; all the Halifax and Finch connexion estranged from the Court; while the Marlborough–Godolphin connexion, on the other hand, was one of the last to relinquish office. It was James's singular achievement to force these divergent elements into temporary union with many of those whom they had bitterly opposed in the Exclusion debates of ten years before.

The Revolution of 1688 was the most important issue in English politics in the years between the Exclusion controversy and the accession of Anne. One might expect to find the various 'Tory' groups at least as united in opposing the deposition of a king as they had been in opposing Exclusion; but this was not the case. Of the 'older' party groups all but one joined in the Revolution instead of opposing it. It will be worth our while to trace briefly the policy of each of the groups during the crisis of 1687–8 in search of further illustration of the functioning of party groups in an actual situation.

Danby's following was the first to belie traditional 'Tory' reverence for royalty and engage in sedition. Among the seven signers of the famous July 1688 'Invitation' to William of Orange, requesting his presence in England, were three Danbyites: Danby himself; his cousin Henry Compton, Bishop of London; and a connexion, Lord Lumley.[2] The idea of the invitation was hatched a year and a half earlier at an interesting meeting in January 1687 at the house of Lord Shrewsbury,

[1] See Foxcroft's *Halifax*, i. 791.

[2] Lord Lumley, a convert from Catholicism and one of the colonels deprived of their regiments by James, was connected through his mother (a Compton) with both Danby and the Bishop of London.

kinsman, ward, and at that time political disciple, of Halifax. There were present: Halifax, Shrewsbury, and Nottingham—of the 'Trimmers'; Danby—of the 'Courtiers'; and Edward Russell, the future Lord Orford, and Mordaunt, Wharton's cousin—both with Junto connexions.[1] Soon after this meeting Shrewsbury and Russell went to Holland, reporting back that the Prince of Orange would come to England if invited by a group of sufficiently important English leaders.

Within the next year the conspirators lost the support of the Halifax–Finch connexion, Shrewsbury excepted; so that the Danbyites were the only group actively engaged in the project prior to William's landing. Seymour, because of his close association with Danby, was early let into the secret, but he remained neutral until some time after the Prince's landing at Torbay. His friend Danby, however, was not only one of the original signers of the Invitation; his early and successful raising of the North for William of Orange was one of the most important military actions taken by any party leader during the crisis.

Danby's action was in contrast to that of his rival Halifax. The great 'Trimmer', together with Nottingham and their cousin Weymouth, was among the first to oppose the illegalities of James II; but the Halifax–Finch connexion avoided any course that could be called treasonable, remaining loyal in deed, if not in heart, to the king—at least until after his second flight from the realm. The policy of the Hydes, the Granvilles, and the Seymours was less forthright, vacillating between Danby's bold treason and the strict neutrality of Halifax and the Finches. Clarendon and Rochester themselves refused to recognize the 'usurper' William—Clarendon for the rest of his life; Rochester, until after the Revolution was an accomplished fact—but a number of their kinsmen and henchmen were among the first to come into the Prince's camp at Exeter.[2] Seymour likewise

[1] For an account of this meeting see Foxcroft's *Halifax*, i. 480–2.

[2] The most prominent of the Hyde connexion to join William were Clarendon's unbalanced heir, Lord Cornbury, and Rochester's Scottish son-in-law, Lord Drumlanrig, subsequently Duke of Queensberry.

took the plunge at this stage. He and his followers were the first important West Country group to 'come over to the Prince'.

The Marlborough–Godolphin connexion, last of the 'older' groups to be considered, played perhaps as decisive a role in the deposition of James as any other group. The superbly timed defection of Marlborough with his regiment and those of his officer friends on the eve of battle forced upon the king the realization that resistance would be hopeless and thus ensured the 'bloodless' nature of the Revolution. The defection of Lady Marlborough was possibly just as decisive. She was responsible for persuading the Princess Anne to forsake her father and take refuge in Danby's north country, accompanied not only by the countess, but also by Danby's kinsman, the Bishop of London. Contemporaries considered the Princess's desertion the final blow that led her father to abandon his kingdom.

Thus it was only the Halifax–Finch connexion and the more responsible leaders of the Hyde connexion who remained loyal to the *de jure* government of James during the Prince's halt at Exeter. During this period the two groups had almost a fortnight in which to frame a common policy; but co-operation between the two proved impossible, and 'ten precious days were lost by a sharp difference between the two wings'.[1] Halifax, Nottingham, and Weymouth refused to work with the Hydes, who had connived in some of the illegal policies of the king.

There was no common Tory policy, then, during the Revolution of 1688; and there is some question whether there is any point in speaking of 'the Tory party' at this time. It remains to be seen whether a united Tory party developed after the Revolution; but first we must enlarge our field to take in the activities of one of the 'younger' party groups, the Junto, most of whom first appeared on the political scene during the crisis of 1687–8.

Just as Danby is usually considered the founder of a long-lived united Tory party, so Shaftesbury has been recognized as 'the principal founder of that great party which, in opposition

[1] Feiling, *Tory Party*, pp. 231–2.

to the prerogative and uniformity, has inscribed upon its banner political freedom and religious toleration'[1]—in other words a lasting and united Whig party. Undoubtedly Shaftesbury did contribute important elements to later 'Whiggism': the idea of political alliance between a section of the aristocracy and the Nonconformist trading element, and the germ of a political philosophy later given classic and lasting definition by the earl's friend, John Locke; but of the actual parliamentary coalition organized and led by Shaftesbury in the 1670's little remained by 1700.

At its height in 1679 that coalition apparently numbered about thirty peers and sixty Members of the Commons;[2] but many of these were ageing veterans of Civil War politics. Of the peers all but three were dead by 1688; and while a number of the younger men in the Commons were still active at the time of the Glorious Revolution, very few of these had owed their seats or their primary allegiance to Shaftesbury himself. The Country party of Shaftesbury, like Danby's Court party, was not a unified party, but included a number of distinct elements. The inner core, Shaftesbury's personal followers in the Lords and Commons, was small—probably only a dozen or so.[3] Far larger was the group, less closely identified with Shaftesbury, which can most conveniently be described as the Sidney–Capel–Howard connexion—an extraordinarily extensive family

[1] Leopold Von Ranke, *English History, Principally in the Seventeenth Century* (Oxford, 1875), iv. 167.

[2] For a list of peers voting for the first Exclusion Bill see the *Lords' Journals* for 15 Nov. 1680. For an earlier list of the Country party in the Lords see *H.M.C. House of Lords MSS.* (9th report, appendix, part ii), p. 79. There is no satisfactory list of the Country party in the Commons. My estimate is based on scattered information in the political correspondence cited in the first note to this chapter.

[3] Nothing of value on the subject of Shaftesbury's activities as a political organizer has been published. W. D. Christie's *Life of Shaftesbury* (2 vols., London, 1871) does not deal with this aspect of the Earl's career. Sir George Sitwell's *The First Whig* (Scarborough, 1894, privately printed; microfilm copy in the Yale University Library) cited by most writers as an authority on Shaftesbury's organizing methods, contains a highly misleading account of the 'Green Ribbon Club'. The whole subject needs investigation.

alliance which included many of the titled houses which at one time or another sided with Parliament during the Civil War and which in the 1670's numbered at least a dozen in the House of Lords and probably twice that number in the Commons.[1] Three leaders of this group did allow themselves to be drawn into the extremist plots of 1681 and died as 'Whig martyrs', but the group as a whole stood to the right of Shaftesbury and did not follow him into the Duke of Monmouth's fatal undertaking.

The third element of Shaftesbury's coalition were the rake-hells: Thomas Wharton, heir to the Puritan lord and a future Junto leader; and five or six young nobles of similar dissolute habits.[2] There was finally a lunatic fringe: Wildman and Ferguson 'the Plotter', and young Hampden, among others. Some of this last group had personal ties with Wharton and his cronies, who in turn had ties with Lord Cavendish and Lord Wiltshire of the Capel–Sidney–Howard connexion. This made it easy for Court spokesmen to stigmatize the entire Country coalition as 'phanaticks' and 'Commonwealth men'; but actually very few men from the Country groups followed Shaftesbury into treason, the great majority hoping instead for a new day under an Orange dispensation.

By 1687 Shaftesbury was dead; most of his following had deserted him, had died, or had dropped out of sight; and only

[1] A detailed account of the personnel of this group lies outside the field of this study. In the Lords it included: the Earls of Essex, Leicester, Bedford, Devonshire, Suffolk, Carlisle, and Stamford; the Marquis of Winchester; and Lords Howard of Escrick, Eure, and Delamere. In the Commons it included, among others, Henry Capel (Essex's brother), Algernon and Henry Sidney (Leicester's brothers), Lord Russell (Bedford's son), Lord Cavendish (Devonshire's son), and Lord Wiltshire (Winchester's son). These families were all tied into a single network of relationships, which can only be indicated by a genealogical chart much too complicated to be reproduced here. Such a diagram is interesting because it shows remarkable correlation between family relationship and common political action, both in the Civil War period and during the 1670's.

[2] Beside Wharton the group included Lord Lovelace, Lord Mordaunt (later Earl of Peterborough and Monmouth), Lord Colchester (later Earl Rivers), Lord Gerard (later Earl of Macclesfield), and Gerard's nephew Lord Mohun, the notorious duellist who figures in Thackeray's *Henry Esmond*.

a fraction of the old Country coalition participated in the Revolution of 1688. Some Country veterans did, but alongside them appeared a group of younger men: Edward Russell, John Somers, and Charles Montagu, among others. These new recruits joined forces with Wharton, Lord Wiltshire (later Duke of Bolton), and one or two older members of the Russell family, to form what was essentially a distinct new group—easily recognizable as the Junto connexion of 1700.

This group was obviously active in the Revolution. Lord Wiltshire and Wharton's cousin Mordaunt were among the first Englishmen to join William in Holland. So was Edward Russell, and he and his kinsman Lord Cavendish were signers of the Invitation. Later the group acted as though they had brought in William and Mary with no help from the Tory groups; and the impression that the Revolution was 'a Whig affair' and that William III was 'the Whigs' king' gained strength from the fact that within a year of James II's forced 'abdication' the various Tory groups were doing their best to disavow the revolution they had done so much to bring about. Virtually all the party groups had agreed that James must go and had helped him on his way. They were agreed, also, in accepting the Prince of Orange as *de facto* ruler for the time being; but how to settle the government on satisfactory new legal foundations was a problem on which they violently disagreed.

The issue did little to divide the Country groups, who argued that William and Mary should now be declared king and queen by parliamentary right, James having forfeited the crown by subverting the original contract between sovereign and people. The older Tory groups were united in opposition to any such 'commonwealth' theory of contract, and they voted together against a Country-inspired declaration that the throne was 'vacant', with its implication that parliament was free to fill the throne as it saw fit.[1] To declare the throne vacant was to

[1] One hundred and fifty-one Members of the Commons voted to agree with the Lords that the throne was not vacant. They were listed in a contemporary

transgress the sacred principle of indefeasible hereditary right; but how to remain loyal to this principle and yet place the government where nearly everybody agreed it must be put—in the hands of the Prince and Princess of Orange—was a problem for which the older party groups had different answers.

The solution offered by Danby and his party rested upon the fiction that James II was legally 'demised', with the additional assumption that the throne had thereby devolved not upon James's Catholic son, but upon the Princess Mary, presumed his rightful heir.[1] This strained interpretation of plain fact was too much for the Finches to swallow. To them James was still legally king; and while the Princess and Prince of Orange must in practice rule for him, it must be as regents. This solution became the favourite of the Churchmen and was ultimately supported by all the older party groups except the Danbyites and Lord Halifax, who on this point parted company with the Finches and even his own children.

When the regency proposal came before the Lords for a vote, it was defeated by two voices, Halifax and Danby both voting against it. The regency advocates then joined forces with the Danbyites in an attempt to declare the Princess Mary sovereign in her own right; but they were unable to win over either Mary herself—who refused to reign without her husband as co-ruler—or a majority of the Commons. There followed a week-long deadlock, broken finally when nearly all the groups concurred in the famous 'vacancy declaration'. This combined a complete absence of logic with a fine practicality—gratifying each group in turn with a reference to its favourite constitutional premiss

pamphlet (printed in Feiling's *Tory Party*, pp. 496–8) as 'those that were against making the Prince and Princess of Orange King and Queen'. The list includes virtually every member of the Hyde, Seymour, Granville, Churchill, Marlborough, and Finch connexions then sitting in the Commons, and the sons of both Danby and Halifax. See also my article on division-lists, in *Bull. Inst. Hist. Research*, xiv, no. 5, p. 25.

[1] A group of Danbyite peers had hit upon the useful fiction of a demise, even before the Convention met, and tried to convert the Princess Mary to this school of thought. See Clarendon's diary for 24 Dec. 1688, in *Clarendon Correspondence*, ii. 235.

—and concluded by vesting the government in William and Mary jointly as King and Queen of England.[1]

The debates in the Convention mark an epoch in party history. If ever there had been a united Tory party, it disintegrated under the stresses of the years 1688–9. 'The change in the Tory party', writes Feiling, 'was so great as to destroy its inner coherence.'[2] Certainly there was little evidence of Tory unity during most of William III's reign, to which we now turn.

In his first choice of ministers William gave some indication of his attitude toward the party groups; for he recognized the assistance given him by many of them and showed that he did not consider himself the candidate of any single one. Halifax's help, for example, though late, had been important; and his group received a share of office: Halifax, at his own request, taking the Privy Seal; his disciples, Nottingham and Shrewsbury, becoming Secretaries of State.[3] The share of the Danbyites was much less than their leader had expected. Refused the office of Lord Treasurer, Danby had to content himself with the Presidency of the Council; and the numerous lesser honours and places given to him and members of his family did little to lessen his disappointment or his jealousy of Halifax.[4] As for the Seymours and Granvilles, they were passed over entirely, as were their allies the Hydes, for whom William had no use whatever.[5]

[1] The division of opinion among the Tory groups appears clearly in the debates in the Convention parliament, reported by Anchitel Grey in his *Debates*. For secondary accounts compare Feiling's *Tory Party*, pp. 245–54, and Macaulay's *History of England* (ed. Sir Charles Firth, 6 vols., London, 1914), iii. 1261–97.

[2] Feiling's *Tory Party*, p. 245.

[3] In addition three of Halifax's kinsmen were called to the Admiralty; and he himself was offered the Garter and a dukedom, but refused. See Foxcroft's *Halifax*, ii. 63–68.

[4] Danby was made Marquis of Carmarthen and was given numerous territorial honours; but he was so aggrieved that for some months he sulked in the country. Strictly, he should be termed Carmarthen from this time until 1694, and Duke of Leeds thereafter; but we shall continue to refer to him by the more familiar title, Danby.

[5] William told Halifax that Nottingham was 'an honest man, but for Lord

The claims of the Junto leaders who had been active in William's cause could not be overlooked; but their expectations were not fulfilled, either. The two seats at the Treasury board, the three Household posts, the large number of peerages given to members of this group[1] hardly disguised the fact that in royal favour and political influence they ranked below Halifax and Nottingham, Danby, and Godolphin (who was chosen to head the Treasury).

Under the circumstances the Junto leaders could hope to win a larger share of policy-making posts either by co-operating heartily with the Court and so proving their usefulness; or by opposing the Court they could try to blackmail the king into giving them the offices they coveted. It was the second alternative which they adopted, as was indicated, among other things, by their support of the 'Sacheverell clause'.

This was a provision excluding from municipal office for a period of seven years all those who had participated in the surrender of borough charters during the last years of Charles II's reign. Had the clause been accepted, it would have caused a purge on such a scale as to enable the Country groups to recover much of the electoral influence which they had lost during the royalist reaction of 1681–7. The attitude of the Court on this issue was that the war with France was the main concern of parliament, which should confine itself to granting supply and to other pressing business; and that the Sacheverell clause, by reviving party feuds, might easily hold up important legislation. Fortunately, with the help of the various Tory groups the government was able to block this explosive proposal, though only after furious debate.

The division on the Sacheverell clause is an interesting one. Included in the minority which favoured it were three distinct groups: old lieutenants of Shaftesbury and various non-Junto

Clarendon and Rochester, they were Knaves' (Spencer House Journals, in Foxcroft's *Halifax*, ii. 202).

[1] The Treasury posts went to Mordaunt and Hampden, of Wharton's clique; the Household posts to Wharton (Comptroller), Devonshire (Lord Steward), and to Devonshire's brother-in-law, Lord Bradford (Treasurer).

Country Members; younger Country Members, associated with the Junto; and a group of Foleys, Harleys, and their kin, who were soon to part company with the Junto leaders. Though part of the government coalition, the Junto lords did not hesitate to muster their following against the Court on this issue.[1]

Such action—the culmination of more than a year of frequent co-operation in attacks on various members of his government—convinced William that the Junto leaders were not fit to help manage his business. Accordingly, he followed Danby's suggestion that parliament be dissolved and the Country leaders be dismissed from their posts to be replaced by Danbyites and by veteran placemen who might have voted against making William king, but would give him more loyal service than the men they supplanted. The result was a new parliament, less Country than that of 1689–90; and an administration dominated by Danby, who now moved into apartments near Whitehall and became in fact the leading minister.

Feiling calls this administration (1690–4) the 'Second Danby Ministry'; but whatever one calls it, it was certainly not a unified administration representing a united Tory party; and Feiling himself cites as a characteristic of this period 'the extraordinary uncertainty in politics—comparable only to the fog in which our modern parties' pioneers groped during the middle years of George III'.[2] This Danby ministry, for example, never enjoyed general 'tory' support. The Finch connexion voted with the government; but the Hydes seem constantly to have voted against it, as did the Seymours—until Sir Edward was won over by a place in the Treasury. Danby and his lieutenants in the Commons faced a formidable opposition made up of Halifax's following, the Hydes, the Junto connexion, the older Country element, and a squadron of Harleys and Foleys. These groups combined so effectively against Danby—pushing

[1] The division-list is printed in John Oldmixon's *History of England under King William, Queen Mary, Queen Anne, and George I* (London, 1735), pp. 36–37. See my discussion of this division in my article in *Bull. Inst. Hist. Research*, xiv, no. 49, pp. 25–26.

[2] Feiling's *Tory Party*, pp. 275–6.

through, among other things, a bill against placemen and one making general elections obligatory every three years—that the king finally decided to bring over at least one important section of this opposition: the Junto.

As a result the Junto leaders were given office. Montagu became Chancellor of the Exchequer; Somers, Lord Keeper; and Russell, head of the Admiralty. Danby remained as Lord President, but lost much of his influence; Secretary Nottingham returned the seals rather than serve with his arch-enemy Russell; and Seymour was replaced at the Treasury by a Junto man. The administration so remodelled has gone down in history as the 'Junto ministry', hailed by Macaulay as the prototype of the modern cabinet.[1]

This Junto administration (1694–8) is interesting, but hardly for the reasons stressed by Macaulay. It was certainly not the executive committee of the majority party in the Commons —the cabinet of modern times. In the first place, the Junto ministers were appointed *before* the general election of 1695, not as a consequence of their successes in that election; secondly, this administration was made up only partly of Junto politicians;[2] and finally, even with the support of the government interest it could count only on a minority of the Commons.[3] However, with Court backing the Junto managed this parliament with phenomenal success during its first two sessions. Supplies were granted with dispatch, and parliament approved the recoinage and the establishment of the Bank of England and the national debt.

Despite these successes the Junto leaders could not retain

[1] Macaulay's *History*, v. 2384–404.

[2] Besides Danby, his follower Pembroke continued in office as Privy Seal; Godolphin remained as head of the Treasury; Shrewsbury, Secretary of State, was not a Junto leader, though often classed as such; and one of the most influential members of the government at this time, the elder Sunderland (Lord Chamberlain), was not a Junto leader like the younger Sunderland, but a political broker for which a two-party system could have no need.

[3] The election of the anti-administration Member, Paul Foley, as Speaker, and the pluralities gained by opposition M.P.s in the balloting for Commissioners of the Public Accounts are both evidence of this fact.

their hold on the government. The peerages given to three of the leaders (Montagu, Somers, and Russell) came nowhere near satisfying their demands; and the size of their appetite and their insistence on having it gratified eventually alienated Godolphin and the elder Sunderland, the two most influential Court managers. The resignation, in 1697, of these two lords was an indication that the Junto was about to lose the support of the Court and would soon lack the votes needed to carry on the king's business. Sure enough, in the 1697–8 session the Junto leaders were not able to keep the opposition from cutting the army down to 10,000 troops—a setback that the king was not willing to overlook, even though peace with France had just been concluded. William decided, instead, to break off the Junto alliance and dissolve parliament. In the ensuing general election of 1698 the Junto leaders lost their government support; many of their followers lost their seats; and while most of the Junto ministers clung to office for some time, the Junto administration had fallen, to all practical purposes, by the end of the year 1698.

The fall of the Junto was due in some measure to Robert Harley, who now emerges as an important political leader. To a considerable degree his rise was due to the disappearance from the Commons during the 1690's of almost the entire older generation of Country leaders.[1] Harley had himself first entered the Commons under the auspices of two veteran Exclusionists; but he soon broke with them and the Junto lords,[2] and set out

[1] Sixteen prominent Country Members in the Commons died during the decade 1691–1700: John Birch, Hugh Boscawen, William Garroway, Richard and John Hampden, William Harbord, Sir Robert Howard, William Jephson, Sir Thomas Lee, Sir William Leveson-Gower, Henry Powle, William Sacheverell, Sir Richard Temple, Sir John Trenchard, William Waller, and Sir Francis Winnington. We know from Grey's *Debates* that these sixteen veteran Exclusionists carried the main burden of debate on the Country side during the first part of William's reign. Their absence left a real political vacuum.

[2] In the Convention Harley represented the Cornish borough, Tregoney, thanks to its patron, Hugh Boscawen the Elder, to whom Harley was recommended by his uncle John Hampden. The failure of these two gentlemen (one of them a kinsman of Wharton) to recommend Harley for re-election probably

on his own to capture the Country Members who had hesitated to follow the Junto or co-operate with the Court. To these 'old Whigs' he offered himself as a new prophet, calling upon them to follow *him* rather than the Junto or Williamites like Shrewsbury, who were renegade 'new Whigs' that had forsaken true Country principles to become the courtiers of a Dutch ruler. Harley's 'appeal from the new Whigs to the old' was not without effect; and on such issues as opposition to a standing army, to placemen in the Commons, and to a 'Whig' national bank, a number of independent Country Members followed his lead.

The support of Country back-benchers and of his own family and friends gave Harley considerable political influence, which he greatly increased by a *rapprochement* with the older Tory groups. By 1695 he was on increasingly close terms with the Granvilles, the Seymours, and the Hydes;[1] and from this understanding there developed a new coalition—sometimes referred to as the 'New Country Party'—combining the three old Cavalier connexions with the ex-Presbyterian Harley–Foley group. It was this coalition that led the opposition to the Junto, finally driving it from the government; but the resignation of the Junto leaders did not result in the appointment of Harley and his New Country allies. Instead, a combination of Danbyites, Sunderland's followers, and various 'official Whigs' was patched together to fill the gaps in the administration. Harley had a number of conferences with Sunderland and Shrewsbury, the two chief 'cabinetmakers'; but another eighteen months were to elapse before the New Country party won a place in the government.

In the meantime Harley and his allies set out to show the Court that no administration could succeed without them. In the 1699–1700 session of parliament they handed the government a decisive defeat in the matter of the Irish forfeited

helped divide him from his old Country associates. See *H.M.C. Portland MSS.* iii. 435–45.

[1] See Harley's political correspondence with various Tory leaders during this period, in *H.M.C. Portland MSS.* iii. 351–625, *passim.*

estates—thousands of acres forfeited to the crown by Irish Jacobites and granted by William III to Dutch favourites and his English mistress. So strong was the popular current against these grants and against William's 'foreigners' that Harley was able to push through parliament legislation providing for the administration of the Irish estates by trustees named by the Commons, most of them Country Members hostile to the Court. At this point William's advisers persuaded him that further reverses could be avoided only by an accommodation with the New Country Party.

Accordingly, the ministry was rearranged during the summer of 1700. Rochester, one of Harley's Tory allies, was given the government of Ireland; and one of Nottingham's disciples was made Secretary of State in order to secure the support of the Finch connexion, which by this time had also joined the New Country coalition. Finally, the return of Godolphin to head the Treasury was designed to bring over the Marlborough–Godolphin connexion, which had likewise co-operated with Harley since Godolphin's resignation two years before. Harley was not himself included in the ministry, but very few measures were concerted by the new managers without his active participation.[1]

The final step in the new arrangements was the dissolution of parliament and government support for the New Country party in the ensuing elections. These resulted in very little change; but the Court–New Country coalition did succeed by a narrow margin in electing Harley Speaker in place of the former incumbent, a friend of the Junto. Another example of successful co-operation was the passage *nemine contradicente* of the important Act of Settlement, which named the head of the house of Hanover as heir to the English throne in default of issue to the Princess Anne, whose only surviving child had just died.

As a matter of fact the Act of Settlement did much more

[1] See the numerous letters between Harley and Godolphin during this period, in *H.M.C. Portland MSS.* iv. 4–34, *passim.*

than settle the succession; and many of its other provisions were emphatically not a part of the government's programme. Drastic restrictions on the prerogative (to take effect upon the accession of the Hanoverian line), such as the exclusion of foreigners from the Council and, above all, the exclusion of placemen from the Commons, were written into the act despite government opposition, which was not strong enough to sidetrack these pet objectives of the Country groups.[1]

Apart from the succession, foreign affairs were the chief preoccupation of the government. The New Country members of the administration had been critical of the Partition Treaties, by means of which the king hoped to avoid a general war over the question as to who should inherit the Spanish throne and its extensive dominions; but when Louis XIV disregarded these arrangements and accepted the entire Spanish inheritance for his grandson, the New Country leaders, like most Englishmen, recognized the threat to English interests. William's last great diplomatic objective—a 'Grand Alliance' of anti-French powers —was undertaken during the summer of 1701 with the active assistance of Godolphin and especially Marlborough, both associated closely at this time with Harley and his friends of the New Country party. The latter did not object so much to the king's foreign policy as to the part in it played by the Junto lords. Discovering that Somers, the Junto Lord Keeper, had illegally attached the Great Seal to a blank commission for the First Partition Treaty, they started impeachment proceedings against him.

Somers's impeachment touched off a series of explosions more suited to a Polish Diet than to the House of Commons. Orford and Halifax were impeached with less reason than Somers; and the 'Kentish petitioners' who ventured to complain to the House of these proceedings were treated with a severity out of all

[1] Certain other provisions, such as the requirement that the sovereign not leave the kingdom for extended periods nor engage the nation in war for the defence of foreign territory, were opposed by the courtiers as reflections on King William.

proportion to the offence. The government was aghast at the uproar. Harley seems to have counselled moderation, but he was overridden by his friends in the older party groups, who effectively showed that they were more troublesome in the government than they had been out of it. At this point Sunderland and the king wisely decided to break off the New Country alliance.

It was an ideal time for a change. James II had just died, and Louis XIV immediately recognized his son as 'James III', provoking a wave of patriotism in England on which the government hoped to capitalize by calling for the election of a new parliament. In the midst of the elections Godolphin resigned, Rochester and Secretary Hedges (Nottingham's friend) were dismissed, and the New Country groups fought the election stripped of government support. Their Junto opponents, in a series of election pamphlets, accused them of pro-French sympathies or worse;[1] and while the label didn't stick in most cases, it helped the Junto to win back a number of seats lost three years before. When the new parliament met in December 1701 the party groups were very evenly balanced.

In the election of Speaker, for example, Harley was re-elected, but only by four votes; and succeeding divisions on party questions were equally close. The most crucial of these came at the end of February 1702, on a New Country motion attacking the Lords for their failure to act on the Commons' impeachment of the Junto leaders. Both sides brought up every available voter. Two hundred and twenty-one Members divided in favour of the motion; but there were 235 who voted against it.[2] Harley and his friends had made their maximum effort and had failed.

[1] A number of leading New Country Members were supposedly observed dining with the French envoy, M. Poussin. They were blacklisted as 'Poussineers', and most of the group lost their seats, in some cases to Junto candidates.

[2] For this division and the debate leading up to it see the dispatches of the Dutch envoys, in Add. MSS. 17677, xx, ff. 51–52, 232–5; also the Imperial Resident's dispatch of 27 Feb. 1702, in Ono Klopp, *Der Fall des Hauses Stuart, und die Succession des Hauses Hanover* (Vienna, 1887) (hereafter cited as Klopp), ix. 523–4. See also my article on division-lists, in *Bull. Inst. Hist. Research*, xiv. 27.

Already the Court managers had made approaches to the Junto. Carlisle, who often co-operated with Wharton, both in the Lords and in North-Country elections, was given Godolphin's old place at the Treasury; and Lord Manchester, Halifax's Montagu stepson, succeeded Hedges as Secretary. Coffee-house politicians confidently predicted another administration dominated by the Junto, with Wharton as the other Secretary; but the king's fatal accident at the end of February changed everything. On 8 March 1702 the Princess Anne succeeded her brother-in-law on the throne of England.

What general conclusions can we draw from this analysis of the politics of the party groups in the period down to Anne's accession? First, we can probably accept the traditional interpretation of party politics to this extent: if the party groups are considered as forming a continuum, ranging from a republican Nonconformist Left to a royalist Anglican Right, the older party groups will in general fall to the right, the younger party groups to the left of some undetermined centreline. At any rate this would seem to be the case during such periods of political stress as the Exclusion controversy, the attempted Stuart counter-revolution, and the Revolution of 1688.

Can we go farther? Can we assume that, because there was a position later called 'Whig', and one later called 'Tory', in each of these crises, and because certain long-lived Members of both Houses took one of these positions in all three crises, therefore there must have been a united Whig and a united Tory party? We think not, mainly because such a thesis leaves too many factors out of account.

In the first place it dodges the important question of the 'excluded middle'. Certain leading Members can be classed as 'either–or', as Whig or Tory on the basis of their voting record in a number of important divisions; but the more one studies the party history of the period, the more Procrustean such a procedure will seem. A number of party groups may have coalesced into a larger entity under the pressure of some clear threat to the Church or the succession, but during the intervals between such periods of crisis the components of such coalitions were constantly dividing against each other. During these intervals the 'either–or' analysis simply doesn't work: too many Members turn out to be neither consistently Whig nor consistently Tory. This was the situation under Charles II and again under James.

No doubt Feiling and others would say that such eccentric political behaviour does not invalidate the two-party thesis, but is a natural consequence of the newness of the parties. Such dismissal of the inconsistencies shown by the various 'wings' and 'factions' becomes more difficult when one moves into the post-Revolution period. With the establishment of the New Country party by Harley and of its rival the reconstituted Whig party of the Junto inconsistencies in party politics should practically disappear, when in actual fact they do not. Danbyite Tories refuse to co-operate with Seymour Tories, and Country Whigs divide against Whigs of the Court. There are still 'Courtiers' and 'Country Members' in William's later parliaments; and 'as late as 1702 it was commonly assumed that "Court" and "Country" were the normal divisions of politics'.[1]

The difficulty, it seems to us, lies in the inadequacy of the conceptual framework, the Left–Centre–Right continuum used by Feiling and Trevelyan; for this concept, though apparently logical, is misleading. Members who do not vote regularly with the Left or Right are lumped in the Centre, whereas in actuality they belong in two very different groups: those who have voted both 'Whig' and 'Tory' but usually *with* the Court; and those who have voted both 'Whig' and 'Tory' but usually *against* the Court. These irregulars need a more descriptive label than 'Centre', one to indicate their attitude towards the administration *qua* administration. In speaking of a Member—or of a group—we should indicate whether he is 'Court' or 'Country' as well as whether he is 'Tory' or 'Whig'.

In order to map the political position of the party groups,

[1] Feiling's *Tory Party*, p. 277.

then, we need all four terms. 'Whig' and 'Tory' will be the 'east' and 'west' points; 'Court' and 'Country', the 'north' and 'south' points of our political compass. We can think of parliament as a compass card that can be divided into a number of different segments, and in any one session we can expect to see it divided differently on different issues. Thus on a straight party issue like the contest between a Whig and a Tory for Speaker there will be an 'east-west' division; but on a standard Country issue like a bill barring placemen from the House there will be a 'north-south' division—Court against Country.

There will thus be four main segments: Whig, Tory, Country, and Court. In addition there will be subdivisions within each main segment: a nucleus of stalwarts (courtiers who always vote Court, and Whigs who always vote Whig), together with other groups—Court Tories, and Country Whigs, for example —which occupy an intermediate position.[1] In succeeding chapters we shall interpret party politics within this general conceptual framework. If it will serve to explain some of the inconsistencies in the usual interpretation, if it will clear up some of the confusion in the party history of Anne's reign, we can accept it as a useful working hypothesis. Before examining the party history of Anne's reign, however, it might be useful to look first for significant changes in constitutional practice during the preceding reign.

In this connexion the effects of the Revolution of 1688 seem commonly to have been exaggerated. The Bill of Rights did restrict the prerogative by specifically outlawing certain questionable devices used by William's Stuart predecessors and made it virtually impossible to upset the Anglican establishment so as to reintroduce Catholicism. Furthermore, the Revolution Settlement made it impracticable for the monarch to get along without frequent sessions of parliament; but to say that the necessity for frequent meetings of parliament 'established

[1] I have restated here in much the same terms the hypothesis sketched in my 'English Party Politics (1688–1714)', in *Essays in Modern English History: in Honor of Wilbur C. Abbott* (Cambridge, 1941), pp. 83–85.

the supremacy of the House of Commons over the king'[1] is to jump to a conclusion not reached for a century.

The more one studies the history of the years just before and just after 1688, the more one is impressed by the absence of such a break in continuity as is usually assumed. William III had as high a view of the prerogative as the Stuarts and intended to rule like Charles II—selecting his own ministers, conducting his own foreign policy, and consulting parliament only when it had to be called to grant funds. Ministers appointed by the king still believed it their duty to carry out the sovereign's wishes without respect to the party make-up of the House of Commons; and parliament still seemed wedded to its traditional role of a permanent opposition. Sovereignty, as it had been ever since 1661, was still divided between executive and legislature.

The solution to the problem of divided authority—ministers responsible to the majority of the House of Commons, and the corollary, an organized majority party responsive to its leaders in office—lay far in the future. If some slight progress in this direction was registered during the decade after the Revolution, the financial exigencies of war-time were largely responsible. William experimented with ministries of every party hue: old Country, Danbyite, Junto, New Country, and back to Junto; but gradually he and his advisers came to understand that a successful administration must include party leaders as well as 'king's servants'. The former were necessary to line up blocs of votes for government supply bills and against the inevitable Country insistence on redress of grievances at the expense of the government's programme. The time had passed when the conduct of the king's business could be monopolized by courtiers with no parliamentary party behind them.

Court managers of this type could, of course, count on the bloc of 'government Members' in the Commons; but that was never large enough to ensure a working majority; and alliance with some of the organized party groups was a necessity. Hence

[1] See the references in the Introduction, above, p. 1.

the government was always a coalition—built up, altered, demolished, and rebuilt, usually *between* elections.[1] William finally saw the necessity of employing party leaders in order to gain the indispensable parliamentary reinforcements; but he did not feel bound constantly to change his ministries so as to bring them into conformity with the balance of parties in the Commons.

That every general election should be followed automatically by the appointment of an administration chosen from the party groups most successful in that election would have struck William III as absurd. It remains to be seen whether significant steps in that direction would be taken under his successor.

[1] For example, the Junto administration was constructed during the course of the 'Tory' parliament elected in 1690, and began to lose ground during the course of the 'Whig' parliament elected in 1695. Defeated in the 1698 elections, this same Junto group managed to keep hold of some of its offices until 1700.

CHAPTER VI

The General Election of 1702: A Case Study of the Party Groups in Action

THE general election of 1702, held in the summer of that year, was not the first important political development of Anne's reign. It was preceded by the formation of a new ministry and by a final session of the old parliament. We have chosen the 1702 election as a case study of the way the party groups operated in one specific area of politics, but before turning to the election itself we must review briefly certain important changes in the government.

In the early eighteenth century the death of one sovereign and accession of another changed the whole complexion of politics. The country did not have to await the outcome of a general election to discover who its new governors would be. This was certainly the case in 1702; for the personal preferences of the new monarch were immediately reflected in an entirely new administration.

Queen Anne, though a woman of average intelligence, was not a nonentity. Her chief traits were her piety and devotion to the Church of England and a generous share of Stuart stubbornness. On questions that concerned the Church or affected her husband and personal friends she had decided opinions and made her influence felt; but in the everyday work of government she naturally deferred to her chief advisers. Few doubted who these would be: Lord and Lady Marlborough and Lord Godolphin—the 'Mr. and Mrs. Freeman' and 'Mr. Montgomery' of her private correspondence.

This general opinion was confirmed when the queen attended parliament for the first time accompanied only by the

Churchills;[1] and within a few days the pre-eminent position of the Marlborough–Godolphin connexion was made official. Nominated Captain-General of the military forces, Master-General of the Ordnance, and a Knight of the Garter, Marlborough took charge of the army and of diplomatic relations with England's allies; the Admiralty came under a new board dominated by Marlborough's brother George Churchill; and most of the important Household posts went to Lady Marlborough and members of her circle. Finally, the most important civilian post in the gift of the crown—that of Lord Treasurer—was revived,[2] and the treasurer's staff given to Godolphin. In control of both the armed services,[3] of foreign relations, and of the Treasury, the Marlborough–Godolphin connexion clearly dominated the new administration.

Feiling quite properly calls the new government the 'Marlborough–Godolphin Ministry';[4] but of course it contained other elements. The dominant group did not have enough experienced administrators nor did it have anything like enough parliamentary support to carry on the queen's business without allies. These would hardly be recruited from the Junto or other Whig groups, but rather from the New Country party, with which Godolphin and the Churchills had frequently co-operated during the past few years.

Rochester, the queen's uncle, himself expected the Treasurer's staff and was greatly chagrined to receive only a new patent as Lord Lieutenant of Ireland; and his disappointment was little mitigated by the inclusion in the government of a number of his followers: Seymour as Comptroller in place of Wharton,

[1] Narcissus Luttrell's *Brief Historical Relation of State Affairs* (6 vols., Oxford, 1858) (hereafter cited as Luttrell), v. 151. For a contemporary reference to Marlborough as 'Grand Vizier' see a letter of Under-Secretary Ellis to George Stepney, 10 Mar. 1702, in Add. MSS. 7074, f. 242.

[2] William III had kept the Treasury constantly in commission; and in fact Queen Anne was the last ruler to have a Lord Treasurer.

[3] Titular command, as distinct from effective command, was vested in the queen's ineffective consort, George of Denmark, who was made Generalissimo of the Army, Lord High Admiral, and Lord Warden of the Cinque Ports.

[4] Feiling's *Tory Party*, chap. xiii.

Granville as Steward of the Duchy of Cornwall together with various other Cornish places, Gower as Chancellor of the Duchy of Lancaster, and Normanby as Privy Seal.[1]

Six members of the Hyde–Seymour group were included in the new list of Privy Councillors, but the Finch section of the New Country party was given a much larger share of policy-making posts. Nottingham was made Secretary of State for the more important areas, and at his insistence[2] the other secretaryship went to his friend Sir Charles Hedges; his kinsmen Weymouth and Dartmouth got seats at the Board of Trade; six seats at the Council Board were assigned to Nottinghamites; and a number of less important posts went to members of that group.[3] Very few positions were assigned to the Harleian connexion; but Harley's close relationship with Godolphin, who insisted that he should continue as Speaker, assured him of a real influence in the new government.[4]

An alliance of courtiers,[5] Nottinghamites, Rochesterites, and

[1] John Sheffield, Marquis of Normanby, married a niece of Seymour and should be classed as one of the Hyde–Seymour connexion.

[2] I see no reason to doubt Burnet's statement to this effect. See Burnet's *History*, v. 10.

[3] Nottingham's Finch cousin, Lord Winchilsea, became Deputy Warden of the Cinque Ports and Lord Lieutenant of Kent; his ally Abingdon got command of the Tower plus the posts of Chief Justice in Eyre (South of Trent) and Lord Lieutenant of Oxfordshire (both formerly held by Wharton); and Sir George Rooke, a connexion and follower, was made a member of the Admiralty.

[4] The most important post to go to a Harleian was that of Solicitor-General, which went to Harley's friend and follower, Simon Harcourt. Another friend, Robert Price, got an English judgeship. Harley's influence in the new administration appears clearly in the correspondence between him and Lord Treasurer Godolphin. See *H.M.C. Portland MSS.* iv. 35 et seq.

[5] With Anne's accession the Churchills became the chief 'courtiers'. Other courtiers in the Marlborough–Godolphin ministry were: Pembroke, an old Danbyite, Lord President; Somerset, Master of the Horse; Devonshire, a Court Whig peer now in his seventies, who continued as Lord Steward of the Household; and Henry Boyle, who seems to have been more 'Court' than 'Whig', continued as Chancellor of the Exchequer. Sir Nathan Wright (Lord Keeper) and Lord Jersey (Lord Chamberlain) are classed by Feiling with the 'Tory Right' and usually voted with Rochester; but I have found no personal connexion between them and the Hyde–Seymour connexion.

Harleians, such was the administration set up by the Churchills in the queen's name. In a good many respects it resembled the administration of 1700–1, which also had Godolphin at the head of the Treasury, Rochester as Lord Lieutenant of Ireland, Hedges as one of the Secretaries of State, and Harley as Speaker. There is a further parallel: Marlborough and Godolphin virtually adopted William's policies and had the same difficulties—and for the same reasons—getting parliament to implement them. Supply, union with Scotland, and preparations for the now inevitable war with France, on each of these issues the two chief ministers thought as William would have; but in each case like William they faced opposition from the Country groups supposedly allied with the Court, but obviously more interested in purely partisan matters.

Both in the cabinet and in the closing session of the old parliament the New Country leaders frequently failed to follow the course set by Marlborough and Godolphin. In foreign affairs, for example, a disagreement between Marlborough and Rochester held up the declaration of war against France. If declaring war meant costly involvement in Continental land campaigns, Rochester was opposed, favouring instead purely naval action. Marlborough, like William III, believed in fighting in the Netherlands and had the support of a majority of the Council; but it was two months before Rochester's opposition was overcome and war actually declared.[1] Similarly, with the projected Union with Scotland, Marlborough, like William, favoured such a step; but many among the Hyde and Finch groups were opposed. Nearly a hundred Members voted against the government bill to appoint commissioners to treat with the Scots; and this minority included a number associated with the New Country groups.[2] Finally, the appropriation of funds for

[1] See the dispatch of the Austrian envoy, Wratislaw, 1 May 1702, in Klopp, x. 43; and Abel Boyer's *History of the Reign of Queen Anne, Digested into Annals* (London, yearly, 1702–10) (hereafter cited as Boyer, *Annals*), i. 28.

[2] See L'Hermitage's dispatch of 20 Mar. 1702 in Add. MSS. 17677, xx, f. 259; and *C.J.* xiii. 812. The tellers for the minority were James Brydges, a

40,000 English troops was constantly delayed by leaders of the organized Tory groups in the Commons, who succeeded in postponing this important business to pursue some partisan policy of their own.

Examples of this last were sometimes trivial, but none the less exceedingly annoying to the government managers. Attacks on William's Irish grants, on the employment of any but native-born Englishmen as officers in the new regiments, and the revival of a parliamentary commission of public accounts—these all stirred up party feeling and consumed valuable time that would have been better devoted to the work of supply.[1] The attack on 'foreigners', aimed at Dutchmen and French Huguenots who had come to England to fight with William III against Louis XIV, was helped along by the queen's first speech, with its phrase, 'I know my own heart to be entirely English'. Taken by the Country groups as a dig at the late king, this passage was probably Rochester's work.[2]

The commission of public accounts leads us to the Speaker, Harley. The idea of such a body first took shape in William's reign, and it might have led to fruitful co-operation between the Commons and the Treasury—even some parliamentary initiative in framing the budget. Instead, the commission was dominated from the first by Harley and his friends, who used it to attack ministers they disliked,[3] or later capitalized on their nuisance value as commissioners to win posts in the government. The newly elected commission—a New Country list of seven chosen in an election suddenly sprung on the House—had no time during the remainder of the session to

Harleian, and Robert Byerly, an independent Yorkshire Member who voted consistently with the Finch connexion.

[1] The government even arranged for the queen to administer a public rebuke. See her message of 30 Mar. 1702 in *C.J.* xiii. 830.

[2] Referring to Rochester, the Dutch agent wrote: 'c'est lui qui fit mettre dans la première harangue de la Reine le mot du cœur entièrement Anglois. . . . Marlborough ne fut pas de cet avis' (L'Hermitage's dispatch, quoted in Morgan's *English Political Parties*, p. 63 note).

[3] For a good account of this body see Dr. Shaw's introduction to the *Calendar of Treasury Books, 1689–1700*.

show its hand, but its make-up is interesting. It included three, or possibly four, Harleians; two Nottinghamites; and a henchman of Sir Edward Seymour.[1]

The tendency of the New Country groups to desert the Court on such issues as the commission of accounts, Union with Scotland, and especially on strategy for the war made the task of the two chief ministers more difficult; and they gave some indication of this when they made the queen tell parliament, 'I wish that no difference of opinion among those that are equally affected to my service may be the occasion of heats and animosities.' These words were part of Anne's speech closing the session, a speech that ended on a different note: 'My own principles must always keep me entirely firm to the Interests and Religion of the Church of England and will incline me to countenance those who have the truest zeal to support it.'[2]

This was taken as a plain declaration of Court favour towards the Hyde and Finch connexions, which professed to speak for the Church and all loyal churchmen. Fortified by such evidence of royal support and by the offices carrying electoral influence which had gone to their leaders, the Rochester and Nottingham groups went into the forthcoming elections more confidently perhaps than any of their party rivals.

By the middle of August 1702 the results of the first general election of Anne's reign were a matter of record, but their significance is still disputed. Bishop Burnet believed that in the new parliament the Tories 'were at least double the number of the whigs',[3] while Trevelyan tells us that the Whigs were reduced to 'a shadow of their former strength'.[4] Marlborough's

[1] Henry St. John, Thomas Coke, and James Brydges (for whom see above, p. 68) were members of Harley's group, while Sir Godfrey Copley, originally a follower of Danby, to whom he was related, later joined Harley; William Bromley and Robert Byerly voted consistently with the Finch connexion; and the seventh member, Francis Scobell, was a relative and follower of Seymour.

[2] For the text of the speech see *L.J.* xvii. 150. That it had been discussed by Godolphin and Harley is clear from Godolphin's letter to Harley, 21 May 1702 in *H.M.C. Portland MSS.* iv. 38.

[3] Burnet's *History*, v. 45.

[4] Trevelyan's *Blenheim*, p. 209.

descendant and biographer, on the other hand, considers the 'election of 1702 no landslide';[1] while Morgan concludes that 'the results were probably closer than they had been ten months before, although it is difficult to obtain satisfactory data'.[2] Actually, the returns provide plenty of satisfactory data, if they are properly used.

The first point to determine is the actual number of changes resulting from the election. The returns show a total of 150; but since fifty of these represent normal 'succession'—the new Member replacing a relative in some family borough, or a noble's nominee giving way to another nominee at the same constituency—there remains a total of about 100 changes to be analysed. Instead of trying to classify these changes simply as gains or losses for either the Whigs or the Tories, we shall show instead how they affected the strength of the individual party groups—those associated with the government and those hostile to it or independent. We shall begin with the government interest itself and move on logically to the Marlborough–Godolphin, Hyde–Seymour, Finch, and Harley connexions associated with it. We shall continue with an analysis of the returns as they affected the organized Whig groups and conclude with a brief estimate of the changes effected in the unorganized and independent groups.

Turning first to the government interest, we note that eleven of the thirty-eight government Members in the old parliament lost their seats in the 1702 elections.[3] Since most of them represented safe government boroughs like Rochester and Harwich and since the government rarely lost an election, this decline in straight government strength is puzzling. The explanation lies in the fact that some of the groups allied with the government used official influence to replace government nominees with candidates of their own.

[1] Churchill's *Marlborough*, ii. 90.

[2] Morgan's *English Political Parties*, p. 82.

[3] Detailed documentation of this election would so encumber the text that it is given instead in Appendix IV. Though eleven lost seats, one government man gained a seat. The *net* loss was ten.

This was not true of Marlborough and Godolphin, who in effect were the Court and who naturally welcomed the re-election of all government Members. Their own personal following was small—twelve in the old parliament, increased to eighteen in the new. Three of these six additional Members were returned for Cornish constituencies, but not at the expense of government Members.[1] The case was very different with Godolphin's New Country allies, particularly the Nottingham–Finch connexion.

In the 1702 elections the most effective use of official influence was made by Nottingham, notably in the Cinque Ports and nearby boroughs traditionally subject to pressure from the government. At these constituencies the new Deputy Lord Warden of the Cinque Ports and Lord Lieutenant of Kent, Nottingham's cousin Lord Winchilsea, worked energetically with Nottingham to replace sitting government Members with men tied closely to the Finch connexion.[2] Five Finch candidates were returned: two in Rochester and one each in Hastings, Rye, and Sandwich. In other government boroughs Nottingham turned the same trick. In Harwich the sitting Member, a navy commissioner, was ousted to make room for an under-secretary of state, and in Weymouth the Surveyor of the Works resigned his seat to admit Winchilsea's nephew. Only two of these seven new Members held official positions.[3]

A gain of seven seats may seem trifling, but one must remember that the whole Nottingham–Finch connexion numbered but thirty-one in the old parliament. The total gain registered by the group in the 1702 elections was fourteen seats, of which half were won by Nottingham through the use of official influence in government boroughs; while another, in Norwich,

[1] A fourth Godolphin nominee was returned for one of the Cinque Ports, the other two in constituencies in Yorkshire and Suffolk. See Appendix IV, Part II.

[2] For this electioneering see Add. MSS. 29588 (Finch Papers), especially Winchilsea's letter to Nottingham, 12 July 1702, and Edward Southwell's to Nottingham, 22 July 1702 (Add. MSS. 29588, ff. 94, 102).

[3] Ellis, the Under-Secretary (Harwich), and Southwell, the Irish Secretary (Rye), were the only ones in office. See Appendix IV, Part III.

was won by a Finch nominee largely out of deference to Her Majesty's Secretary of State.[1] Of the remaining half dozen seats won by the group four were gained by Nottingham's allies Lord Abingdon and Lord Bruce (in Wiltshire and Oxfordshire constituencies where the Bruces and Berties had family interests); one, for Cheshire, by Nottingham's prospective son-in-law Mostyn (who was also re-elected for Flint); and one, at Cambridge University, by a member of the Annesley family, who succeeded Sir Isaac Newton as second Member for Cambridge University.[2]

The Hyde–Seymour group also strengthened its position, partly through official influence. The election of two of Rochester's followers for Westminster, in place of the government Members who represented it in the old parliament, was due largely to Rochester's official position and influence. These two recruits plus the single additions contributed by his sister-in-law Lady Sandwich and his kinsman Sir John Pakington increased Rochester's following from twelve in the old parliament to sixteen in the new.[3]

Colonel Granville used his official influence, as Lord Lieutenant of Cornwall and Warden of the Stannaries, to even better effect. He could boast of ten Members among the Cornish delegation elected in 1702 and of two from Devon—an increase of five. His nephew Sir John Leveson-Gower also used his official influence, as Chancellor of the Duchy of Lancaster, for the benefit of the family connexion, bringing in three new members of the group for Lancashire boroughs where the Duchy had influence.[2]

Sir Edward Seymour and his friends also made gains, but not apparently through government influence. As a matter of fact, Seymour's son was dropped by the Duke of Somerset, who replaced young Seymour at Cockermouth with a government

[1] For Nottingham's efforts to get his nominee returned at Norwich see Add. MSS. 29588, f. 115.

[2] See Appendix IV, Part IV.

[3] See Appendix IV, Part IV. The group gained a seat by the election of Robert Hyde for Wiltshire; but this was offset by Kendall's replacement by a Godolphin at West Looe.

candidate; but Seymour's ally, Jack Howe, was elected for no less than four constituencies (one of them a Cornish borough where Granville had an interest); and Sir Christopher Musgrave recovered three seats in Cumberland and Westmorland, so that he no longer needed the seat for Totnes which Seymour had kept for him.[1] Taken as a whole, the gains made by Rochester and his lieutenants amounted to nineteen new seats and gave the Hyde–Seymour connexion sixty-six Members in the new parliament as against forty-seven in the old. This was about three times as many Members as were grouped in the Harley–Foley connexion, last of the groups allied with the government. In the 1702 elections all seven Harleys and Foleys were re-elected; and while two kinsmen were unseated, another three came in for other constituencies, so that the total for the group was twenty-one, one more than in the old parliament.[1]

To what degree did the government and the party groups associated with it win the election? In the old parliament the straight 'government interest' totalled thirty-eight; in the new, only twenty-eight: a *loss* of ten. Even if the Marlborough–Godolphin connexion is included with the Court, where it properly belongs, there is still a government loss of four seats. The groups allied with the government, on the other hand, did make extensive gains—a total of thirty-three more votes than before. In the old parliament the New Country party had ninety-eight votes; in the new it could count on 131. It was not the Court, then, that won the 1702 election, but the party groups allied with it and taking advantage of Court influence.

What of the organized party groups associated less closely or not at all with the government? Were the thirty-three seats gained by the Rochester and Nottingham groups won largely at their expense, and if so, which suffered most heavily? To answer these questions we need to survey briefly each of the other organized connexions, starting with the five little Court groups centred on Stamford, Carlisle, Somerset, Radnor, and Pembroke. Of these the first two were the heaviest losers.

[1] See Appendix IV, Part IV.

Carlisle was first Lord of the Treasury during the 1701 elections, and this no doubt assisted him in returning six followers to William's last parliament. In 1702, now ousted from office, he managed to re-elect only two of these, the Members for the family borough of Morpeth. Three of the four who lost their seats were replaced by Musgraves, the clan headed by Seymour's friend, Sir Christopher.[1]

Stamford was in a similar position. Chancellor of the Duchy of Lancaster in William's last government, he returned three Members on the Duchy interest. In the 1702 elections all three were dropped by Gower, the new Chancellor of the Duchy, who put in men who would vote with the Hyde–Seymour connexion. Stamford suffered a further loss, the defeat of a nominee at Leicester; and like Carlisle was able to re-elect only two of his group: the Members for his family borough of Beeralston in Devon.[2] These two ex-ministers, both Court Whigs, together lost eight seats, six of them to the Hyde–Seymour connexion.

The other three Court peers were not allies of the Junto, and two of them retained office in the new government. Radnor did not, and he, significantly, lost three Cornish seats: one to an independent merchant; one to Godolphin; and one to Granville, his successor as Lord Lieutenant of Cornwall.[3] Somerset, kept in the government, as Master of the Horse, had returned only two Members to William's last parliament; and he returned two to Anne's first one, though not the same two.[4] Pembroke, Lord President of Anne's Council, had returned three Members to William's last parliament. One of his Members, for the family borough of Wilton, was apparently defeated in 1702; but the election was controverted, and the man would probably

[1] See Appendix IV, Part VI.

[2] See Appendix IV, Part VI. Stamford's nominees for Preston and Wigan could be classed as 'government Members', but they seem to have been henchmen of Stamford rather than straight government officials.

[3] Granville replaced one of Radnor's family by Jack Howe. See Appendix IV.

[4] At Cockermouth Somerset replaced one of Sir Edward Seymour's sons with General Stanhope, later identified with the Newcastle–Townshend group. See also Appendix IV.

be seated on petition.[1] Of the five Court peers those that remained closest to the Court did best in the 1702 elections.

No part of William's last government nor yet of Anne's first one, the Newcastle connexion was not regarded with any particular animus by the new Country elements in the administration.[2] This group had returned sixteen Members to William's last parliament. In the 1702 elections it won the same number of seats, single losses by the Pelhams, Fanes, and Townshends being made up by a gain of three scored by Newcastle himself in Yorkshire and Nottinghamshire.[3] This family connexion, which stood somewhere between the Court and the Junto, was not a loser in the election. In fact none of the organized Court and Court Whig groups, except for Carlisle's and Stamford's, lost heavily in the general election of 1702.

The case was rather different with the Junto, as one might expect. Wharton's name had been struck from the list of Privy Councillors, his Comptroller's staff was given to Seymour, and his territorial honours to Nottingham's friend Abingdon. In the face of such obvious signs of royal displeasure Wharton was not able to return twenty-five nominees to the Commons, as he had in 1701; but he managed to elect eighteen followers to Anne's first parliament, a remarkable feat under the circumstances.[4] Orford and Sunderland suffered to about the same degree. Together they returned seventeen Members to William's last parliament. They would have three less in the new House of Commons. Percentage-wise Halifax was hardest hit. Managing the Montagu interests, he had returned seven nominees in 1701. In the 1702 elections four of these were defeated—two of them Montagus.[5] Of the Junto leaders only Somers held his own, returning six Members to the new parliament as he had in the old; while the 'sixth Junto peer', the Duke of Bolton, did

[1] See Appendix IV, Part VI.

[2] At all events, none of the leaders of this group lost the territorial honours held under William III.

[3] See Appendix IV, Part VII.

[4] See Appendix IV, Part VIII, for details.

[5] See Appendix IV, Part VIII.

almost as well, with a net loss of only one seat, from nine in the old parliament to eight in the new. As a whole the Junto connexion lost fifteen seats—a considerable drop, from sixty-four in William's last parliament to forty-nine in the first of Queen Anne.[1]

No one party group benefited significantly from the Junto losses. Nottingham picked up four seats from the Junto; Rochester two; and the Harleian group one. The other nine seats lost by the Junto went to Members who belonged to none of the organized party groups. Nearly half the House was made up of such men, who are difficult to classify with any accuracy; but they fall into five fairly distinct categories: unorganized Court Whigs, who voted on the Whig side in party matters, but usually *with* the government on other issues; unorganized Court Tories, who voted Tory in party divisions, but otherwise with the Court; Country Whigs, Whig on party issues, but usually opposed to Court measures; Country Tories, Tory in party questions, but anti-administration in general; and finally, High Church Members, zealous Anglicans, whose concern for the Establishment was more decisive in determining their politics than either a Whig versus Tory or Court versus Country orientation.

In William's last parliament the relative strength of these five groups was: Court Whigs, 68; Country Whigs, 34; Court Tories, 33; Country Tories, 60; and High Church, 48.[2] In the 1702 elections the two unorganized Whig groups lost a dozen Members apiece; while the three Tory groups gained corre-

[1] See Appendix IV, Part VIII.

[2] My classification is based on each Member's voting record and what information I could gather on his personal connexions. The evidence for classing a Member as Court Whig, Court Tory, or High Church is reasonably definite. In the case of the Country groups information is often very scanty, and many of them have no voting record. However, we can be reasonably sure that such obscure figures *were* probably 'Country'; and whether they were inclined to the Whig or Tory side makes relatively little difference. Errors in assigning them to one position or the other in many cases must cancel, and in any case I hardly believe that quantitatively they are of a magnitude to affect the general picture.

spondingly: the High Churchmen, 14; the Country Tories, 4; and the Court Tories, 6.

Considering the election of 1702 as a whole, one notes in the first place that, numerically, the change in the strength of any one group was small—a gain or loss of seventeen being the maximum. Cumulatively, these changes add up to a considerable shift, which *can* be interpreted in terms of over-all Whig and Tory strength. If we include as 'Whig': the Junto and Newcastle connexions, the nominees of the Court Whig peers Carlisle and Stamford, and the unorganized Court and Country Whig Members, we get a total of 149 for this 'Whig party' in the 1702 parliament. Similarly, a combination of the organized 'Tory' groups—those of Godolphin, Nottingham, Rochester, Harley, and the three Court Tory peers (Pembroke, Radnor, and Somerset)—and the unorganized High Church, Country, and Court Tory Members would give a total 'Tory party' of 321.

This exercise in addition suggests that Bishop Burnet was right in speaking of the 'tories as double the strength of the whigs'; but it would be a mistake to attach much significance to these totals. For one thing, they leave room for a government interest of only forty-three Members, men who cannot somehow be classed either as Whig or Tory. It would be just as logical to add up all the groups with a pro-government attitude and arrive at a 'Court party' of 181 Members. In other words, the parliament of 1702, like any other in this period, can be divided into a number of different two-, three-, four-, or *n*-way divisions, as was suggested somewhat earlier in this essay.[1]

Bearing these considerations in mind, we can say that there were about fifty more 'Tories' in Anne's first parliament than there were in William's last; but of much greater significance were the changes in the relative strength of the chief 'minority interests'. Just as a modern corporation is often controlled by a few large stockholders who seldom individually own more than a tenth of the voting stock, so an early eighteenth-century

[1] See above, pp. 92–93.

parliament was often controlled by its chief 'minority stockholders'—the seven principal interests or connexions described in Chapter IV.

Queen Anne's first ministry was a combination of five such interests: the Court, Marlborough–Godolphin, Finch, Hyde–Seymour, and Harley connexions. In the 1702 elections this combination gained only twenty-seven votes; but these, added to the 161 held over from the previous parliament, gave an over-all voting strength of 188. Moreover, since this combination of interests acted for the government, it could usually expect the support of about a hundred unattached Court Members (Whig and Tory), who normally voted with any administration. There was thus a total of 288 Members attached to the administration or willing to follow its lead, and this should be enough for effective control of the Commons, given the lack of effective organization among the independent or unattached Members who made up a large part of the balance of the House.

This 'majority' of 288 was very unlike the majority of a present-day party administration, however, since it merely reflected the combination of groups enlisted at the particular time in the government or allied with it. The ministry constituted in 1702 'was from the first a coalition', Professor Feiling quite properly points out; and he goes on to explain that 'the intensity of party feelings in the next few years was destined to destroy it'.[1] At the end of six years little remained of the original combination of 1702; but the coalition was not so much 'destroyed' as reconstituted year by year in such gradual fashion that it is difficult to say exactly when the decisive shift took place. The final stage in that reconstitution—the replacement of the last remaining 'Tory' ministers by men drawn from the Whig groups—was closely connected with the events of the parliamentary session of 1707–8. We have chosen that session as a second case study illustrating the way in which the party system functioned in a specific situation, and an account of that session will follow in the next chapter; but first, by way of

[1] Feiling's *Tory Party*, p. 366.

introduction, it will be necessary to summarize the chief political developments of the intervening period.

During the five years that followed the election of 1702 the position of the various party groups *vis-à-vis* the government changed significantly. The alliance between the Marlborough–Godolphin group and the Hyde–Seymour and Finch connexions was predicated on the expectation that the latter would work with the government interest to further the queen's business in parliament. Instead, these two connexions jeopardized the government's programme by constantly pursuing objectives not positively opposed by the Court, but viewed rather as inexpedient, since they would undoubtedly 'raise party heats' and distract both Houses from their primary task—implementation of the administration war programme.

From the beginning of Anne's first parliament, for example, the Finch connexion threw most of its energies into the fight for the 'Occasional Conformity Bill', which would exclude from municipal office Nonconformists who 'conformed' once a year in order to get around the disability imposed on them by their separation from the Established Church. The Hyde–Seymour group also supported the bill, which would effectively destroy the electoral interests built up by their party opponents in many boroughs through alliance with leading local Nonconformists; while the Junto leaders, conversely, did all they could to kill the bill. Church sentiment against 'occasional conformity' was so strong that the practice could not be defended. Instead, the Junto manœuvred the Rochester and Nottingham groups into provoking a deadlock between the two Houses on the issue,[1] a deadlock so awkward for the government that Godolphin shifted from lukewarm acceptance of the bill to outright opposition.

[1] For the parliamentary history of the Occasional Conformity Bill see *C.J.* xiv. 76–77, 238, 247; *H.M.C. House of Lords MSS.* (N.S.), v. 297–300 (for the text of the bill); and Oldmixon, p. 323 (for a summary of the debates). The best report of the proceedings is by Thomas Johnson, M.P. for Liverpool, in a letter of 10 Dec. 1702 in *Norris Papers* (Chetham Soc. Publ., ix), p. 102.

The Occasional Conformity Bill was only one of the inconvenient issues raised by the Finch and Hyde–Seymour groups. They also revived the parliamentary commission of public accounts, the impeachment of the Junto leaders, and the attack on William III's grants—all of them highly explosive.[1] In connexion with the last Seymour and Musgrave, of the Rochester connexion, even quashed Anne's proposed grant to Marlborough—this despite private assurances that no difficulties would be raised by the groups associated with the Court.[2] There was finally the case of Ashby *v.* White, arising out of Wharton's efforts to get a judicial decision reversing the disfranchisement of some of his voters at Aylesbury, a borough disputed between him and the lord of the manor, a cousin and follower of Rochester. Wharton managed to get the 'Aylesbury Case' before the Lords, who handed down a decision in his favour, thereby precipitating a quarrel with the Commons that was just as bitter as the one over Occasional Conformity and served equally to postpone and interrupt public business.[3]

In fighting over these party issues Rochester and his followers had constantly ignored Godolphin's advice. Finally losing his patience, Godolphin persuaded the queen to order her uncle to his government in Ireland. Rather than leave, Rochester tendered his resignation—which was thereupon accepted. This was the first breach in the government coalition; but it was a small crack, concealed by the appointment in Rochester's place of his son-in-law and by peerages given to three of his lieutenants.[4]

[1] See above, pp. 88, 89, 99–101, for the earlier history of these issues.

[2] For the 'private assurances' see Godolphin's letter to Harley, 10 Dec. 1702, in *H.M.C. Portland MSS.* iv. 53. The debate on Marlborough's grant is reported by Johnson, in letters of 10, 12 Dec. in *Norris Papers*, pp. 103–7. Significantly, Nottingham's brother, Heneage Finch, and his prospective son-in-law Mostyn both spoke in *favour* of the grant.

[3] For the parliamentary history of the Aylesbury Case see *C.J.* xiv, *passim*; *L.J.* xvii, *passim*; Boyer's *Annals*, iii. 189; Luttrell, v. 380, 524; and the *Parliamentary History of England from the Earliest Period to the Year 1803* (London, 1806–20; compiled by William Cobbett), vi. 253–64 (hereafter cited as *Parl. Hist.*).

[4] Namely Granville, Leveson-Gower, and Seymour-Conway (soon to marry Rochester's daughter). Heneage Finch was given a peerage at this time, also.

A more serious division in the government appeared a year and a half later, when Nottingham was forced out. During the first session of the 1702 parliament he had sinned by 'being so impertinent as to join with Sir Edward Seymour and others to obstruct business';[1] and after the second session the Court heard that he was party to a scheme to force through the Occasional Conformity Bill during the next session by tacking that bill to the Land Tax. When Nottingham unwisely chose this moment to insist on the dismissal of certain Court Whig peers who had criticized him in the Lords, Godolphin was able to persuade Anne to refuse that request; and Nottingham perforce resigned. Seymour and Musgrave left the government at this same time, also; but neither of them voluntarily or as a gesture of sympathy either with Nottingham or with their own chief, Lord Rochester. The dismissal of Seymour, a ringleader in every fracas that had upset the government's time-table, was long overdue;[2] while Musgrave forestalled dismissal by dying.

In the final session of Anne's first parliament the line-up of party groups was quite altered. The Harley connexion was now more strongly represented in the government, Harley himself taking the secretary's seals from Nottingham; and some additional parliamentary support for the government coalition was secured through an alliance with the Newcastle connexion. On the other hand, most of the leaders of the Hyde–Seymour and Finch connexions were now in opposition, ready to stake everything on a 'Tack' of the Occasional Conformity Bill, only to be defeated in the crucial test by a vote of 251–134.

The published list of the minority[3] in that division shows

[1] Marlborough to Godolphin, undated; and see also another letter to Godolphin, 3 June 1703; both in Coxe's *Marlborough*, i. 270, 275.

[2] See Godolphin's complaint: 'I am so out of patience with Sir Edward Seymour that I can meet him nowhere but to scold' (letter to Harley, 4 Nov. 1702, in *H.M.C. Portland MSS.* iv. 50); and that of Marlborough: 'We are bound not to wish for anybody's death, but if Sir Edward Seymour should die, I am convinced it would be no great loss to the queen nor the nation' (letter to Godolphin, 5 June 1702, in Coxe's *Marlborough*, i. 275).

[3] For this division-list see my article in *Bulletin of the Institute of Historical Research*, xiv. 28–29.

clearly not only the division between the 'moderate and ministerial Tories' (as Feiling and Trevelyan call the Court Tories and Harley's group) and the 'Tory Right' (the elements led by Rochester and Nottingham), but more significantly the divisions *within* the Tory Right itself. Of the total membership of the Finch and Hyde–Seymour connexions less than half voted for the Tack.[1] By forcing a division on an issue that had been made a test of allegiance to the government, Rochester and Nottingham forced their followers still in office to choose between loyalty to them and loyalty to the Court; and it is significant that the magnetic pull of the Court proved more powerful than that of party.

The dissolution of Anne's first parliament in the spring of 1705 was followed by the dismissal of the leading Rochester and Nottingham lieutenants still in office.[2] The break between Godolphin and the Finch and Hyde–Seymour groups was now complete; but as yet the Treasurer made no approach to the Junto, although that group had guaranteed the success of the last session by voting with the Court on all crucial issues. Instead, it was the Newcastle connexion that was brought into the administration: the duke, as Privy Seal; and Walpole, as a Councillor for the Admiralty; while other vacant posts were shared between lesser figures of that group and clients of Godolphin and Marlborough. So reconstituted, the government rested on a narrow basis and could not hope successfully to carry on the queen's business in the next parliament unless it made significant gains in the forthcoming elections.

[1] Of forty-four members of the Finch connexion twenty-seven voted for the Tack; but a much smaller proportion (twenty-three out of sixty-one) of the Hyde–Seymour connexion were 'Tackers'. Almost everyone in both groups who still had a place was a 'Sneaker', i.e. voted against the Tack.

[2] The chief casualties in the Hyde–Seymour connexion were Seymour's nephew by marriage, the Duke of Buckingham (Lord Privy Seal), and Granville (Lord Warden of the Stannaries and Lord Lieutenant of Cornwall); and in the Finch connexion, Lord Winchilsea (Deputy Lord Warden of the Cinque Ports and Lord Lieutenant of Kent), Sir George Rooke (Admiralty), and Under-Secretary Ellis. Secretary Hedges voted against the Tack and was spared for a while.

Fortunately, Godolphin was able to register such gains. The government interest, for example, picked up twenty-two additional seats—some in Kent and the Cinque Ports, at the expense of Finch nominees; some in Devon and Cornwall, where Godolphin had the assistance of Bishop Trelawny—and Godolphin himself returned six more followers than before. His chief allies did not do so well; but together the government coalition increased its parliamentary following by twenty-eight Members: a total of 132 administration votes. Conversely, the Finch and Hyde–Seymour connexions suffered together a net loss of thirty-seven votes, cutting their combined strength from 116 to 79 Members. As for the Junto connexion, that group did almost as well as the government interest, winning twenty new seats. Numbering sixty-four, the Junto connexion was the largest single organized group in the new parliament.[1]

With this strength the Junto leaders could argue that their assistance was essential and should be secured by giving them a real share in the government. Political logic was on their side, but Godolphin's position was not so weak that he had to capitulate. Instead, partly by taking advantage of the queen's and Harley's opposition to such an accommodation, he managed to hold off the Junto leaders without losing their support for over

[1] The table below gives the results of the 1705 election in tabular form:

Party Group	*Old Parliament*	*New Parliament*
Government Interest	36	58
Marlborough–Godolphin	17	23
Harley–Foley	20	14
Newcastle–Pelham–Walpole	20	24
Court peers	10	13
Total of gov't coalition	103	132
Court Whig	56	64
Court Tory	39	33
	95	97
Total pro-admin. groups	198	229

Party Group	*Old Parliament*	*New Parliament*
Nottingham–Finch	50	39
Hyde–Seymour	66	40
High Church Indep.	62	49
Country Tory	51	44
Total of opposition	229	172
Junto connexion	44	64
Country Whig	42	48
Total non-admin. Whig	86	112
Total non-admin. groups	315	284
Total pro-admin. groups	198	229
Total House	513	513

four years. The efforts of the Junto, in and out of parliament, to gain their share of policy-making posts, and Godolphin's efforts to keep them from outright opposition by conceding the absolute minimum—this is the key to the party history of the next few years.

For example, in the choice of a new Speaker to succeed Harley and of a new Lord Keeper to replace an ineffectual Churchman who was dismissed at this time Godolphin promoted men who, while not members of the Junto connexion, were yet much friendlier to the Junto than the candidates favoured by Harley and the queen. Anne would have preferred a Churchman as Speaker, and the Finch and Hyde–Seymour groups did their best to oblige her; but the government and Junto joined forces and won over enough independent Whig Members to elect the government candidate by a vote of 248 to 205.[1] The first trials of strength over disputed elections went the same way—seven opposition Members were unseated in favour of administration candidates—and the Junto and Court groups combined just as effectively in the proceedings over supply, which went more smoothly than in any previous session.

The principal issue of the session was the opposition proposal to invite over the Electress Sophia, heir presumptive to the English throne. By moving for such an 'invitation' Nottingham and Rochester thought they could not lose. If the ministers supported the motion, they would forfeit the favour of the queen, to whom the idea was anathema; but if they opposed it, they would alienate the Whig groups and a large section of the electorate, who would construe opposition to the invitation as opposition to the 'Protestant Succession'.

[1] On the election of a Speaker, see *C.J.* xv. 5; letter of Lewis, Under-Secretary, dated 26 Oct. 1705, in Add. MSS. 4743, f. 47; Lady Granby's letter to the Duke of Rutland, in *H.M.C. Rutland MSS.* ii. 183; and the newsletter in *H.M.C. Portland MSS.* iv. 268.

Government Members who voted against John Smith, the government candidate, were immediately disciplined. See the case of George Clarke, Admiralty Secretary, described in his autobiography, in *H.M.C. Leyburne-Popham MSS.*, p. 283.

The government's successful counter-strategy, concerted beforehand with the Junto,[1] was to sidetrack the invitation without a vote, on the grounds that it was not expedient at the moment.[2] Quashing the invitation in this manner had a double effect: not only was the queen grateful to her chief ministers, she actually transferred to the leaders of the Finch and Hyde–Seymour connexions much of the hostility she had formerly shown towards the Junto lords.[3] The Junto and the government then spiked the argument that they were 'against the Protestant Succession' by introducing a measure setting up automatic machinery to ensure the accession of the Hanoverian heir. Caught in their own snare, the Finch and Hyde–Seymour groups did not dare oppose the 'Regency Bill' directly, but concentrated their strength on adding one particular clause.

This clause specifically spelt out the exclusion of placemen from the House of Commons, following up the provision written into the Act of Settlement by Country groups in 1701.[4] The Court had hoped to circumvent that provision; but Rochester and Nottingham joined forces with the Country groups to keep it on the statute book and to strengthen it; and the chances for victory looked bright, since the same combination had successfully introduced a regular 'place bill' earlier in the session by a vote of 220–134.[5] Actually, the 'clause' was too popular to be defeated outright, and the Court was forced to concede the exclusion from the Commons of all pensioners and those holding new offices and to accept the requirement that Members accepting office must in future stand immediately for re-election. The Finch and Hyde–Seymour groups opposed this compromise

[1] See Godolphin's letter to Newcastle, 13 Nov. 1705, in *H.M.C. Portland MSS.* ii. 191. At the strategy meeting Bolton was spokesman for the Junto.

[2] For proceedings on the 'invitation' in the Lords, see *L.J.* xviii. 19; *H.M.C. House of Lords MSS.* (N.S.), vi. 322, quoting MS. minutes; and Boyer's *Annals*, vi. 192–6; for the Commons, James Brydges's letter to Marlborough, 4 Dec. 1705, in Add. MSS. 9094 (Coxe Transcripts), ff. 221–2.

[3] See the queen's letter to Lady Marlborough, in *Conduct of the Duchess*, pp. 159–60.

[4] See above, pp. 88–89.

[5] *C.J.* xv. 64.

and carried with them a number of Country Members, but they were outvoted by the government forces, 208–196.[1]

This qualified victory for the Court was the high point of the session, which was marked also by the government's success in laying the groundwork for a treaty of union with Scotland. In both cases the government would have been defeated except for the support of the Junto, and the Treasurer realized he must pay for that support. To find posts for the Junto lords in the government would involve a long controversy with the queen, backed by Harley; but Godolphin avoided this and satisfied the Junto leaders for the time being by naming eight of them to the commission for negotiating the treaty with Scotland.[2]

In those negotiations (summer of 1706) the Junto lords played a conspicuous part; and their industry, patience, and skill—particularly Somers's—contributed in large measure to the successful framing of a treaty. They were unwilling to continue their efforts, however, and pilot the Union Treaty through parliament without some recognition; and they now asked that Sunderland should be made Secretary of State in place of Nottingham's old friend and associate, Sir Charles Hedges. Sunderland was chosen, rather than Somers, because he was Marlborough's son-in-law; and in pressing his claims the Junto believed they were 'driving the nail that would go'.[3]

The nail finally did go, but only after a long struggle with the queen. Coached by Harley, Anne insisted that to dismiss Hedges, who had not been disloyal to her, and to advance Sunderland, whom she did not like, would be to 'fall into the

[1] *C.J.* xv. 153, 159–60. The parliamentary proceedings in both Houses were extremely complicated and cannot be unravelled here. For a contemporary blacklist of the Court majority see my article in the *Bulletin of the Institute of Historical Research*, xiv. 29–33. For the final version of the 'whimsical clause', as Godolphin called it, see *Statutes of the Realm* (folio edn.), viii. 502.

[2] All five Junto lords, the Duke of Bolton, and Orford's two nephews, the Marquesses of Granby and Hartington, were among the twelve commissioners who were not members of the government. The official members of the commission: both archbishops, the two chief justices, and twelve members of the government, were not nearly so faithful nor so active as the Junto commissioners.

[3] *Conduct of the Duchess*, pp. 160–1.

hands' of a 'faction'.[1] Her stubborn resistance was not overcome for four months, until just before the meeting of parliament and then only because Marlborough and Godolphin both threatened to resign unless Sunderland were given the seals. Coming after such a long delay, the appointment only partly mollified the Junto lords; and the earldom given to Wharton, together with his reappointment as Justice in Eyre in place of his rival Abingdon, which would have been a 'mighty right compliment' in July, was rather grudgingly accepted in December.[2]

The most significant business of the 1706–7 session of parliament was the Union with Scotland, which came before the English parliament in January 1707. Opponents of the Union had counted on the treaty being rejected by the Scottish Estates; but after a stormy four-months' session that body did ratify it. Nottingham and Rochester counted on similar difficulties and delays in the English parliament; but the Court and Junto forces in the Commons steam-rollered the treaty through that House in record time, amid cries of 'post-haste!' from the opposition.[3] Approval of the many complicated articles of the treaty was completed in two sittings, and these provisions were then lumped together in a long preamble—as matters of fact—by the Court managers who drafted the Union legislation, leaving only a short enabling clause as target for the opposition. The committee stage of this bill was finished in a single long sitting; and soon after the bill received its third reading by a vote of 274–116.[4]

At first the Lords did not move so fast, and Nottingham and Rochester had time to argue that the Union would endanger

[1] The queen to Marlborough, 10 Sept. 1706, in Coxe's *Marlborough*, iii. 90–92. The story of the struggle over Sunderland's appointment can be followed in the correspondence printed in Churchill's *Marlborough*, chap. xi; and in *Conduct of the Duchess*, pp. 161–73.

[2] Sunderland to Lady Marlborough, undated, in *Private Correspondence*, i. 39.

[3] Boyer's *Annals*, v. 439–40; and see also Luttrell, vi. 136–7. For the text of the bill see *Statutes of the Realm* (folio edn.), viii. 566–77.

[4] For the parliamentary history of the bill see *C.J.* xv. 272–317, *passim*.

the Church of England by yoking it with the Scottish Kirk; but it soon appeared that this leisurely pace was designed simply to give the Commons time to complete and send up their Union bill.[1] When the bill arrived, the government majority hurried it through all its stages in less than three days, over the protests of some twenty peers connected with Rochester and Nottingham.[2] It received the royal assent early in March, and on 1 May 1707 the realms of England and Scotland were united as a single 'United Kingdom of Great Britain'.

Passage of the Union was the high point of what Godolphin called 'the best session of parliament that England ever saw'.[3] For this happy issue he had the Junto lords to thank, but their reward was small. Most of the Junto leaders were now called to the new 'Privy Council of Great Britain', while all fifteen Nottingham and Rochester partisans among the old Privy Councillors were passed over; and various members of the Finch and Hyde–Seymour connexions still in office were also ousted at this time, leaving vacant a number of important places: the government of Ireland, the post of Attorney-General, and two seats at the Board of Trade—but none of these went to the Junto.[4] This suggests that Godolphin's position was not so desperate as is often pictured. At any rate the Junto leaders could not coerce him into thrusting another Junto man into the ministry over the protests of the queen.

[1] So Sir David Nairne in a letter to the Earl of Mar, 20 Feb. 1707, in *H.M.C. Mar and Kellie MSS.*, p. 378; see also Burnet's *History*, v. 295–6.

[2] The best report of proceedings in the Lords is in Boyer's *Annals*, v. 429 ff. See also *H.M.C. House of Lords MSS.* (N.S.), vii. 20; *L.J.* xviii, *passim*; and the dispatches of L'Hermitage and Bonnet, 1, 8 Mar. 1707, in Von Noorden, ii. 494 (note), 495 (note).

[3] Godolphin to Marlborough, undated but obviously spring 1707, in Coxe's *Marlborough*, iii. 149.

[4] These were the more important changes: Ld.-Lieut. of Ireland, Pembroke (Court Tory) *vice* Ormonde (Rochester's son-in-law); Board of Trade, John Pulteney (government) and Robert Monckton (Newcastle) *vice* Weymouth (Nottingham's kinsman and follower) and Dartmouth (Nottingham also); Attorney-General, Simon Harcourt (Harley) *vice* Sir Edward Northey (Court Tory).

The only office of any importance secured for the Junto was Harcourt's former position, that of Solicitor-General, which went to Halifax's brother.

A battle with the queen soon did develop, but on another issue: preferment in the Church. The Bishops of Winchester, Ely, and Chester had died, as also the Regius Professor of Divinity at Oxford, and two deans of cathedrals. The vacancies on the bench of bishops were particularly important, since they carried a vote in the Lords; and Godolphin wanted them filled with men who would support the government—men like Bishop Trelawny of Exeter and Moore of Norwich, whom he now recommended for the wealthier sees of Winchester and Ely, respectively. He also wished to advance his brother, the Dean of Peterborough, and two friends of Marlborough: his chaplain and Dr. Potter, a protégé at Oxford. For the last Godolphin got the queen's promise of the Regius Professorship, and he expected no difficulty with his other recommendations.

Initially there was no trouble. Moore and Trelawny were duly translated to Ely and Winchester; but then something went wrong. Godolphin, after consulting with the Archbishop of Canterbury and Lord Somers, decided to recommend his own brother and two divines suggested by the Junto[1] for the three sees now vacant; but when these recommendations were brought to the queen for her approval, she brought Godolphin up short with the shocking news that two of the bishoprics had been privately promised already to candidates suggested by the Archbishop of York, a High Churchman and friend of Lord Nottingham.[2] For the queen to have done this without consulting or even informing her chief ministers was bad enough; but

[1] Namely Dr. Charles Trimnell, head of a large London church and formerly family chaplain to the Spencer family at Althorp, in which capacity he had served as tutor to Lord Sunderland; and Dr. White Kennett, Archdeacon of Lincoln, a client of the Russells and Cavendishes. For these two men see the *D.N.B.*; and for this whole controversy see especially the Rev. Norman Sykes's article on 'Queen Anne and the Episcopate', in *E.H.R.* l (July 1935), 433–64; also his 'The General Election of 1705 and the Cathedral Chapter of Exeter' (ibid. xlv (April 1930), 260–72), and his *Church and State in England in the Eighteenth Century* (Cambridge, 1934), chaps. 1, 2, and 4.

[2] See A. T. Hart, *The Life and Times of John Sharp, Archbishop of York* (London, 1949); also the two-volume *Life of John Sharp* (London, 1825) by his son, Thomas Sharp, useful for its excerpts from the Archbishop's diary, which has since disappeared.

that was not all. Apparently she was also planning to dispose of the Regius Professorship and certain other ecclesiastical positions in the same fashion—disregarding the Treasurer's advice or wishes in these matters.

Marlborough was so obviously upset to hear that his friend Dr. Potter, despite the queen's promise, was not sure of the Regius Professorship, that the Junto leaders absolved him and Godolphin of treachery—their first thought upon learning that their candidates for the episcopate might be passed over—and they concluded that Secretary Harley must be the villain. In particular they suspected that Harley had privately coached his cousin and confidante, Abigail Hill, now the queen's favourite bedchamber woman;[1] and that Abigail had then encouraged Anne to show her 'independence of faction' by promising bishoprics to two sound High Churchmen recommended by Archbishop Sharp rather than to politically minded Low Churchmen favoured by Marlborough and Godolphin. Whether Harley or Abigail actually tendered such advice to the queen we do not know; but certainly Harley did his best to obtain the Regius Professorship for an Oxford friend, Dr. Smalridge,[2] while in certain minor affairs he and Abigail did persuade the queen to follow her own inclinations without consulting her chief ministers—in one case, a regimental matter initiated without the knowledge of Marlborough, the Commander-in-Chief.[3] In any case, the damage was done; Anne refused to change her mind about the two bishoprics already

[1] For the well-known story of the rise of Abigail Hill, originally introduced into the queen's household by Lady Marlborough, see the Duchess's account (*Conduct of the Duchess*, pp. 176–90), which for all its partisanship is accurate in matters of fact as distinct from interpretations drawn from them.

[2] For Dr. George Smalridge, see the *D.N.B.*, and his letter to Harley of 8 Jan. 1708, in which he thanks Harley for 'having been so heartily recommended by you to her Majesty' (*H.M.C. Portland MSS.* iv. 473–4).

[3] This last was a private arrangement whereby the regiment commanded by Samuel Masham, recently married to Abigail, was to be kept in Ireland and not sent to the Continent. For the evidence, see three letters of Anne to Harley, in *H.M.C. Bath MSS.* i. 86, 97–98, and 189. The first two, dated 6 Aug. and 2 Sept. without the year, were misdated '1706' by the editor; and for this reason their significance has, I believe, hitherto been overlooked.

promised; and it took a six-months' campaign by the chief ministers, backed by Lady Marlborough and the Junto, to get Anne to concede the third bishopric, the Regius Professorship, and the deanship of St. Pauls to the candidates supported by Godolphin and the Junto.[1]

The final decision on appointments in the Church was not made until January 1708—two months after the opening of parliament; and the long delay had its effects on the relations between the party groups. Harley was unsuccessful in getting promotions for any of his particular friends in the Church; but in the long run he strengthened his position. In the first place, through Abigail and by his welcome advice to the queen that she follow her own inclinations in promoting Churchmen, he consolidated his position in the royal closet. Secondly, by working, although secretly, for High Church candidates he laid a foundation for later approaches to the High Church leaders. Thirdly, he helped widen the breach between the queen and Lady Marlborough and so, indirectly, between Anne and her two chief ministers; and finally, one paradoxical result of his activities was the break-down of mutual trust—not between Godolphin and Marlborough and himself, but between the two chief ministers and the Junto.

From the beginning the Junto leaders seem to have been much more acute about the Secretary's part in the bishoprics question than were Marlborough and Godolphin. The Junto lords simply could not believe that the chief ministers were really doing all they could to overcome the queen's apparent stubbornness. They suspected Godolphin of playing both ends against the middle, and Sunderland frankly warned Marlborough that unless he and the Treasurer made a determined stand—threatening to resign, if necessary—the Junto leaders would definitely go into opposition, signalling their new role

[1] The final disposal of these posts was: Dr. Trimnell to be Bishop of Norwich; Dr. Potter, Regius Professor; Dr. Godolphin, Dean of St. Paul's; and Francis Hare, Marlborough's chaplain, to succeed Dr. Godolphin as residentiary at St. Paul's.

vis-à-vis the government by attacking Admiral Churchill's administration of the Admiralty.[1] What with the Junto's fear of being double-crossed and the Treasurer's irritation at being pushed, relations between the two groups could hardly help being strained; and until the bishoprics question was finally settled, the Junto leaders refused to commit themselves to support of the government, preferring to make their co-operation conditional on Godolphin's getting the bishopric of Norwich for Sunderland's old tutor, Dr. Trimnell. It was with no easy confidence that Godolphin faced the opening of the parliamentary session of 1707–8, to which we now turn as a second case study of the party system at work.

[1] See the letters between Sunderland, Marlborough, and Godolphin, in Coxe's *Marlborough*, iii. 364–5.

CHAPTER VII

The Parliamentary Session of 1707–8: A Second Case Study of the Party Groups in Action

THE opening session of the 'First Parliament of Great Britain' began on 23 October 1707. Technically this was a new parliament, for the one chosen in 1705 had been 'determined' by the Union; but of course it was actually not a new parliament. Everyone elected in 1705 kept his seat in this first Union parliament, and the only new Members were the sixty-one Scots—sixteen representative peers and forty-five commoners—sent to Westminster for the first time since the Interregnum. These Scottish Members were a new factor in English parliamentary politics. How should they be classified in party terms?

Scottish political sentiment was divided over certain basic religious and political issues, but this does not mean that there were organized national parties in Scotland; and in fact the two-party concept is even less applicable north of the Tweed than south of it. The factors which promoted the formation of personal connexions in England operated still more strongly in Scotland. Aristocratic influence was more deeply entrenched, family loyalty was stronger in a society that knew the clan system, political loyalties were more personal, and the attraction of the Court—the one political group organized on a non-family basis—was more powerful. In Scotland, as in England, there was a well-organized government interest, a relatively unorganized Country opposition, and a number of distinct smaller groups based on family connexion.[1]

[1] For the general character of Scottish parties see P. Hume Brown, *Legislative Union of England and Scotland* (Oxford, 1914); W. Law Mathieson, *Scotland and the Union, 1695–1745* (Glasgow, 1905); A. V. Dicey and R. S. Rait, *Thoughts on the Union between England and Scotland* (London, 1920);

The Scottish Court party, like the English, had a nucleus of men in government posts, around which were gathered the friends and dependants of the more influential ministers. In Queen Anne's time the most powerful minister was the Duke of Queensberry. Associated with him were the Earl of Seafield and the Earl of Mar, each of whom had a small personal following, and, more important, the young duke of Argyll, lord of the Western Isles and chief of the Campbells, one of the greatest Scottish clans. Made High Commissioner in 1705, Argyll and his followers joined with Queensberry and the other courtiers in the difficult task of carrying through the Union.

The two major opposition groups were the 'Cavaliers', mostly Jacobites and Episcopalians; and the Country Party, chiefly Presbyterians who accepted the Revolution Settlement but resented being excluded from office. Both groups 'patriotically' opposed any subordination to England and accepted the common leadership of the Duke of Hamilton, by birth and fortune the most important single member of the Scottish aristocracy. Hamilton maintained contact with the exiled Stuarts, but he was too cautious to give his distant cousins over the water more than lip service. In the last Scottish parliament, chosen in 1703, he headed the combined Cavalier and Country opposition and was at first the leading opponent of union with England. Then

and Trevelyan's *Ramillies and the Union.* Among general sources the most useful are *The Acts of the Parliament of Scotland* (1824), especially the Appendix, pp. 162–205 (proceedings of the commissioners for a Union); and DeFoe's *History of the Union of Great Britain* (Edinburgh, 1709).

For the personal and family connexions of Scottish politicians Paul's *Scots Peerage* (Edinburgh, 1909) is invaluable. The most useful contemporary correspondence and papers are the following: reports of the H.M.C. on the Atholl, Mar and Kellie, Marchmont, and Seafield MSS.; *The Lockhart Papers*, ed. A. Aufrere (London, 1817); *Letters relating to Scotland in the Reign of Queen Anne*, ed. P. Brown, for the Scottish Historical Society (Edinburgh, 1815); *The Correspondence of George Baillie of Jerviswood*, ed. Lord Minto, for the Ballantyne Club (Edinburgh, 1842); *The Papers of the Earls of Marchmont*, ed. G. H. Rose (London, 1831); *Annals and Correspondence of the Viscount and First and Second Earls of Stair*, ed. J. M. Graham (Edinburgh, 1875); and the family papers printed by Sir William Fraser in *The Earls of Cromartie* (Edinburgh, 1875), *Memorials of the Earls of Haddington* (1889), and *The Melvilles and the Levens* (Edinburgh, 1890).

he astonished his followers by suddenly shifting from opposition to the very idea of naming commissioners to treat with the English and made the motion—successful, as it proved—that the queen be empowered to name the Scottish group.[1]

Hamilton's change of front helped along the cause of union, but equally important was the breaking away from the Country opposition of a group of men, nicknamed the *squadrone volante*, a flying squadron of some two dozen, led by the Marquesses of Tweeddale and Montrose, and the Earls of Haddington, Marchmont, Roxburgh, and Rothes, six peers closely connected by blood or marriage, with a following of some twenty untitled followers among the commoners of the parliament. Placed in office by the London government in 1704, at a time when Queensberry was hopelessly discredited, the *squadrone* leaders only made things worse for the Court. They were soon replaced by Queensberry and Argyll; but instead of going back into opposition, as was expected, they joined with their old foes of the Court party to work for passage of the union. The votes of this 'New Party', as it called itself, were enough to put the treaty through; and for this service its leaders were promised a share of Scotland's representation in the first Union parliament.

The Scottish Members in the first parliament of Great Britain, like the English, were not returned at a general election. Instead, the Scottish parliament which had passed the union selected forty-five from its own membership to represent the Scottish commons at Westminster. If it could hold together, the same majority that passed the union could elect all forty-five, and for this reason the opposition bitterly objected; but this of course did not change the Court's resolution 'not to swallow a cow, and stick at the tail'.[2]

The election went as the Court hoped, and the opposition feared. By giving the *squadrone* a third of the places on an

[1] See Trevelyan's *Ramillies and the Union*, pp. 258–60.

[2] The phrase is George Lockhart's, a Jacobite of the Cavalier opposition; see *The Lockhart Papers*, i. 221.

administration list, the government secured the support of that faction; and the two groups joined forces to elect all but four of their combined list. Consequently the forty-five elected included: fifteen clients of Queensberry; thirteen *squadrone* members; five dependants of Lord Chancellor Seafield; four henchmen of Argyll, all of them Campbells; two clients of the Lord Justice-General, Lord Cromarty; and two brothers of Lord Stair, aide-de-camp to Marlborough and one of his favourite officers. Only four were unconnected with the Court or the *squadrone*; and of these one had supported the union, one was doubtful, and two had opposed it.[1]

In the election of sixteen representative peers the Court was even more successful. The successful candidates were: Queensberry himself and six of his followers, all of them ministers; two administration peers less closely allied with Queensberry; Argyll and two more of that group; and four *squadrone* peers.[2] The election both of peers and commoners was gratifying to Queensberry, who controlled the greater part of them; and also to Godolphin, who counted on the Scottish courtiers' voting with the English government interest. The *squadrone* element, which formed more than a fourth of the Scottish delegation, was a less certain quantity; but it had voted with the administration on the Union issue, and Godolphin hoped for its continued co-operation, just as he hoped for the continued co-operation of the Junto.

In the early stages of the parliamentary session of 1707–8 the Treasurer had the support of both Junto and *squadrone*. Both joined in voting six millions for the war; with their help the land- and malt-tax bills were completed with remarkable dispatch; and the work of finding ways to raise the balance of the six millions was speedily undertaken. The elaborate finance

[1] For a more detailed description of the Scots chosen to sit in the first British parliament see Appendix V.

[2] For a detailed account of the election of Scottish representative peers see the letters of Lord Mar to Sir David Nairne, 5, 13 Feb. 1707, in *H.M.C. Mar and Kellie MSS.*, pp. 370–2, 373–7.

bills that finally emerged from the Committee on Ways and Means passed with little opposition.[1] Meanwhile the Commons had turned to the work of 'completing the Union', coupled with supply in the queen's opening speech as one of the most important tasks for the session.

As far as Godolphin and Queensberry were concerned, 'completing the Union' meant passage of legislation continuing a separate Privy Council for Scotland and establishing under its jurisdiction a system of local law enforcement and a militia system like England's. The second of these objectives presented some difficulties, for it would not be easy to set up a Scottish system of Justices of the Peace without encroaching on the heritable jurisdictions enjoyed by many leading Scots families. Some of the Scottish Court Members were doubtful of the advisability of such a step, and, curiously enough, it was a *squadrone* spokesman who proposed the introduction into Scotland of a system of J.P.s on the English model.[2] This motion was not, however, introduced at Godolphin's request as part of the government's scheme for completing the Union. On the contrary, it was the opening move in a gambit by Junto and *squadrone* leaders to force the Court on the defensive and win from it some concessions.

That the *squadrone* and the Junto—both compact and well-disciplined groups, both active in putting through the Union, and both denied any real share in the government of their respective countries—should have come to some working agreement was quite natural. Leading members of the two parties had been exchanging ideas for almost a year, when the arrival in London of the *squadrone* lords provided the opportunity to follow up these early contacts.[3] The joint decision of the two

[1] For proceedings on the money bills see *C.J.* xv. 397–485, *passim*; and Boyer's *Annals*, vi. 257–301, *passim*; for the revenue measures themselves, see *Statutes* (folio edn.), viii. 730–6, 765–76.

[2] The *squadrone* spokesman was John Haldane of Gleneagles. For a report of this debate see Mar's letter to his brother, Lord Grange, undated but obviously written 6 Dec. 1707, in *H.M.C. Mar and Kellie MSS.*, p. 424.

[3] See the letters between Marchmont and Somers, and Wharton and Marchmont, November 1706 to March 1707, in *Marchmont Papers*, iii. 303–26, *passim*.

groups to oppose both the English and the Scottish Court on the issue of continuing the Scottish Privy Council was good practical politics. That Council was unpopular with most Scots, who considered it a creature of the English government and of the Duke of Queensberry—which was precisely why Godolphin and Queensberry wanted it continued. Without the support of the *squadrone* and the Junto that was to prove impossible.

The debates over continuing the Edinburgh Council are most interesting from the point of view of party politics. The motion to abolish the Scottish Council was made and seconded by *squadrone* Members, and at first the proposition was opposed only by Scottish Court Members. English Members did not seem particularly interested, and at this stage Queensberry's followers could probably have killed the motion by moving to adjourn; but when Harley and one or two other Englishmen connected with the government spoke up in favour of the Edinburgh Council, things began to happen. The Junto delegation moved into action beside the *squadrone* and were soon followed by some of the Country Members and then by spokesmen for the Finch and Hyde–Seymour connexions, who scented an opportunity to hand the government a defeat. When the Court finally did move an adjournment, it was too late. They were defeated by eight votes, and after that there was no sense risking another defeat on the main question. The resolution to abolish the Scottish Privy Council was allowed to pass unopposed, as was the resolution to introduce a bill coupling abolition of the Council with the introduction of a system of J.P.s for Scotland.[1]

Final passage of that bill was not effected until two months later, and in the meantime the government made extraordinary efforts to save the Edinburgh Council. All failed. In the Commons, one administration amendment to the bill was defeated

[1] This debate is reported by James Vernon, in a letter to Shrewsbury, 9 Dec. 1707, in *Vernon Corresp.* iii. 288–90. See also *H.M.C. Lonsdale MSS.*, p. 117, for an undated letter from 'H.M.'. A comparison with Vernon's letter shows clearly that this is another report of the same debate, written to Wharton probably by his cousin Harry Mordaunt.

by thirty-eight votes after long debate, and a final attempt by the Court forces during the third reading to continue the Council for at least one more year was voted down by more than sixty votes.[1] If the Scottish Council were to be saved, it would have to be in the Lords; and here 'the Court appeared with more warmth' than the Earl of Mar had seen it display on any previous occasion.[2] Among the English ministers who defended the Council was Godolphin himself, while Mar and Seafield were its principal Scottish defenders. The *squadrone* peers and Halifax, Sunderland, and especially Somers, of the Junto, were the leading speakers on the other side, together with Bishop Burnet, himself a Scot. The division ending the debate was extraordinarily close. The three *squadrone* peers and a lone Scottish ally voted against continuing the Council, as did the whole Junto delegation. They were joined by most of the Finch connexion and by all of the Hyde–Seymour group except for Rochester himself. The Court might still have carried the day, had it not been for the bishops. Those who were High Church followed Nottingham into the opposition lobby; and when their Low Church brethren marched with Bishop Burnet into that same lobby, the government's cause was lost. Only Trelawny and one other bishop stood by the government; while Dr. Moore, recently translated to Ely, abstained. On the final count the Court lost by five votes.[3]

Two days later the Court tried once again. This time they were defeated by seven votes, whereupon twenty-seven of the minority signed a protest. Among the signatories were Court

[1] For the first of these defeats see *C.J.* xv. 461; and Vernon to Shrewsbury, 11 Dec. 1707 (*Vernon Corresp.* iii. 290–2); for the second, *C.J.* xv. 512; Luttrell, vi. 259–60; and Addison to Manchester, 29 Jan. 1708, in *Court and Society*, ii. 274.

[2] Mar to his brother, Lord Grange, 5 Feb. 1708, in *H.M.C. Mar and Kellie MSS.*, pp. 426–7.

[3] For reports of this debate and division see Mar to Lord Grange, 5 Feb. (as above); Addison to Lord Manchester, 6, 10 Feb. (in *Court and Society*, ii. 275, 278–9); and Vernon to Shrewsbury, 7 Feb. (in *Vernon Corresp.* iii. 341–2). There is a draft of Somers's speech against the Scottish Privy Council in *Hardwicke State Papers*, ii. 473–8.

Whigs like Somerset, Radnor, and Rivers; and three members of the Newcastle connexion: Townshend, Dorchester, and Cowper, recently advanced from Lord Keeper to Lord Chancellor. Historians have not distinguished between these two groups and the Junto, treating all three as indistinguishable parts of a single Whig party; whereas on this and many other occasions the groups divided against each other—further evidence of our thesis that instead of one Whig party there were several distinct Whig groups which frequently pursued different policies.

Continuation of the Scottish Privy Council was not the only issue on which the Junto and the Newcastle and Court Whigs voted on opposite sides. The same division occurred during the debates on the Admiralty. Marlborough and Godolphin had been warned by the Junto to expect an attack on the Admiralty if the vacant bishoprics were not disposed of satisfactorily. This was not done until long after parliament convened, and meanwhile the Junto leaders had started to make good on their threat. Marlborough was particularly sensitive on this issue, since his brother George Churchill was the leading member of Prince George's Council for the Admiralty; and at one time during the summer Marlborough had made a real effort to forestall trouble by suggesting to his brother that he should resign.[1] Admiral Churchill stayed on, however, to become a target for the Junto lords, who hoped to replace him with their own candidate, Lord Orford.

The attack on the Admiralty came suddenly, at the very beginning of the session, on the occasion of the Lords' debate on the queen's opening speech. Instead of joining with the administration to move an address of thanks—the usual procedure—the Junto lords turned instead to an attack on the Admiralty for its failure to safeguard adequately English shipping against French privateers. Wharton and Somers began

[1] See Godolphin's letter to Marlborough of 27 June 1707, and Marlborough's reply, 18 July (N.S.); also Marlborough's letter to his wife, 22 July (N.S.)—all in Coxe's *Marlborough*, iii. 274–5, 277–9, 280–1.

the attack and were joined by Rochester, Buckingham, and Guernsey (Lord Nottingham's brother). In the face of this combination the government unwillingly agreed to postpone debate on the address and to set aside time within the next few days for full discussion of the issue which the Junto lords had raised.[1]

On the day appointed Wharton once again opened the debate, this time by presenting a giant petition from some 200 London merchants, praying for more effectual naval protection for their convoys. He was followed by Lord Haversham, a disgruntled ex-Williamite Whig who was frequently more extreme in his attacks on the Court than any of the hottest Rochester or Nottingham Tories. Haversham started by laying blame on the Admiralty, but ended by attacking the government as a whole. This was no part of the Junto strategy, which for the moment aimed only at a change in the Admiralty; and Halifax quickly diverted the debate by moving for a committee of inquiry. Godolphin seconded this motion, foreseeing a reprieve—at least until the committee reported—and the Lords concurred. The House then rose, but it was observed that Marlborough, nettled by the course of the debate, 'took the Earl of Wharton aside, and there passed some warm expostulations between them'.[2]

The Admiralty inquiry, begun so warmly in the Lords, thereafter subsided. The committee of inquiry accumulated masses of testimony and reported from time to time, but its reports never occasioned such lively debate as during the opening days of the session. Marlborough's principal biographer suggests that the Junto leaders intentionally moderated their attack, once they learned that some at least of the vacant positions in the Church would go to men they approved.[3] The proceedings

[1] *L.J.* xviii. 338; and for a summary of the debate, see Boyer's *Annals*, vi. 252.

[2] For a report of the debate see Boyer's *Annals*, vi. 252–7. The incident of Marlborough's encounter with Wharton comes from Oldmixon (*History*, i. 385).

[3] This is Archdeacon Coxe's view, but he cites no specific evidence for it. See Coxe's *Marlborough*, iv. 16–17.

in the Commons suggest a different explanation. There the leading speaker against the Admiralty was Richard Hampden, Buckinghamshire neighbour and friend of Wharton; and Hampden followed almost identical tactics, relying on the London merchant Members to provide evidence of Admiralty mismanagement. Admiral Churchill spoke in his own defence; and he was supported not only by regular government Members, but by Newcastle Whigs like Walpole—himself a member of the prince's Council—and by a number of independent merchants who ordinarily voted with the Country opposition or with one of the organized Tory groups.[1]

Hampden repeatedly moved that 'the merchants had made good their allegations against the Admiralty', but the House would not concur. The best Hampden could do was to win consent for a bill providing more cruisers for the protection of convoys. Annoyed, he publicly deplored the fact that 'the Admiralty of Great Britain was so destitute of Council', that he, a private Member, had to take the initiative.[2] In all of this there was no noticeable moderating of the Junto attack. It simply could not be pressed home. The Finch and Hyde-Seymour connexions refused to join forces with the Junto; and they declined to do so, one may reasonably conclude, because they sensed that this manœuvre was not so much designed to embarrass the government as to procure Admiral Churchill's place for Lord Orford. They showed no such reluctance in the proceedings over the third important issue to come before parliament that session—the war in Spain.

The war in Spain had begun well with the seizure of Gibraltar and the occupation of Barcelona and all the eastern provinces by the Allies; but during the year 1707 these successes were offset by a disaster: the defeat at Almanza. The Allies designed to capture Madrid that summer as part of a larger operation

[1] See the reports of these debates by Vernon, in *Vernon Corresp.* iii. 283–4, 286–7, 292–4, 326. Among the merchants supporting Admiral Churchill were the two Hernes, both of whom had voted for the Tack.

[2] Vernon to Shrewsbury, 27 Jan. 1708, in *Vernon Corresp.* iii. 326.

that was to include taking the great French naval base at Toulon. The attack on Toulon started much too late and then failed—owing to a variety of complications in the Italian theatre—and the French, instead of having to withdraw troops from Spain, as was expected, were able instead to reinforce their army around Madrid.

The three Allied commanders in Spain: the Austrian Archduke, Lord Galway, and the Earl of Peterborough, could not agree whether to attack Madrid at once, before the French reinforcements arrived, or to remain on the defensive. The final compromise was disastrous. While the Archduke Charles, the most cautious, dispersed his forces in garrisons along the east coast; Galway, the boldest, marched the English, Dutch, and Portuguese contingents off towards Madrid. Peterborough, meanwhile, had been relieved of his command and was thus able to dissociate himself from Galway's terrible defeat, late in April, at Almanza. That battle was fought on very uneven terms. When the Portuguese fled at the first shock of battle, Galway found himself outnumbered nearly three to one, and he was lucky to fight his way out with 1,500 foot and a few squadrons of horse—all that escaped of his original army of over 15,000. With exceptional skill Galway kept up the morale of his troops and saved Valencia, but Spain was lost beyond recovery.[1]

A parliamentary inquiry into the Spanish débâcle was inevitable, and the government made no effort to avoid it. It began in the Lords, as an investigation of Lord Peterborough's conduct. That eccentric peer had been recalled not so much for his failure in the field as for his irregular behaviour as envoy: he had used the queen's name to float a large unauthorized loan in Italy. Peterborough returned to London by way of half the courts of Europe, at odds with the chief ministers and anxious to get his side of the case before the public—which he did by publishing an elaborate *Account of the Earl of Peterborough's*

[1] For an account of the war in Spain see Trevelyan's *Ramillies*, chaps. 2, 4, 8, and 15.

Conduct.[1] His cause was immediately taken up by the Rochester and Nottingham groups, who saw an opportunity to embarrass the government. The Lords devoted numerous sittings to Peterborough's case and called for all the relevant papers, including instructions to the commanders in Spain and accounts of the number of troops in that theatre. Peterborough himself engrossed the stage in most of these debates. 'He bids open defiance, and fires very thick at the ministry', reported one observer, 'and sometimes with a good deal of wit', so that 'people attend it as they do a play—for entertainment.'[2] Like any show that runs too long, however, it grew tiresome; and Peterborough and his backers never succeeded in getting the Lords to vindicate their hero.[3]

At only one stage in these debates did the opposition seriously threaten. That was on the second day, when Nottingham raised the basic question of the proper strategy in the struggle against France. He declared that concentration upon the Netherlands theatre was a mistake; that Marlborough should remain on the defensive there, so that fifteen or twenty thousand troops could be diverted to Spain. Rochester emphatically seconded this point, complaining that Spain was being 'in a manner abandoned'.[4] This criticism was too much for Marlborough, who replied with some heat that it was absolutely necessary to have *more* rather than fewer troops in the Netherlands. Then in an effort to spike the argument about Spain, he conjured up the vision of a great Spanish expedition, on the order of 40,000 troops under the command of Prince Eugene, which he said was being planned with the emperor. This dramatic disclosure

[1] Written by Peterborough's physician, Dr. Freind, and belittled by Whig wits as 'The Earl of Monmouth's Vindication of the Earl of Peterborough'—Peterborough being also Earl of Monmouth.

[2] Mr. Edwin to Lord Manchester, 6 Feb. 1708, in *Court and Society*, ii. 277.

[3] For accounts of Peterborough's performance see Addison's letter to Manchester, 16 Jan. 1708 (*Court and Society*, ii. 277); and Vernon's letters to Shrewsbury, 15, 18 Jan. (*Vernon Corresp*. iii. 307–8, 316–17).

Vernon thought the inquiry was intentionally being 'industriously spun out' (letter of 5 Feb. 1708 in *Vernon Corresp*. iii. 339).

[4] See Boyer's report of this debate, in *Annals*, vi. 298.

had a remarkable effect. Rochester, taken aback, professed himself satisfied; and the opposition threat appeared to have been neatly parried.[1]

Unfortunately, the matter was not allowed to rest there. The grandiose expedition mentioned by Marlborough did not exist as yet except in his own mind. He had mentioned it on the spur of the moment in order to divert the dangerous course of the debate; but in no time at all the Junto leaders gave the idea independent life. After Somers's motion—'that no peace can be safe or honourable' which left Spain and the Indies in the possession of the Bourbons—had been passed, Wharton moved that the Lords thank Her Majesty for her pains in planning such an expedition as Marlborough had mentioned; and Halifax added a final motion that the queen be asked to continue her efforts to induce the Emperor to do his part.[2]

The last two motions were particularly awkward. They would place the government on record as favouring, in fact as having initiated preparations for, a grand descent on Spain. England's allies were in no way prepared for such a move, which would involve protracted negotiations with the Imperial court; and Marlborough foresaw considerable difficulty in extricating himself from the position into which he was being manœuvred. For this reason he and Godolphin opposed the motions made by Wharton and Halifax, but without success. Both those motions were embodied in an address to the queen, in which the Commons speedily concurred.[3] In this curious fashion the exclusion of the Bourbons from the Spanish throne became a definite objective of government policy. It proved to be an impossible goal, and for its failure to recognize this fact the Marlborough–Godolphin administration was to pay dearly before two years

[1] I follow here Winston Churchill's interpretation of Marlborough's part in this debate, which seems to me best to fit the facts. See Churchill's *Marlborough*, iii. 339–47.

[2] For reports of this debate see Vernon's letter to Shrewsbury, 20 Dec. 1707 (*Vernon Corresp.* iii. 300–2); Sir John Perceval's letter of 27 Dec. (*H.M.C. Egmont MSS.* ii. 219–22); and Boyer's *Annals*, vi. 296–300.

[3] Vernon to Shrewsbury, 23 Dec. 1707 (*Vernon Corresp.* iii. 302–3).

were out; but at the moment this turn in the debate over the war in Spain did not seem particularly damaging. It was certainly far less dangerous to the Court than the course which the debate on the Spanish campaign took in the House of Commons.

In the Commons followers of Rochester and Nottingham, acting 'in conformity with their friends in the House of Lords',[1] were the first to move for an investigation of the war in Spain; but unlike their leaders in the Upper House they showed more interest in the Almanza disaster than in Peterborough's grievances. The first call for papers—from a Northern Member associated with the Hyde–Seymour group—was for an account of the number of English troops at the Battle of Almanza; and further material along the same lines was called for by two High Church disciples of Nottingham.[2] On 17 January 1708, when the House resumed the inquiry on Spain, the government countered by calling for documents bearing on the year 1706. These would bring Peterborough's dilatory tactics of that year within the scope of the inquiry; and various Court speakers—Walpole among them—argued that these papers would place the Almanza defeat in proper perspective as 'a misfortune owing to the neglect of the former year', when Peterborough delayed so long in marching on Madrid that the Allies had to give up the city 'after having been in possession of it six weeks'.[3]

The organized Tory groups were for having only the Almanza accounts read, arguing that investigation of this defeat was the original purpose of the inquiry; but the government forces won their point, and the rest of that day's sitting was taken up with reading the papers for 1705 *and* 1706, together with the accounts

[1] For the quotation see Vernon's letter to Shrewsbury, 18 Dec. 1707, in *Vernon Corresp.* iii. 298.

[2] See *C.J.* xv. 454, 465; and Vernon's letters of 9, 18 Dec. in *Vernon Corresp.* iii, 288, 298. In his 18 Dec. letter Vernon identifies the leading instigators of the Almanza inquiry as James Graham, a friend of the Musgraves; and two Tackers, William Bromley and Ralph Freeman, the first of whom led the struggle for the Occasional Conformity Bill.

[3] So Vernon, describing the debate in his letter to Shrewsbury of 17 Jan. 1708 (*Vernon Corresp.* iii. 313).

called for by the organized Tory groups.[1] If the government tactics were designed to distract attention from the Almanza accounts, they were successful. The significance of two of the documents bearing on Almanza and read at that time seems generally to have been overlooked; but the oversight was far more serious on the part of the Court managers, who should have been on the alert, than it was for the opposition leaders, who were the first to wake up to the damaging implications that could be drawn from these two accounts.

The two papers in question—which were read together with long instructions to the commanders in Spain, and the like—were Secretary-at-War St. John's estimate of the number of English troops at the Battle of Almanza and Paymaster Brydges's account of the funds disbursed for the payment of the English forces in Spain and Portugal. The number of troops given by Brydges was over 29,000, whereas St. John estimated the number of English effectives at Almanza at less than 9,000! The glaring discrepancy between the two figures apparently went unnoticed by the government leaders in the Commons—particularly Harley and St. John—for nearly two weeks.[2] At all events, when the House resumed the Spanish

[1] *C.J.* xv. 503; and Vernon to Shrewsbury, 17 Jan. 1708 (*Vernon Corresp.* iii. 311–16).

[2] That this was the actual sequence of events seems clear from a careful reading of the *Journals* and of Vernon's reports, supplemented by other accounts. St. John's account was presented to the House and the title read on 12 Jan. (*C.J.* xv. 491–3, where the text may be found); while Brydges's account was presented and the title read four days later (*C.J.* xv. 500–1, where the text is given). The *Journals* for the following day, Saturday, 17 Jan. record that 'all the letters, . . . accounts, and papers, which have been laid before the House, relating to the war with Spain, were read' (*C.J.* xv. 503). Vernon, in his account of that day's proceedings, says that 'great attention was given' to the papers read, but summarizes only those for 1706, which seem chiefly to have interested him and presumably the rest of the House (*Vernon Corresp.* iii. 311–14).

I had worked out this sequence independently, before I saw Dr. Godfrey Davies's paper on 'The Fall of Harley in 1708', in *E.H.R.* lxvi (1951), 246–54. Dr. Davies suggests that St. John's estimate of 8,660 men may have been presented to the Commons as early as 13 Dec., and he cites the *Journals* for that day, which state that Mr. St. John presented 'an account of Her Majesty's

inquiry twelve days later on 29 January, St. John and the other government spokesmen were obviously caught completely off guard by the motion, made by a Nottingham Tory, 'that of the 29,395 English forces provided by the Parliament for the service of Spain and Portugal in the year 1707, there was but 8660 in Spain and Portugal at the time of the Battle of Almanza'.[1]

The Nottingham and Rochester groups had obviously worked out their strategy in advance, for their motion came at the end of a set speech by Sir Thomas Hanmer; and 'there seemed to be another question to follow it of mismanagement and misapplication of money'.[2] The brunt of the government's defence fell upon Harley, Brydges, and particularly St. John—none of whom was prepared. St. John tried to explain that his estimate of effectives did not include several thousand men in various categories; but this did little to erase the unfortunate first impression conveyed by the opposition motion. The House in fact began to 'grow warm'. The Country Whigs, led by Peter King, who had already caused the government endless trouble by joining with the organized Tory opposition to block the government's programme for recruiting, now joined the attack. The debate got out of control, and the government was not able finally to extricate itself until three o'clock in the morning.[3]

The Court might well have suffered a serious defeat if the Junto delegation had not come to its rescue. During this debate,

forces that were at Almanza' (*C.J.* xv. 465). This account, however, probably consisted only of a list of regiments; because five days later it was ordered that 'an account be laid before this House what *numbers* [italics mine] the several regiments consisted of that were in English pay at the time of the Battle of Almanza' (*C.J.* xv. 473). It was the numbers that gave St. John trouble, and I doubt if he had time to get information on the actual strength of English regiments in the field before 12 Jan., when this second account was presented to the House.

[1] *C.J.* xv. 520; Vernon to Shrewsbury, 29 Jan. 1708 (*Vernon Corresp.* iii. 328–30); Addison to Manchester, 3 Feb. 1708 (*Court and Society*, ii. 272); and Luttrell, vi. 262.

[2] This was Vernon's conclusion (*Vernon Corresp.* iii. 329).

[3] *C.J.* xv. 520; and see the reports of Vernon, Addison, and Luttrell, as above, n. 1.

and in fact throughout the Spanish inquiry, the Junto connexion appears to have taken a line of its own, independent of both Court and opposition. No Junto spokesman arose to defend the government until early in the morning, when Somers's brother-in-law moved to adjourn the debate. The government was only too glad to support the motion. With the help of Junto votes the motion was carried by 188–172—a close division in a House still remarkably full for that time of night.[1] The adjournment, of course, did not save the government for long. Five days later the opposition returned to the attack. By this time St. John had prepared a fuller explanation of the discrepancy between his figures and those of Brydges, but the House was not impressed. It refused to let the original motion drop and was not even disposed to soften it—except to add the phrase 'besides officers and servants' after the damning total '8660'.

For this slight modification the Court again had the Junto to thank, for it was Somers's brother-in-law who offered this amendment. On the main question, so amended, the government did not dare risk a division, and it passed unopposed. The opposition leaders then tried to follow up this victory. They planned to use the resolution as the basis for some severe reflections on the ministry; but with the assistance of the Junto the government managed to prevent things going as far as that. Sir Joseph Jekyll,[2] the Junto spokesman who had been so active in these debates, suggested simply that the resolution should be included in an address to the queen, praying for a fuller explanation why there were not more men in Spain at the time of the Battle of Almanza and exhorting her government to a more vigorous prosecution of the war in that theatre. This by no means satisfied the opposition speakers, who foresaw nothing but more accounts and papers; but their efforts to persuade the House to take stronger action were shut off by the Court and

[1] *C.J.* xv. 520; and see the reports of Vernon, Addison, and Luttrell, as above, p. 140, n. 1.

[2] Brother-in-law to Somers, and the Member already twice mentioned.

the Junto. Acting together, the two groups moved the previous question and carried it; voted down an opposition motion to have the address framed by a committee—which would have entailed more debate; and finally carried a motion to adjourn.[1]

The two debates on Hanmer's motion, which was intended as a vote of censure against the government for its mismanagement of the Spanish war, were the climax of a session that saw the government forced into an increasingly precarious position. At the very beginning of the session a majority of the Lords took the unprecedented step of refusing to answer their sovereign's opening speech, turning instead to an attack on the Admiralty, headed by the queen's husband and managed by Marlborough's brother. Then came the first Spanish debates in the Lords, the criticism of Marlborough's concentration on the Netherlands theatre, and finally a concerted opposition to the government's plans for 'completing the Union' with Scotland.

After the Christmas adjournment the situation grew worse rather than better. On 16 January the Commons rejected the government's proposed recruiting programme without a division and four days later defeated the government again on the same issue—this time by a majority of eight votes.[2] Three days later, on 23 January, the government's plan to continue the Scottish Privy Council was voted down by a majority of seventy-nine. On 29 January came the first disastrous Almanza debate, followed five days later by the second—which was little better; and on the day after that (4 February) the Court's last-ditch effort to save the Edinburgh Council was defeated by a majority of four in the House of Lords. As if all this were not enough, Godolphin learned at the very end of 1707 that a clerk in the

[1] *C.J.* xv. 524–5; Luttrell, vi. 264; Addison to Manchester, 3 Feb. 1708 (*Court and Society*, ii. 272); and for the fullest report, Vernon to Shrewsbury, 3 Feb. 1708 (*Vernon Corresp.* iii. 335–7).

[2] *C.J.* xv. 499–500, 506, 508. The best report of these proceedings is to be found in Vernon's letters of 17, 20 Jan. 1708 (*Vernon Corresp.* iii. 309–11, 318). Addison's account, in his letter to Manchester, 29 Jan. (*Court and Society*, ii. 273), is misleading in that it combines several days' proceedings.

office of Harley, the Secretary of State, was carrying on treasonable correspondence with France; and finally it became increasingly clear to Godolphin during the month of January that he could not trust the leading minister in the Commons, Harley himself!

The series of parliamentary crises just mentioned coincided in fact with a prolonged crisis within the government. This extremely interesting episode has never been satisfactorily explained or even described by historians—possibly it never can be.[1] Be that as it may, it is clearly impossible in this brief study to review all the evidence, and only a few indisputable facts can be set down here. On the night of 29 January—either during or after the crucial Almanza debate—Harcourt, the Attorney-General, officially informed Harley that he (Harley) had come under the Treasurer's displeasure. Harcourt gave no particulars, but Harley apparently learned these in an interview which he managed to get with Marlborough on the following morning. He then wrote a characteristic letter to Godolphin, trying to clear himself; but his letter does not reveal the nature of the charge against him.[2] That he was guilty—and of a serious offence—seemed obvious to Godolphin, who replied: 'I have received your letter and am very sorry for what has happened to lose the good opinion I had so much inclination to have of you, but I cannot help seeing and hearing, nor believing my senses. I am very far from having deserved it of you. God forgive you!'[3]

What had the Treasurer seen and heard that could inspire such a message? It is natural to conclude that it must have been something connected with the Almanza debate of the previous evening; and some historians have jumped to the conclusion

[1] See Note A at the end of the chapter.

[2] Harley to Godolphin, 30 Jan. 1708 (*H.M.C. Bath MSS.* i. 189–90). In this letter Harley refers both to Harcourt's message and to his interview with Marlborough.

[3] Godolphin to Harley, no date, but endorsed by Harley 'January 30' (*H.M.C. Bath MSS.* i. 190).

that Harley and St. John intentionally paved the way for the government's difficulties in that affair. They suggest that the two ministers planned their treachery in advance and that St. John's estimate was 'planted' with the knowledge and expectation that the opposition would use it, presumably to bring down the government.[1] Such a Machiavellian scheme seems most unlikely, especially in view of St. John's letter to Harley of 14 January (two days after he had presented his first estimate of 8,660 men to the House), which contains no hint of such a plot.[2] Moreover, it does not fit in with Harley's constant efforts in behalf of every government measure during the previous months of the session. It is hard to see how a parliamentary crisis like that of 29 January could help Harley's plans—and in fact that episode helped to wreck them.

Actually St. John and Harley were probably innocent of treachery in that affair; and while it is possible to argue that Godolphin none the less believed them guilty, it is more likely that he attributed the government's difficulties in the Almanza business to the worst kind of carelessness on the part of two responsible ministers who should have known better. If this was his attitude, his anger would hardly be tempered by the suspicion that Harley for some time had been so engrossed in undercover efforts to change the ministry that he had probably been neglecting his duties in the Commons.

We cannot attempt here to unravel Harley's schemes for a new administration similar to the one which he himself headed only two years later; but we can be fairly certain that Godolphin was aware of them. Whether or not he considered them 'disloyal', he could hardly ignore them. Eventually he must decide whether to fall in with Harley's ideas and break off with the Junto; or whether to break with Harley and work more closely

[1] This view was first suggested by C. von Noorden, in his *Europaische Geschichte, im Achtzehnten Jahrhundert* (Dusseldorf, 1870–82), iii. 219–20; and was adopted wholeheartedly by Churchill, in his *Marlborough*, iii. 351–2. Trevelyan and Feiling, though more cautious, incline to the same theory. See Trevelyan's *Ramillies*, p. 327; and Feiling's *Tory Party*, p. 399.

[2] St. John to Harley, 14 Jan. 1708 (*H.M.C. Bath MSS.* i. 189).

with Somers, Wharton, and the rest of that group. In reaching a final decision Godolphin would have to take many factors into account, and surely one of them must have been the parliamentary situation. One can see, then, how the course of the 1707–8 session would have a direct bearing on the changes in the government which actually did take place in the few days after the Almanza crisis.

Assuming that this interpretation is correct, we can say that Godolphin postponed reaching a decision until the beginning of the year 1708. The discovery of treachery in Harley's office would have weakened Harley's position, and so we find Godolphin inclining towards a Junto alliance. This would explain the final compromise reached early in January on the bishoprics question, when Sunderland's old tutor was finally named Bishop of Norwich. This would also explain why the Junto leaders, though they continued to oppose the Court on the issue of the Scottish Council—on which they were already deeply committed—displayed a rather conspicuous neutrality in the debates on the war in Spain. Then came the disastrous Almanza debate. In this affair it was St. John and Harley who got the government into trouble, while the Junto helped to get them out of it. The choice was now clear. Godolphin and Marlborough immediately broke with Harley, informing the queen that they could no longer serve with such an untrustworthy fellow.

The events of the next ten days (30 January to 8 February) showed how firmly Harley was entrenched in the queen's favour. Anne would not abandon him, even after a final interview with the two chief ministers which resulted in their actually laying down their offices and absenting themselves from Court, Council, and Cabinet. Meanwhile Harley worked feverishly to mature plans which were not yet ripe, confident that he could form an alternative government. He counted on the neutrality at least of Newcastle and the important Court peers in the government, but he proved to be mistaken in this calculation. When the Cabinet Council met without Marlborough or Godolphin, on Sunday, 8 February, Somerset, after an uneasy silence, told the queen he could no longer serve her if that fellow, pointing to Harley, was going to be allowed to treat of the affairs of the war without either the General or the Treasurer being present. This seemed to be the consensus of most of the lords present. At any rate the meeting broke up in confusion.[1] The queen was still unwilling to let Harley go, but his position was hopeless. A few days later he and his three principal followers resigned.

The Cabinet crisis did not quite interrupt the meeting of parliament. Rumours of the struggle between Harley and the chief ministers reached the Commons, and for a day or two the House simply marked time; but it soon returned to business, and it was at once apparent that there was a new temper there. This was particularly evident, two weeks after Harley's resignation, when the Commons resumed the debate on Spain. The opposition, reinforced now by Harley's group, once more tried to press home their attack on the government—accusing it of 'too little and too late' in dispatching fresh troops to the Spanish theatre. When the question was put, Harley, Harcourt, and Mansell voted against the Court; but the opposition motion was defeated, 230–175.[2] In the division the Junto voted in a body with the government and drew most of the Country Whigs with them. Moreover, it was a Junto leader, the Duke of Bolton's brother, who followed up the victory by moving for an address to the queen, thanking her for the measures her government was taking for the recovery of Spain. The motion passed without opposition, and the sitting 'ended very much to the satisfaction of the court, tho' many of their friends were very apprehensive'.[3]

[1] I follow here Swift's account, the most nearly contemporary. He is borne out by Burnet and Lady Marlborough. See Swift's letter to Archbishop King, 12 Feb. 1708 (in *Correspondence of Jonathan Swift*, ed. F. Elrington Ball (London, 1910), i. 74); Burnet's *History*, v. 354; and *Account of the Conduct of the Duchess of Marlborough*, p. 212.

[2] *C.J.* xv. 569; Addison to Manchester, 24 Feb. 1708 (*Court and Society*, ii. 292); Vernon to Shrewsbury, same date (*Vernon Corresp.* iii. 355–6). The figures on the division are given in Vernon's letter as 230–145. This may be an error in transcription.

[3] The quotation is from Addison's letter, as above.

The wholehearted co-operation of the Junto in this debate suggests that this group and the Treasurer had finally come to terms. The question is, what sort of terms? According to the leading authorities on the period Godolphin was forced to surrender virtually without conditions. The Junto was now 'in the saddle', we are told.[1] 'The real victory lay not with the *duumvirs* [Marlborough and Godolphin], but with the Whigs.'[2] With the dismissal of Harley the government changed from 'a non-party group of the Queen's servants' to a 'Whig Government' in which no one 'would oppose the policies of the Junto'.[3] Such is the verdict of the authorities, but does the evidence bear them out? Did the concessions won by the Junto outweigh so heavily the concessions which Godolphin won in return?

The advantages gained by the Treasurer were by no means inconsiderable. In the first place he was taken off the tenterhooks in parliament. During the remainder of the session and throughout the next parliament he was not once faced by the same hostile combination of Junto, Country Whig, and organized Tory which had made the first half of the 1707–8 session so very difficult. In fact the rest of that session went so smoothly that there is no need to follow its proceedings in detail. Nothing more was heard about Spain after the successful debate already described; and an attempt by Nottingham and his following among the Churchmen to strike at the power of the bishops by increasing the autonomy of their cathedral chapters, though supported by the whole Harley connexion, was defeated by the Court and Junto combined.[4]

Meanwhile the work of supply went on smoothly, and by early March the Commons had finished the last important money bill and were expecting to be prorogued. Then came news that a French fleet, bearing the Pretender, was on its way

[1] W. T. Morgan, *English Political Parties*, p. 315.

[2] Feiling, *Tory Party*, p. 400.

[3] Trevelyan, *Ramillies and the Union*, p. 327.

[4] *C.J.* xv. 580; Luttrell, vi. 270, 283; Vernon to Shrewsbury, 19 and 28 Feb. 1708 (*Vernon Corresp.* iii. 352–3, 357–8); Addison to Manchester, 20 Feb., 2 Mar. 1708 (*Court and Society*, ii. 284, 296–7).

to invade Scotland. When the news was first officially communicated to the Commons, a Junto Member took advantage of the occasion to launch a thinly veiled attack on Harley and his friends, moving that the House include in its loyal address to the queen a passage attacking those who had tried to 'raise jealousies in Her Majesty of those who have served her in the most eminent and distinguishing manner'.[1] Court and Junto combined to vote through this vindication of Marlborough and Godolphin; but thereafter, for three weeks, the sobering news from the north put a quietus on party quarrels.

By the end of March the danger was over, the French fleet beaten off, and the Pretender back in France. It was now the opposition that tried to capitalize on the invasion attempt with a motion to thank the Admiralty, the particular target of the Junto. That group lacked the votes to kill the motion single-handed and the best they could do was to put through an amendment, suggested by Wharton's friend Hampden, in praise of Orford's friend Admiral Byng, who had commanded the fleet that intercepted the French squadron.[2] The Commons had leisure for such skirmishing, since they had completed all the money bills and were waiting for the Lords to approve them. Later that same day (1 April 1708) the Upper House had done its part, and Black Rod knocked, signalling the expected prorogation. The session of 1707–8 was at an end, and so was this parliament. Soon afterwards it was dissolved.

The successful conclusion of the session was certainly a relief to Godolphin and suggests that his decision to throw overboard Harley and his friends was both wise and practical. Historians have argued that the decision may have been the expedient one, but that it meant surrender to the Junto. It is impossible within the limits of this particular case study to deal satisfactorily

[1] *C.J.* xv. 602; Addison to Manchester, 12 Mar. 1708 (*Court and Society*, ii. 315). Addison writes that the passage quoted was suggested by Mr. Wortley Montagu, a kinsman and follower of Halifax.

[2] *C.J.* xv. 649; Luttrell, vi. 286; Addison to Manchester, 2 Apr. 1708 (*Court and Society*, ii. 331).

with this interpretation, but it should be pointed out that the changes made in the administration down to the end of 1708 hardly support such a generalization.

At the beginning of that year the Junto had two men in the ministry: the Secretary of State, Sunderland, and the Solicitor-General, Montagu, Halifax's brother. In February four members of the Harley connexion quitted the government, two others—Paymaster Brydges and Vice-Chamberlain Coke—electing to stay with the Court. No doubt the Junto leaders were jubilant over Harley's fall, but they did not themselves profit by it. Montagu, significantly, did not receive the expected promotion to Attorney-General in place of Harcourt—at least for many months—and in the meantime he had to do the work of both offices. Sunderland no doubt would have welcomed a Junto colleague as the other Secretary of State—someone like Lord Manchester—but the seals which Harley had returned went to Henry Boyle, Chancellor of the Exchequer.

Boyle was a Court politician, once intimate with Harley but now closely associated with Walpole and others of the Newcastle connexion. His promotion was followed by that of his friend Walpole, who succeeded St. John as Secretary at War; while another politician of the same persuasion, John Smith, the Speaker, succeeded Boyle as Chancellor of the Exchequer. None of these was a Junto man; all three had been working closely with Godolphin for the past three years or more; and they had all done yeoman service for the Court in the first part of the session, frequently in direct opposition to the Junto, who referred to them scornfully as 'Lord Treasurer's Whigs'. To assume, as so many historians do, that the favour shown to this element was a significant concession to the Junto is to misunderstand the party situation. At no time were the Junto and the Newcastle–Court Whig groups more at odds than during the session of 1707–8. In fact for a while the rivalry between them was stronger if anything than their joint hostility to the organized Tory groups. Godolphin's action in promoting 'Treasurer's Whigs' while passing over the Junto was particularly significant in view of the approaching general election. The end of a parliament usually saw extensive changes, particularly in the lesser offices; and a whole series of such changes was announced on the eve of the 1708 election. Yet once more the Junto was almost entirely passed over,[1] and the Junto leaders fought that election with little more official influence than they had enjoyed three years before.[2] Obviously, no accommodation had been reached between the Court and the Junto prior to the election, which in fact was as much a contest between Godolphin and the Junto as it was between Court and Country or between Tory and Whig.

The election of 1708 is worth a case study in itself, there are so many incidents that throw light on the relations between the party groups; but such a study falls outside the scope of this essay. We can only suggest here that the 1708 election was hardly the 'Whig landslide' pictured by most historians. It certainly was no Junto landslide, for that group failed to return as many Members as it had had at the end of the old parliament. Disappointed in the English elections, the Junto leaders plunged into the Scottish elections, once again joining forces with the *squadrone*. North of the Tweed the Junto lords, and particularly Sunderland, her Majesty's Secretary of State, directly opposed the Court. Both sides hoped to win support from the Jacobite peers recently implicated in the invasion attempt; but it was the Junto and *squadrone* leaders who got to

[1] The only Junto promotion was that of Orford's friend Admiral Byng to the Council for the Admiralty; but that was offset by the retention of Admiral Churchill and the advancement of four 'government' admirals: Queensberry's brother-in-law and three navy men who went over to Harley in 1710.

In other changes Godolphin's nephew took over the Stannaries, a post important for its influence in Cornish elections; and two members of the Newcastle connexion (Craven Peyton, the Duke's nominee at Boroughbridge; and Walpole's brother-in-law, Sir Charles Turner) got positions at the Mint and the Board of Trade respectively.

[2] Sunderland was now Secretary, and Montagu Solicitor-General; but the only posts with some real influence in elections gained by the Junto had been given them over a year before: namely, Wharton's appointment as Chief Justice in Eyre South of Trent; and Bolton's appointment as Governor of the Isle of Wight, in succession to Lord Cutts, killed on the battlefield.

them first. When the smoke had cleared, the Junto–*squadrone* alliance was found to have returned about a third of the commoners and over a third of the representative peers.[1]

The success of the Junto in the Scottish elections undoubtedly improved its bargaining position, and the Junto leaders now began actively to press for the concessions first demanded of Godolphin soon after the dissolution. These were moderate: promotion of Halifax's brother to Attorney-General, and the Presidency of the Council for Lord Somers. Godolphin was inclined to accept these terms; but the queen, backed by Harley, absolutely refused. She told Marlborough that she looked upon it as '*utter destruction*' to bring Somers into her service,[2] and she vetoed the compromise suggested by Newcastle and other Court Whig peers in her service, whereby Somers would be invited to attend the Cabinet Council, but without office. As the summer passed with no sign of a break in this deadlock, the Junto leaders grew angry and accused Godolphin of double-crossing them—falsely promising to forward their demands while actually planning a government based exclusively on 'Treasurer's Whigs', who meanwhile were receiving additional marks of Court favour.

The breach between the Junto and 'Treasurer's Whigs' grew wide and deep at this juncture;[3] but Newcastle, at least, was not

[1] The efforts of the Court to secure the electoral influence of the Jacobite leaders can be followed in Lord Mar's correspondence, in *H.M.C. Mar and Kellie MSS.*, pp. 435–534; the more successful efforts of the Junto and *squadrone*, in the letters between Sunderland, Marchmont (for the *squadrone*), and the Jacobite leaders, Hamilton, his brother Orkney, and Lord Annandale, in Add. MSS. 9101–2 (Coxe Transcripts), *passim*.

[2] The emphasis is the queen's; see her letter to Marlborough, 22 Apr. 1708, in Coxe's *Marlborough*, iv. 72–73.

[3] Lord Coningsby, a leading 'Treasurer's Whig', later wrote of the way 'Mr. Smith and myself had carried on the publick business with the greatest success, in opposition to the wild embroilments attempted by the Junto' (in his 'State of Political Parties in the Reign of Queen Anne', reprinted from Lansdowne MSS. 885, ff. 65, 75, by Sir Henry Ellis, in *Archaeologia*, xxxiii. 3–18); while Wharton, in a conversation with Lady Marlborough's chief political informant, referred to 'Mr. Smith whose opinion no man valued, & Mr. Compton, who he believed was of Mr. Harley's' (Arthur Maynwaring to Lady Marlborough, undated (but October 1708), in *Private Correspondence*, i. 157).

willing to see the Junto driven into outright opposition. Accordingly, a representative of his group attended a council of war held by the Junto, at which an ultimatum to the Court was agreed upon by the two groups: either Somers be given the Presidency of the Council and Wharton the government of Ireland, or the two connexions would unite to set up an independent Member as Speaker, in opposition to the Court candidate.[1] Almost certainly the queen would have rejected this ultimatum,[2] since it involved removing her husband from the post of Lord Admiral; but the sudden death of Prince George at one stroke removed this obstacle and any disposition on the queen's part to continue the struggle—for some time, at any rate. Lord Pembroke succeeded the prince at the Admiralty, making room for Somers to succeed Pembroke as Lord President and for Wharton to replace Pembroke as Lord Lieutenant of Ireland.

The Junto lords had finally succeeded in securing important positions for two more of their number, but did this actually amount to a surrender or result in a purely Junto, or even Whig, administration? The Treasury was still in Godolphin's hands; the conduct of the war and of foreign affairs in Marlborough's; the management of the navy in those of Marlborough's brother, under a new chief, the Court Tory Pembroke; most important of all, the government interest was still loyal to Godolphin and remained so until it became obvious that he no longer had the queen's confidence and would surely be supplanted by a man who did. Historians, picturing Godolphin and Marlborough

[1] See Sunderland's letters to Newcastle, particularly those of 19 and 26 Oct. 1708, in Lansdowne MSS. 1236, ff. 246–7. They were printed by Sir Henry Ellis in *Original Letters* (2nd Series), iv. 249–55, and also by Trevelyan, who was apparently unaware that Ellis had previously printed three of the five letters, in *Ramillies*, Appendix C (pp. 412–16).

[2] The initial effect of the ultimatum was to force Anne to give up her opposition to Montagu's promotion, and he was now made Attorney-General. The concession, 'if done in time', lamented Godolphin, 'would have removed most of our difficulties' (letter to Marlborough, 22 Oct. 1708, in Coxe's *Marlborough*, iv. 318). As it was, the promotion did not 'seem to transport his brother', Halifax, who took it 'rather as a debt paid, than an obligation received' (Maynwaring to Lady Marlborough, 'Thursday afternoon' (21 Oct. 1708), in *Private Correspondence*, i. 165–6).

hemmed into a dangerous no-man's land between opposing Whig and Tory forces, have greatly exaggerated the weakness of the chief ministers' position. They forget that these two still held the citadel—the Court—a much stronger position than that held by any of the party groups trying to storm their way into it. Robert Harley knew better, and his successful assault two years later succeeded initially because it was planned from inside the citadel, with the connivance of the titular and not yet passive commander-in-chief, the monarch herself.

NOTE A

The statement was made in the text that the true story of Harley's fall had never been written and could perhaps never be written. This seems inevitable in view of the fragmentary and inconclusive evidence so far brought to light. Actually almost nothing written at the time by those directly involved is available to form the basis for an accurate reconstruction of the episode.

Of strictly first-hand evidence there are only the following: two notes to Harley from the queen, both summoning him to an interview (*H.M.C. Bath MSS.* i. 189); Harley's letter to Godolphin, 30 Jan. 1708, and Godolphin's immediate reply (ibid. i. 189–90); and Marlborough's letter to the queen, undated but probably 6–8 Feb. 1708 (Coxe's *Marlborough*, iv. 24).

Of much lesser importance are the contemporary accounts by observers who are usually reliable but were not in a position to know what was happening, much less to reveal the motives of the principal actors. Such are the reports of Addison and Sir James Montagu (*Court and Society*, ii. 279–82); of Vernon (*Vernon Corresp.* iii. 343–5); of Lord Mar (*H.M.C. Mar and Kellie MSS.*, p. 427); and of Swift, in his well-known letter to Archbishop King, 12 Feb. 1708 (*Swift's Correspondence*, i. 74). The same is true in even greater degree of the reports of foreign observers, such as L'Hermitage (Add. MSS. 17677, xxx) and the Austrian and Prussian envoys, whose dispatches are printed or summarized by Klopp and von Noorden.

There remain the various accounts drawn up from two to ten years later, none of them by persons directly involved, though some of the narrators profess to be relaying conversations held with Harley and St. John. Such are Cowper's account of a conversation held with Harley on the subject of this incident and recorded in Cowper's *Diary* under date of 18 Sept. 1710 (pp. 42–43); Swift's 'Memoir Relating to that Change Which Happened in the Queen's Ministry in the Year 1710' (*Swift's Prose Works*, ed. Temple Scott (London 1907), v. 370), supposedly based on conversations with Harley and St. John; Edward Harley's account (*H.M.C. Portland MSS.* v. 647–8), also supposedly drawn from conversations with his brother; Lord Coningsby's 'State of Political Parties During the Reign of Queen Anne' (cited above, p. 151, n. 3); Bishop Burnet's account and Lord Dartmouth's note thereon (Burnet's *History*, v. 353–5); and finally, Lady Marlborough's account (*Conduct of the Duchess*, pp. 211–14).

The accounts by Burnet and Lady Marlborough are the most hostile, but were also written after the greatest interval of time. However, they probably reveal pretty accurately the eventual opinion of both Godolphin and Marlborough, namely that Harley had treacherously been trying to undermine them in secret interviews with the queen. Neither of these accounts suggests that there was planned treachery in the Almanza debates. Coningsby's account is interesting as revealing the attitude of a 'Treasurer's Whig' towards the Junto; and it is in general more sympathetic to Harley. The other three accounts—Cowper's, Swift's, and Edward Harley's—all stem from Harley himself. Like most of Harley's utterances they suggest more than they actually reveal and are full of hints about shifting attitudes and voltes-faces on the part of Marlborough and Godolphin.

Any systematic attempt to reconcile all of these accounts, it seems to this writer, breaks down before the silence of all the participants except Harley, whose own testimony, filtered through three different narrators, is full of ambiguities that cannot be resolved in the absence of further as yet unknown evidence.

CHAPTER VIII

Conclusion

IN this study of early eighteenth-century English parties we have taken the term 'party' in a restricted sense, as 'one of the parts into which a legislative body may be divided by questions of public policy or elections of public officers'—to adapt the definition of a contemporary political scientist.[1] Specifically, the object of analysis has been the political party in Parliament. A party, so defined, consisted of men summoned to the House of Lords by patent or returned to the House of Commons through election; and we began this study with an examination of the electoral system as it operated in the early years of the eighteenth century.

Any student who approaches the electoral system of that period through contemporary election correspondence becomes aware of the phenomenon known as 'interest'. To a major degree 'interest' is the clue to an understanding of eighteenth-century elections, and in the second chapter we illustrated the way the electoral system functioned in terms of the electoral interests enjoyed and cultivated by a relatively small number of groups and individuals. We then turned to an analysis of the membership of the House of Commons chosen in 1701, identifying first the occupation or profession of its Members and then the relationships of Members with the peerage and with the Court.

More than half the membership of the Commons, it appeared, was closely connected with the Court or with some important peer or group of peers. In fact upon closer examination it developed that a majority of the Lower House belonged

[1] Professor Arthur N. Holcombe, in his article on 'Political Parties' in Alvin Johnson and others, editors, *The Encyclopedia of the Social Sciences*.

to one or another of seven 'connexions'. These we described in some detail, starting with the 'government interest' and continuing with six other connexions organized on a more personal basis. These we characterized as the 'A, B, C's' of parliamentary politics—in terms of structure, at least—and we suggested that a realistic interpretation of party politics must take account of these individual groups.

The important question of how such groups should be fitted into the traditional Whig and Tory parties that have dominated historical thinking about party politics was then attacked in the second part of the study. In dealing with this question a feasible approach seemed to be a study of the past political behaviour of each group, as determined by its attitude towards the administration and important public issues in the period since it first appeared as a recognizable group in parliament. On the basis of 'age' the six personal connexions fell into different classifications, which made it easier to trace the political course of each group through the rather complex politics of the previous fifteen or twenty-five years.

In following the political course of each group the two-party concept did not prove particularly helpful. On such issues as Exclusion, the position of the Established Church, and the Revolution of 1688 there was a 'Whig' and a 'Tory' position, and there were rival philosophies underlying each position; but the evidence for national parties embodying the rival philosophies and taking the rival positions proved extremely elusive. The various groups tended to be 'Whig' or 'Tory' in general, but on specific issues in parliament and particularly during the intervals between the great debates all the groups followed distinctly individual, though sometimes parallel, courses.

The existence in 1701 of individual connexions seemed to us clearly established on the basis of the evidence summarized in the first part of this essay, but we did not anticipate much difficulty fitting them into one or the other of the two traditional parties. However, the party politics of the 1670's, 80's, and 90's did not fit neatly into the usual Whig-versus-Tory pattern. In fact that interpretation seemed to be developing 'symptoms of acute Ptolemaism', with the addition by historians such as Feiling of a series of 'apologetic epicycles':[1] 'wings', 'sections', 'factions', 'coalitions', and a 'Middle Party'—thereby greatly complicating the original concept of two parties.

These complications are not necessary unless one clings to the idea that Members of Parliament have to be members either of 'the Whig Party' or 'the Tory Party'. As we have pointed out, this concept does not allow for Members who did not vote consistently Whig or Tory, but who did vote very consistently—either for or against the government of the day. One very important connexion in the last parliament of William III, for example, was neither Tory nor Whig, but 'Court'—namely, the government interest. In order to account for the political orientation of this group and of its opposite, the 'Country' opposition, we need something besides the usual set of Whig–Tory co-ordinates. We need a Court–Country frame of reference.

To the argument that a second set of co-ordinates will hopelessly complicate matters and that party politics will lose all meaning, we reply that, on the contrary, they will gain another dimension, bringing out the details more clearly. We can assume that the House of Commons is divided, not into two parts—like a log split down the middle—but into several divisions. Schematically we can represent it as a pie that can be divided into a number of pieces or as a circle with four major segments: Court, Whig, Country, and Tory—forming, as it were, the north, east, south, and west quadrants. Any single division of the Commons will obviously show two 'parties'—the 'ayes' and the 'nays'—but on examination each of these will be found to consist of more than one segment. This particular point was sufficiently illustrated, we would think, in the case study of the parliamentary session of 1707–8.

This general conceptual scheme is useful not only in studying

[1] I have borrowed this metaphor from Professor J. H. Hexter. See his review of *Essays in Modern English History*, in *A.H.R.* xlvii (1942), 329.

a particular session of parliament, but more generally in tracing and explaining changes of government. Our assumption here is that the parliamentary foundation of any administration will be the Court segment, with its solid nucleus of regular government Members. The task of the chief ministers will then be to recruit enough elements from the adjoining Whig or Tory segments—'Court Whigs' and 'Court Tories', for example —so that they and the government Members together will give the administration a working majority. We suggested that Godolphin constructed his ministry in 1702 precisely as though he, too, were acting on our assumption; and in a case study of the Election of 1702 we showed how an early eighteenth-century election could be interpreted in terms far more precise and far more meaningful to a member of the government of the day than the usual guess as to how much of a 'Whig' or a 'Tory' victory it may have been.

As a sequel to our analysis of the 1702 election and as introduction to a second case study, of the parliamentary session of 1707–8, we outlined briefly the chief developments in parliament during the intervening period and connected them with the changes which Godolphin made in the government. This account served also to suggest how a multi-party hypothesis might explain the apparently unorthodox behaviour of the Godolphin ministry, which changed in a period of six years from a 'Tory administration' to a 'Whig' one. We submit that our hypothesis does prove useful in explaining this transformation. It frees us from any difficulty about 'coalitions', for we assume that any administration will inevitably be a coalition, made up of several of the party groups which we have identified. Viewed in this way, the Godolphin administration with its successive reconstructions no longer seems anomalous. Throughout its eight years it rested squarely on the foundation of the government interest plus the personal following of the two chief ministers. In addition it enjoyed the constant support of a considerable pro-administration element in both the Whig and Tory segments of the House. The same Court Whigs and

Court Tories who served in 1702 were still serving in 1710, with but few exceptions.

These Court elements were the heart of the administration, but Trevelyan and Feiling overlook them in their concentration on the strict party elements, which of course did change. Godolphin began by including in his ministry the Finch and Hyde–Seymour groups, with whom he had worked before; but within two years he found them more troublesome than useful and he discarded them in favour of Harley's group and the Newcastle connexion. This brought him closer to the Whig groups on the other side of the Court and gained him some support even from the Junto connexion, particularly during the years 1705–7, when the Junto helped put through the Union with Scotland. For this service the Junto leaders demanded their reward; but Godolphin's position was so secure that he could hold them off year after year, conceding only the appointment of Marlborough's son-in-law Sunderland as Secretary of State.

How much longer Godolphin could have secured the Junto leaders' co-operation without granting them a larger share of office is hard to say, because Harley took a hand in the game and made it a three-cornered contest. Eventually Harley and the Junto forced the Treasurer to choose between them; but this does not mean that Harley's dismissal represented a surrender on Godolphin's part. He ousted Harley, not because the Junto wanted him to, but because he finally decided that Harley was too untrustworthy to keep in office; and he did not replace Harley and his friends with Junto leaders. He still had considerable other support: in Court politicians like Pembroke and Somerset, in 'Treasurer's Whigs' like Smith and Coningsby, and among the Newcastle connexion—all of whom did yeoman service in the 1707–8 session 'in opposition to the wild embroilments attempted by the Junto' and their *squadrone* allies. Godolphin was strong enough to hold off the Junto not only past the 1708 elections—in which the Court improved its position while the Junto did not—but on through the summer, until an act of God, the unexpected death of the queen's husband, finally opened a way into the administration for two more Junto leaders.

The process by which the Godolphin ministry changed from a Court–Churchill–Harley–Rochester–Nottingham coalition into a Court–Churchill–Newcastle–Junto combination is a logical one, if one recognizes that the architects of governments and of parliamentary majorities worked within a multi-party framework. This assumption often fits the facts far better than the two-party interpretation; but the party history of the period 1688–1714 has been explained so universally in terms of 'Whig' and 'Tory' exclusively, that the many similarities between it and the later eighteenth-century political structure have been commonly overlooked. The more one studies the party structure under William and Anne, the less it resembles the two-party system described by Trevelyan in his Romanes Lecture and the more it seems to have in common with the structure of politics in the Age of Newcastle as explained to us by Namier.

APPENDIXES

APPENDIX I

The 1701 Parliament: Occupations of Members[1]

PART I. THE COMMERCIAL INTEREST

Summary:

1. Merchants	
East Indies trade (Old and New East India Companies)	15
West Indies, American, and Colonial trade	11
Turkey and Mediterranean trade	5
Baltic trade	1
Coal trade	1
Coasting trade	2
Local	8
Total merchants	43
2. Bankers	
Directors of the Bank of England	7
Bank directors already included as merchants (subtract) (*minus*)	5
Private bankers, goldsmiths, promoters, &c.	5
Total banking interest (exclusive of those already counted)	7
3. Liquor trade	
Brewers	4
Distiller	1
Total	5
4. Miscellaneous Trades and Manufactures	6
Total commercial interest	61

[1] In this appendix and those that follow it is impossible to give footnote references for each M.P. For documentation see the notes on these M.P.s deposited by me with the History of Parliament Trust, Senate House, London.

1. *Merchants*: listed alphabetically, with residence, trade, and seat.

Ashurst, Sir Henry (of London, W. Indies trade, M.P. Wilton—outsider).

Burridge, Robert (of Lyme, W. Indies trade, M.P. Lyme).

Carr, William (of Newcastle-on-Tyne, coal trade, M.P. Newcastle-on-Tyne).

Champneys, Arthur (of Exeter(?), local merchant, M.P. Barnstaple—owned an estate near by).

Clayton, William (of Liverpool, W. Indies and American trade, M.P. Liverpool).

Cooke, Sir Thomas (of London, E. Indies trade, M.P. Colchester—outsider).

Cotesworth, William (of London, E. Indies trade, M.P. Grimsby—outsider).

Coulson, Thomas (of London, E. Indies trade, M.P. Totnes—Seymour nominee).

Crow, Mitford (of London, Mediterr. and Turkey trade, M.P. Southampton—outsider).

Daines, Sir William (of Bristol, W. Indies and American trade, M.P. Bristol).

*Furnese, Sir Henry (of London, E. Indies trade, M.P. Sandwich—outsider).

*Gould, Nathaniel (of London, Mediterr. and Turkey trade, M.P. Shoreham—outsider).

Hayes, John (of London, mercer and army clothier, M.P. Winchelsea—outsider).

*Heathcote, Sir Gilbert (of London, E. India trade, M.P. London).

Herne, Frederick (of London, E. India trade, M.P. Dartmouth—outsider).

Herne, Nathaniel (of London, American trade, M.P. Dartmouth—cousin of Fred.).

Heysham, Robert (of London, W. Indies trade, M.P. Lancaster—birthplace).

Jeffries, Sir Jeffrey (of London, W. Indies and American trade, M.P. Brecon—his birthplace and owned property there).

Jeffries, John (of London, W. Indies and American trade, M.P. Marlborough—outsider, brother of next above).

Johnson, Thomas (of Liverpool, W. Indies trade, M.P. Liverpool).

Johnson, William (of London, E. Indian trade, M.P. Aldeburgh (Suffolk)—on his brother, Sir Henry's interest (cf. misc. trades, below)).

* Those merchants marked with an asterisk (*) are listed also as bankers. See next section of the commercial interest, below.

Joliffe, William (of London, Turkey and E. Indian trade, M.P. Poole —his father a native of Poole).

Maister, William (of Hull, coastwise trade, M.P. Hull).

Mitchell, Robert (of London, E. Indies trade and a contractor, M.P. Petersfield—an outsider).

Mitford, Michael (of London, Baltic trade, M.P. Bedwin—an outsider).

Molyneux, Thomas (of London, Turkey trade, M.P. Preston—had property there plus the Duchy of Lancaster interest(?)).

Moore, Arthur (of London, E. Indian trade, M.P. Grimsby—an outsider).

Morgan, John (of London, W. Indies trade, M.P. Monmouth—cadet of Morgans of Tredegar, who had interests in Monmouth).

Paice, Joseph (of London, Turkey and Mediterr. trade, M.P. Lyme —an outsider).

Phillips, Richard (of Ipswich, local trade, M.P. Ipswich).

Phippard, Sir William (of London and Poole, Dorset, W. Indian trade, M.P. Poole—native son and benefactor).

Rebow, Sir Isaac (of Colchester, local trade, M.P. Colchester).

Rigby, Sir Alexander (of London, Turkey and Mediterr. trade, M.P. Wigan—some local interest plus the Duchy interest).

*Scawen, Sir William (of London, E. Indian trade, M.P. Grampound —bought an interest there).

Shepheard, Francis (of London, E. Indies trade, M.P. Andover—an outsider).

Snell, John (of Exeter, local trade, M.P. Exeter—leader of Seymour interest).

Styles, Joseph Haskins (of London, E. Indies trade, M.P. Sudbury —outsider).

Swift, Samuel (of Worcester, local trade, M.P. Worcester).

Turner, Sir Charles (of Lynn, Baltic trade(?), M.P. Lynn).

Turner, Sir John (of Lynn, Baltic trade(?), M.P. Lynn—uncle of next above).

Ward, John (of London, E. Indies trade, M.P. Bletchingly—nominee of Sir Robert Clayton (see 'Bankers', below)).

Williams, John (of Fowey, local merchant, M.P. Fowey).

Yate, Robert (of Bristol, W. Indies and American trade, M.P. Bristol).

2. *Bankers*: listed alphabetically, with residence and parliamentary seat.

Abney, Sir Thomas (of London, Bank Director, M.P. London).

Ashurst, Sir William (of London, Bank Director, M.P. London).

Child, Sir Francis (of London, goldsmith and banker, M.P. Devizes —outsider).

Clayton, Sir Robert (of London, Bank Director, M.P. London and patron of Bletchingly (cf. John Ward *sub* 'Merchants')).

Davall, Sir Thomas (of London, private banker, M.P. Harwich—Recorder and owned property in the borough).

*Furnese, Sir Henry (of London, Bank Director, M.P. Sandwich—see 'Merchants').

*Gould, Nathaniel (of London, Bank Director, M.P. Shoreham—see 'Merchants').

Gulston, William (of London, private banker and promoter, M.P. Bridport—an outsider).

*Heathcote, Sir Gilbert (of London, Bank Director, M.P. London—see 'Merchants').

Hopkins, Edward (of London and Coventry, private banker, M.P. Coventry—birthplace and owned property).

*Scawen, Sir William (of London, Bank Director, M.P. Grampound—see 'Merchants').

Woollaston, Richard (of London, private banker and promoter, M.P. Whitchurch—an outsider).

3. *Brewers and Distiller*: listed alphabetically, with residence and seat in Commons.

Bliss, Thomas (of Maidstone, brewer, M.P. Maidstone).

Cholmley, John (of Southwark, brewer, M.P. Southwark).

Cox, Charles (of Southwark, brewer, M.P. Southwark).

Hutchinson, Jonathan (of Berwick, distiller, M.P. Berwick).

Parsons, Sir John (of London, brewer, M.P. Reigate—purchased a moiety of the manor and borough).

4. *Miscellaneous Trades*: listed alphabetically, with residence and seat in Commons.

Burton, John (of Yarmouth in Norfolk, salt-maker, M.P. Yarmouth).

Chase, James (of London, apothecary, M.P. Marlow—an outsider, had Wharton's electoral interest).

Guy, Thomas (of London, stationer, founder of Guy's Hospital, M.P. Tamworth—native son and benefactor there).

Johnson, Sir Henry (of London, shipbuilder, M.P. Aldeburgh (Suffolk)—purchased that Suffolk manor and borough).

Renda, Thomas (of London and Wallingford, manufacturer of copper coins for the Treasury, M.P. Wallingford—owned property there).

Wheeler, William (of Blackpool, ironmonger, M.P. Haverfordwest—local interest).

Note on the London Merchant-Bankers: with regard to residence and seat in Commons.

Total number of London merchants in the Commons . . .	39
Sitting for City of London	4
Sitting for boroughs where they or their fathers were natives	11
Sitting for constituencies where they had bought property and an electoral interest	10
Sitting for constituencies where they were strangers . .	14
	39

PART II. THE ARMED SERVICES

Summary:

Army officers	
Major-generals	4
Brigadier-generals	3
Colonels	10
Lieutenant-colonels	7
Majors	4
Captains	6
Lieutenants and cornets of horse	5
Total of army officers	39
Navy officers	
Admirals	5
Captains	4
Total of navy officers	9

Army Officers: listed alphabetically, with rank and constituency.[1]

Austen, Robert (lieutenant of foot, M.P. Winchelsea—local interest, plus Finch).

Bellasyse, Sir Henry (colonel of a foot regt., M.P. Durham—Bishop of Durham's plus his own interest).

(Berkeley), John, Viscount Fitzharding (colonel of dragoons, M.P. Windsor—Court interest).

Boteler, John (cornet of horse, M.P. Hythe—had gov't interest in 1702, local interest in 1701(?)).

[1] This list is based largely on Charles Dalton's *English Army Lists and Commission Registers, 1661–1714* (6 vols., London, 1892–1904); supplemented by information from Luttrell, Boyer's *Annals*, the published State Papers, &c.

Carew, Thomas (major of foot, M.P. Saltash—local interest).

Churchill, Charles (maj.-gen., colonel of a foot regt., M.P. Weymouth —gov't interest).

Courtenay, William (captain of marines, M.P. Michael—local interest).

Crawford, Robert (colonel, Governor of Sheerness, M.P. Queenborough—gov't interest).

Cutts, John, Lord Cutts (maj.-gen., colonel Coldstream Guards, Governor of the Isle of Wight, M.P. Cambridgeshire—his own interest). (Also returned for Newport, I. of Wight, on the gov't interest.)

Delaval, Sir John (captain in Foot Guards, M.P. Morpeth—Lord Carlisle's interest).

Dodson, Thomas (major, Captain of Bermuda Castle, M.P. Liskeard —own interest).

Dore, Thomas (lieut.-col. of foot, M.P. Lymington—Burrard's interest).

Erle, Thomas (maj.-gen., colonel of a foot regt., Governor of Portsmouth, M.P. Portsmouth—gov't interest, returned also for Wareham—own interest).

Fairfax, Thomas, Lord Fairfax (brig.-gen., colonel of regt. of dragoons, M.P. Yorkshire—own interest, plus that of Lords Carlisle and Wharton).

Fletcher, George (captain of horse, M.P. Cumberland—own interest, plus that of Lords Carlisle and Wharton).

Gibson, John (colonel of a foot regt., Lieut.-Governor of Portsmouth, M.P. Portsmouth—on the gov't interest).

Howard, Philip (lieut.-col. of marines, M.P. Carlisle—on Lord Carlisle's interest).

Howe, Emanuel Scrope (brig.-gen., colonel of a foot regt., M.P. Morpeth—on Lord Carlisle's interest).

King, Thomas (lieut.-col. in the Foot Guards, Lieut.-Governor of Sheerness, M.P. Queenborough—on the gov't interest).

Kirkby, Roger (colonel of foot, Governor of Chester, M.P. Lancaster —his own interest, plus the Duchy interest, probably).

Luttrell, Alexander (lieut.-col. of marines, M.P. Minehead—own interest).

Mordaunt, Harry (colonel of a foot regt., M.P. Brackley—Wharton's interest).

Mordaunt, John, Lord Mordaunt (captain of foot, M.P. Chippenham —Lord Wharton's interest).

Morgan, Anthony (major of horse, M.P. Yarmouth, I. of Wight— own interest).

North, Charles (captain of foot, M.P. Banbury—family interest).
Pope, Roger (major of horse, M.P. Bridgnorth—family interest).
Raleigh, Carew (cornet of horse, M.P. Downton—own interest).
Seymour, William (colonel of a foot regt., M.P. Cockermouth—Duke of Somerset's interest).
Shrimpton, John (major in Foot Guards, M.P. Whitchurch—own interest).
Stanhope, James (lieut.-col. in Foot Guards, M.P. Newport, I. of Wight—gov't (Governor Lord Cutts) interest).
Stanley, James (colonel of foot, M.P. Lancashire—family interest).
Stringer, Thomas (lieut.-col. in Foot Guards, M.P. Clitheroe—own interest).
Temple, Sir Richard (colonel of foot, M.P. Buckingham—own interest).
Thompson, Maurice (captain in Foot Guards, M.P. Gatton—family interest).
Travell, Sir Thomas (captain of horse, M.P. Milborne Port—own interest).
Trelawny, Charles (maj.-gen., Governor of Plymouth, M.P. Plymouth —on the gov't interest).
Trelawny, Henry (brig.-gen., colonel of foot, M.P. Plymouth—gov't).
Webb, John Richmond (colonel of foot, M.P. Ludgershall—own interest).
Wharton, Goodwin (lieut.-col. of horse, M.P. Buckinghamshire—family interest).

Navy Officers: listed alphabetically, with rank and constituency.

Aylmer, Matthew (vice-admiral, Governor of Deal Castle, M.P. Dover —originally Admiralty interest, plus his own).
Bankes, Sir Jacob (captain, M.P. Minehead—his brother-in-law Luttrell's interest).
(Berkeley), James, Viscount Durseley (rear-admiral, M.P. Gloucester —family interest).
Bokenham, William (captain, M.P. Rochester—Admiralty interest).
Churchill, George (vice-admiral, an Admiralty Lord, M.P. St. Alban's —Lady Marlborough's interest).
Greville, Algernon (captain, M.P. Warwick—family interest).
Hopson, Thomas (vice-admiral, M.P. Newtown, I. of Wight—gov't interest).
Rooke, Sir George (admiral, Navy Comm'r, M.P. Portsmouth—gov't interest).
St. Loe, George (captain, Navy Comm'r at Plymouth, M.P. Weymouth—gov't interest).

PART III. THE LEGAL PROFESSION

Summary:

Common-law barristers	
Middle Temple	21
Inner Temple	18
Lincolns Inn	15
Grays Inn	4
Total barristers	58
Chancery lawyers	2
Admiralty and civil lawyers .	2
Total for legal profession	62

Lawyers in the House of Commons: listed alphabetically, with Inn of Court and significant offices. Unless otherwise stated, the man is a barrister.[1]

Acton, Sir Edward (Inner Temple, Recorder of Bridgnorth, M.P. for that).

Anderton, James (Inner Temple, Deputy custos rotulorum for Duchy of Lancashire, M.P. Ilchester—an outsider and Seymour interest).

Ashurst, Henry (Inner Temple, Town Clerk of London, Atty.-Gen. Duchy of Lancashire, M.P. Preston—on the Duchy interest).

Barrell, Francis (Middle Temple, M.P. Rochester—his two brothers held positions in the Cathedral, possibly a Cathedral candidate).

Bertie, Robert (Middle Temple, Recorder of Hertford, M.P. Westbury —family interest).

Birch, John (Middle Temple, M.P. Weobley—own interest).

Blaake, Henry (Inner Temple, M.P. Calne—own interest plus Lord Wharton's).

Brereton, Edward (Inner Temple, M.P. Denbigh—own interest).

Bridges, William (Middle Temple, M.P. Liskeard—probably had Godolphin interest).

Burnaby, Anthony (Middle Temple, M.P. Stockbridge—outsider).

Caesar, Charles (Middle Temple, M.P. Hertford—local interest).

Campion, William (Middle Temple, M.P. Kent—local interest).

Carter, Laurence (Inner Temple, Receiver-Gen. Duchy of Lancs., Dep. Recorder of Leicester, M.P. Leicester—Lord Stamford's interest).

Cocks, Charles (Middle Temple, Clerk of the Patents, M.P. Droit-

[1] This list is compiled principally from the published records of the Inns of Courts, supplemented by other scattered references.

wich—local interest, plus his brother-in-law Lord Somers's interest).

Colchester, Maynard (Middle Temple, M.P. Gloucestershire—local interest).

Compton, Spencer (Middle Temple, M.P. Eye—Lord Cornwallis's interest).

Comyns, John (Lincolns Inn, Recorder of Malden, M.P. Malden—local interest).

Conyers, John (Middle Temple, King's Council, M.P. Grinstead—own interest).

Coward, William (Lincolns Inn, Serjeant at Law, Recorder of Wells, M.P. Wells—his own interest).

Cowper, William (Middle Temple, King's Council, M.P. Beeralston—Lord Stamford's interest).

Coxe, Charles (Lincolns Inn, King's Serjeant, M.P. Cirencester—his own interest).

Crawley, Richard (Admiralty and civilian lawyer, Register to the Admiralty and to the High Court of Delegates, M.P. Wendover—his own interest).

Davy, Robert (Inner Temple, Recorder of Norwich, M.P. for that—own interest).

Dolben, Sir Gilbert (Inner Temple, Judge of Irish Court of Common Pleas, M.P. Peterborough—own interest).

Dormer, Fleetwood (Lincolns Inn, Recorder of Wycombe, M.P. Wycombe—Lord Wharton's interest).

Dormer, Robert (Lincolns Inn, Serj., M.P. Bucks.—also Northallerton—Wharton's interest).

Ekins, Thomas (Middle Temple, M.P. Higham Ferrers—own interest).

Etherege, Sir James (Inner Temple, M.P. Marlow—own interest).

Ettrick, William (Middle Temple, Receiver of Customs at Sunderland, M.P. Christchurch—Lord Rochester's interest).

Eyre, Robert (Lincolns Inn, Serjeant at Law, Recorder of Salisbury, M.P. Salisbury—own interest).

Farrer, William (Inner Temple, King's Council, Deputy Recorder of Bedford, M.P. Bedford—Duke of Bedford's interest).

Finch, Heneage (Inner Temple, King's Council (sometime—1679–86—Solicitor-Gen.), M.P. University of Oxford—Finch interest).

Fleming, Henry (Lincolns Inn, M.P. St. Germans—Eliot's (his uncle) interest).

Gape, John (Lincolns Inn, M.P. Hertford—own interest).

Goulston, Edward (Grays Inn, M.P. New Romney—bought property there).

Harcourt, Simon (Inner Temple, Recorder of Abingdon, M.P. for that —own interest).

Harvey, Stephen (Middle Temple, M.P. Reigate—Lord Somers's interest).

Hawles, Sir John (Lincolns Inn, Solicitor-Gen., M.P. St. Ives—Duke of Bolton's interest).

Hedges, Sir Charles (civilian and Admiralty lawyer, Chancellor and Vicar-Gen. of Diocese of Rochester, M.P. Malmesbury—outsider —elected also for Calne, but unseated on petition).

Hoblyn, John (Middle Temple, Town Clerk of Bodmin, M.P. Bodmin —own interest).

Hooper, Sir Nicholas (Inner Temple, Serjeant at Law, Recorder of Barnstaple, M.P. Barnstaple—own interest).

Jacob, Thomas (Lincolns Inn, M.P. Wootton Bassett—local interest).

Jekyll, Sir Joseph (Middle Temple, Chief Justice of Chester, M.P. Eye—Lord Cornwallis's interest).

King, Peter (Middle Temple, M.P. Beeralston—Lord Stamford's interest).

Lloyd, Henry (Inner Temple, M.P. Cardigan—own interest).

Loraine, William (Lincolns Inn, M.P. Northumberland—Lord Carlisle's interest(?)).

Methuen, John (Inner Temple, Master in Chancery, and Irish Lord Chancellor, M.P. Devizes—own interest).

Morley, George (Lincolns Inn, Master in Chancery, M.P. Hindon—outsider).

Northmore, Thomas (Inner Temple, Master in Chancery, M.P. Okehampton—own interest).

Offley, Joseph (Middle Temple, M.P. Rye—outsider).

Ogle, Samuel (Grays Inn, Comm'r of the Revenue in Ireland, Recorder of Berwick, M.P. Berwick—own interest).

Owen, Thomas (Grays Inn, Attorney of the Common Pleas Office, M.P. Bramber—outsider).

Pitfield, Alexander (Lincolns Inn, a chancery lawyer, M.P. Bridport —outsider).

Powys, Sir Thomas (Lincolns Inn, Serjeant at Law, Recorder of Ludlow, M.P. Ludlow—own interest).

Price, Robert (Lincolns Inn, Welsh judge, M.P. Weobley—own terest).

Proby, John (Middle Temple, M.P. Huntingdonshire—own interest(?)).

Rowney, Thomas (Inner Temple, M.P. Oxford City—local interest).

Scobell, Francis (Middle Temple, M.P. Grampound—Seymour interest).

Topham, Richard (Lincolns Inn, a chancery lawyer, M.P. Windsor—Court interest).

Vaughan, Richard (Grays Inn, Recorder of Carmarthen, M.P. Carmarthen—family interest).

Whitaker, Charles (Inner Temple, King's Serjeant, Recorder of Ipswich, M.P. Ipswich—own interest(?)).

PART IV. OFFICE-HOLDERS IN THE COMMONS

Summary:

1. Members holding responsible offices 8
2. Members holding administrative offices requiring the major part of their time and effort:

Admiralty and Navy Office	8
War Office and Ordnance	3
Treasury and Excise	2
Secretary of State's Office	1
The Mint	1
Post Office	2
Ireland	2
Miscellaneous	4
	23

Total administrative officers of this type . . 23

3. Legal positions 17
4. Military governors of garrisons and garrison-towns 8
5. Household posts, sinecures, and minor positions:

In the royal household	16
Sinecures and part-time offices	33
Pensions	6
	55

Total places of this type 55

Government contractors 2

Total office-holders in the Commons 113

1. *Members holding responsible offices:*

Blathwayt, William (Secretary of War, Clerk of the Privy Council, and a Comm'r of Trade and Plantations, M.P. Bath—own interest).

Boyle, Henry (Chancellor of the Exchequer, M.P. University of Cambridge—own interest).

Churchill, George (Admiralty Lord, M.P. St. Albans—Lady Marlborough's interest).

Fox, Sir Stephen (Treasury Lord, M.P. Cricklade—own interest).

Harley, Robert (Speaker of the House of Commons, M.P. Radnor—family interest).

Hawles, Sir John (Solicitor-Gen., M.P. St. Ives—Duke of Bolton's interest).

Smith, John (Treasury Lord, M.P. Andover—own interest).

Vernon, James (Secretary of State, Northern Dept., M.P. Westminster—gov't interest).

2. *Members holding administrative offices requiring most of their time:*

Aylmer, Matthew (Comm'r of the Navy, and for Registering Seamen, Governor of Deal Castle, M.P. Dover—gov't interest).

Bertie, Charles (Treasurer and Paymaster of the Ordnance, M.P. Stamford—family interest).

Bokenham, William (Dockyard official at Chatham, M.P. Rochester—gov't interest).

Brewer, John (Auditor of the Excise, M.P. New Romney—gov't interest).

Cardonnel, Adam (Chief Clerk in the War Office, M.P. Southampton—gov't interest plus his own).

Cotton, Sir Robert (Joint Postmaster-Gen., M.P. Truro—Boscawen interest).

Crow, Mitford (Governor of Barbados, M.P. Southampton—gov't interest).

Dudley, Joseph (Lieut.-Governor I. of Wight, Colonial Agent, M.P. Newtown, I. of Wight—gov't interest).

Frankland, Sir Thomas (Joint Postmaster-Gen., M.P. Thirsk—own interest).

Gwyn, Francis (Secretary to the Lord Lieutenant of Ireland, Clerk of the Crown for Wales, M.P. Christchurch—Lord Rochester's interest).

Kendall, James (Comm'r of the Irish Revenue and other offices, M.P. West Looe—Seymour–Trelawny interest).

Littleton, Sir Thomas (Treasurer of the Navy, M.P. Woodstock—outsider).

Lowndes, William (Secretary of the Treasury, M.P. Seaford—gov't interest).

Lydell, Dennis (Navy Comm'r, M.P. Harwich—gov't interest).

Markes, Richard (Portsmouth Dockyard official, M.P. Petersfield—local interest).

Mounsher, John (Portsmouth Dockyard official, M.P. Hastings—gov't interest).

Newton, Sir Isaac (Master of the Mint, M.P. Cambridge University—own interest, plus Lord Halifax's support).

Pulteney, John (Secretary to the Master-Gen. of the Ordnance, M.P. Hastings—gov't interest).

Rooke, Sir George (Admiralty Lord, M.P. Portsmouth—gov't interest).

St. Loe, George (Navy Comm'r at Plymouth, M.P. Weymouth—gov't interest).

Sergison, Charles (Navy Comm'r, M.P. Shoreham—gov't interest).

Wren, Sir Christopher (Surveyor-Gen. and Master of the Works, M.P. Weymouth—gov't interest).

Yard, Robert (Under-Secretary of State and Clerk of the Privy Council, M.P. Marlborough—Duke of Somerset's interest).

3. *Members holding legal positions*: unless otherwise noted, all of these Members have already been listed as lawyers, and the note as to their electoral interest in their constituency will be omitted.

Conyers, John (King's Council, M.P. Grinstead).

Cowper, William (King's Council, M.P. Beeralston).

Coxe, Charles (King's Council, Puisne Justice for Wales, M.P. Cirencester).

Crawley, Richard (Register of the Admiralty, and of the High Court of Delegates, M.P. Wendover).

Dolben, Sir Gilbert (Judge of the Irish Court of Common Pleas, M.P. Peterborough).

Dormer, Robert (Chancellor of the County Palatine of Durham, M.P. Buckinghamshire).

Farrer, William (King's Council, M.P. Bedford).

Hedges, Sir Charles (Chancellor and Vicar-Gen. of Diocese of Rochester, M.P. Malmesbury).

Jekyll, Sir Joseph (Chief Justice of Chester, M.P. Eye).

Methuen, John (Irish Lord Chancellor, M.P. Devizes).

Morley, George (Master in Chancery, Sewer of the Chamber, M.P. Hindon).

Northmore, Thomas (Master in Chancery, M.P. Okehampton).

Owen, Thomas (one of the Four Attorneys of the Pleas Office, M.P. Bramber).

Pitfield, Alexander (Chancery Cursitor for Kent and Devon, M.P. Bridport).

Price, Robert (Welsh Judge, M.P. Weobley).

Stringer, Thomas (Chancery Filazer for Yorkshire—this man was an army officer (see 'Armed Services'), M.P. Clitheroe).

Whitaker, Charles (King's Serjeant and Foreign Opposer in the Court of Exchequer, M.P. Ipswich).

4. *Members holding governorships of garrison-towns*: unless otherwise noted these Members are army officers and are listed as such already.

Crawford, Robert (Governor of Sheerness, M.P. Queenborough).

(Cutts), John, Lord Cutts (Governor, I. of Wight, M.P. Cambridgeshire).

Dodson, Thomas (Captain of Bermuda Castle, M.P. Liskeard).

Erle, Thomas (Governor of Portsmouth, M.P. Portsmouth).

Gibson, John (Lieut.-Governor of Portsmouth, M.P. Portsmouth).

King, Thomas (Lieut.-Governor of Sheerness, M.P. Queenborough).

Kirkby, Roger (Governor of Chester, M.P. Lancaster).

Trelawny, Charles (Governor of Plymouth, M.P. Plymouth).

5. *Members with sinecures, pensions, minor part-time posts, &c.:*

Ashe, Edward (Comptroller of Customs at Plymouth, M.P. Heytesbury—own interest).

Ashurst, Sir Henry (Comm'r for Duties on Hackney Coaches, M.P. Wilton—Lord Pembroke's interest).

Ashurst, Henry (Atty.-Gen. of the Duchy of Lancs., M.P. Preston—Duchy interest).

(Berkeley), John, Viscount Fitzharding (Exchequer Teller—also an army officer—M.P. Windsor—Court interest).

Bertie, Peregrine (Vice-Chamberlain, Receiver of Rents for the Duchy of Cornwall, M.P. Boston—family interest).

Booth, George (pension of £600 per annum, M.P. Lostwithiel—Lord Radnor's interest).

Chase, James (Apothecary to the Court, M.P. Marlow—Wharton's interest).

Churchill, Charles (Gent. of the Bedchamber to Prince George—also an army officer—M.P. Weymouth—gov't interest).

Cocks, Charles (Clerk of the Patents—also a lawyer—M.P. Droitwich).

(Coningsby), Thomas, Lord Coningsby (Joint Paymaster-Gen. in Ireland, and Vice-Treasurer there, M.P. Leominster—own interest).

Croker, Courtenay (Governor of the Fort and Castle of Dartmouth, M.P. Plympton—local interest).

Drake, John (Register of the Chirographer's Office—sinecure owned by the family—M.P. Amersham—family interest).

Duncombe, Anthony (Comm'r of Transport, M.P. Hedon—family interest).

Ettrick, William (Receiver of Customs for Port of Sunderland, M.P. Christchurch—Lord Rochester's interest).

(Fairfax), Thomas, Lord Fairfax (pension of £600 per annum, M.P. Yorkshire—also in the army).

Farrer, William (Receiver-Gen. for Cambridgeshire—also King's Council—M.P. Bedford—Duke of Bedford's interest).

Forester, Sir William (Clerk of the Board of Green Cloth (Household post), M.P. Wenlock—family interest).

Fox, Charles (Joint Paymaster of the Forces in Ireland, Treasurer to the Queen Dowager, M.P. Salisbury—local interest).

Gauntlett, John (Clerk of the Signet Office, M.P. Wilton—Lord Pembroke's interest).

Godfrey, Charles (Master of the Jewel Office—Household post, M.P. Wycombe—Lord Wharton's interest).

Godolphin, Francis (Teller of the Exchequer, Joint Registrar of Chancery—both sinecures, M.P. Helston—family interest).

Godolphin, Sidney (Governor of the Scilly Isles, M.P. Helston—family).

Goodricke, Sir Henry (Lieut.-Gen. of the Ordnance, M.P. Boroughbridge—Duke of Leeds's interest(?)).

Gwynne, Sir Rowland (Treasurer of the Chamber, Clerk of the Board of Green Cloth—both Household posts, M.P. Brecknockshire).

Henley, Anthony (pension of £2,000 per annum, M.P. Weymouth—gov't(?)).

Herbert, James (Receiver-Gen. of Prizes, M.P. Aylesbury—Sir John Pakington's interest).

Howard, Philip (pension of £400 per annum—also an army officer—M.P. Carlisle).

Howe, Emanuel Scrope (Groom of the Bedchamber—also an army officer—M.P. Morpeth—Lord Carlisle's interest).

Hutton, John (Physician-in-Ordinary to the King, M.P. Richmond—outsider).

(Jones), Richard, Earl of Ranelagh (Paymaster-Gen. of the Army, Vice-Treasurer of Ireland, M.P. West Looe—Trelawny interest).

Lowther, James (Clerk of the Deliveries of the Ordnance, M.P. Carlisle—family interest, and Lord Carlisle's).

Marsham, Sir Robert (Clerk of the Court of Chancery—sinecure—M.P. Maidstone—local interest).

Mason, Charles (Joint Comptroller of the Mint, M.P. Bishop's Castle—Lord Macclesfield's interest plus his own).

Molyneux, Thomas (Joint Comptroller of the Mint, M.P. Preston—Duchy interest plus his own).

Montagu, Charles (Constable of the Castle of Durham, M.P. Durham—Bishop of Durham's interest).

Mordaunt, Harry (Treasurer of the Ordnance—also an army officer—M.P. Brackley—Lord Wharton's interest).

Musgrave, Sir Christopher (Master of the Robes to the Queen Dowager, M.P. Totnes—Sir Edward Seymour's interest).

Ogle, Samuel (Comm'r of the Irish Revenue, M.P. Berwick—also a lawyer).

Pauncefort, Edward (Cashier of the Paymaster's Office, Yeoman of the Jewel Office, M.P. Malmesbury—Sir C. Hedges's interest).

Pope, Roger (Equerry to the Master of the Horse—also an army officer—M.P. Bridgnorth).

Powlett, Lord William (Farmer of the Green Wax—a sinecure—M.P. Winchester—family interest).

Raleigh, Carew (pension of £120 per annum and a royal page, M.P. Downton—own interest).

Rigby, Sir Alexander (Clerk of the Crown for the Duchy of Lancaster, M.P. Wigan—Duchy interest plus his own).

Robartes, Francis (Comm'r of the Irish Revenue, M.P. Tregoney—Lord Radnor's interest).

Russell, Lord Edward (Treasurer of the Chamber, M.P. Bedfordshire—Duke of Bedford's interest).

Russell, Lord Robert (Clerk of the Pipe—a sinecure—M.P. Tavistock—Duke of Bedford's interest).

Saunderson, James (Comm'r of the Alienation Office, M.P. Newark—family interest).

Sayer, George (pension of £500 per annum, M.P. Canterbury—own interest).

Spencer, William (of the Band of Gentleman Pensioners, M.P. Bedfordshire—Duke of Bedford's interest).

Stanley, James (Groom of the Bedchamber, M.P. Lancashire—family interest).

Topham, Richard (a grant out of the Windsor rents, and contractor for the Berkshire fee-farm rents—a chancery lawyer—M.P. Windsor).

Tredenham, Sir Joseph (Captain and Governor of St. Mawes Castle, M.P. St. Mawes—own interest).

Vane, Lionel (Joint Master of the Subpoena Office, M.P. Durham—family interest).

Vincent, Henry (Comm'r of the Victualling Office, M.P. Truro—own interest).

Weston, John (Receiver-Gen. of Surrey and Kent, Gentleman of the Privy Chamber, M.P. Surrey—local interest).

PART V. MEMBERS OF THE COMMONS RELATED TO ENGLISH PEERS

Summary:

Eldest sons and heirs apparent to an English peer	13
Younger brother and heir presumptive	1
Younger son	1
Younger brothers	19
Uncles	13
Nephews	8
First cousins	17
First cousins by marriage (where obviously politically significant)	4
Second cousins (where obviously politically significant)	3
Fathers-, sons-, and brothers-in-law	18
Total Members related thus to English peers	97

Note: of these relationships fifteen seem to have been without political significance: two among the brothers, eight among the first cousins, and five among the in-laws. The fact is noted in the list below. In the remaining eighty-two cases the relationship seems to have had a bearing on the Member's presence in the House or on his political affiliation.

Members related to English peers: listed alphabetically—in case of a title, the man is listed under his surname—with name of English peer and the relationship, together with the Member's constituency:

Ashe, Sir James (Viscount Townshend's uncle, M.P. Downton—own interest).

Ashley, Maurice (Earl of Shaftesbury's brother, M.P. Wiltshire, returned also for Weymouth—family interest in both cases).

Barrington, Sir Charles (Earl of Nottingham's nephew by marriage, M.P. Essex—local interest).

(Berkeley), James, Viscount Durseley (Earl of Berkeley's eldest son and heir apparent, M.P. Gloucester—family interest).

(Berkeley), John, Viscount Fitzharding (Lord Godolphin's first cousin, M.P. Windsor—Court interest).

Bertie, Charles (Earl of Lindsey's uncle, M.P. Stamford—family interest).

Bertie, Henry (Earl of Abingdon's uncle, M.P. Westbury—Lord Abingdon's interest).

Bertie, James (Earl of Abingdon's brother, M.P. Woodstock—Lord Abingdon's interest).

Bertie, Peregrine (Earl of Lindsey's brother, M.P. Boston—Lord Lindsey's interest).

Bertie, Robert (Earl of Abingdon's brother, M.P. Westbury—Lord Abingdon's interest).

Booth, George (Earl of Warrington's brother, Earl of Radnor's brother-in-law, M.P. Lostwithiel—Lord Radnor's interest).

Boyle, Charles (Countess of Sandwich's first cousin, M.P. Huntingdon —Lady Sandwich's interest).

Boyle, Henry (Earl of Burlington's brother, first cousin of the Duke of Somerset (Chancellor of Cambridge Univ.), M.P. Cambridge Univ.—Somerset's interest(?)).

(Boyle), Lionel, Earl of Orrery (Earl of Dorset's first cousin, M.P. Grinstead—Lord Dorset's interest).

Brydges, James (Lord Chandos's eldest son and heir apparent, M.P. Hereford—own interest).

Cavendish, Lord James (Duke of Devonshire's brother, M.P. Derby —family interest).

(Cavendish), William, Marquis of Hartington (Duke of Devonshire's eldest son and heir apparent, M.P. Castle Rising—Walpole interest).

Cecil, William (Earl of Exeter's brother, M.P. Stamford—family interest).

(Cheyne), William, Viscount Newhaven (Earl of Kingston's brother-in-law—of no political significance—M.P. Amersham—own interest).

Churchill, Charles (Earl of Marlborough's brother, M.P. Weymouth —gov't interest).

Churchill, George (Earl of Marlborough's brother, M.P. St. Albans —Lady Marlborough's interest).

Cocks, Charles (Lord Somers's brother-in-law, M.P. Droitwich—his own interest plus Lord Somers's).

Coke, Thomas (Earl of Chesterfield's son-in-law, M.P. Derbyshire—his own interest plus Lord Chesterfield's).

Compton, Spencer (Earl of Northampton's brother—but their politics were different—M.P. Eye—Lord Cornwallis's interest).

Dunch, Edmund (Earl of Marlborough's nephew, kinsman and follower of Lord Wharton, M.P. Cricklade—own interest plus Wharton's).

Dunch, Wharton (Lord Wharton's nephew, M.P. Appleby—Lord Wharton's interest).

Egerton, Charles (Earl of Bridgwater's uncle, M.P. Brackley—family interest).

Finch, Heneage (Earl of Nottingham's brother, M.P. Oxford University—Lord Nottingham and the Church interest).

Forester, Sir William (Earl of Salisbury's son-in-law—of no political significance—M.P. Wenlock—his own interest).

Godfrey, Charles (Earl of Marlborough's brother-in-law, but a follower of Lord Wharton at this time, M.P. Wycombe—Wharton's interest).

Godolphin, Francis (Lord Godolphin's eldest son and heir apparent, M.P. Helston—the Godolphin interest).

Godolphin, Sidney (Lord Godolphin's second cousin and namesake, M.P. Helston—on the Godolphin interest).

Goodricke, Sir Henry (Earl of Dartmouth's uncle by marriage—of little, if any, political significance—M.P. Boroughbridge—own interest).

Graham, Henry (Earl of Berkshire's brother-in-law—of little political significance—M.P. Westmorland—family interest).

Granville, John (Earl of Bath's uncle and heir presumptive, head of the Granvilles, M.P. Cornwall—Granville family interest).

Greville, Algernon (Lord Brooke's younger son, M.P. Warwick—family interest).

Greville, Francis (Lord Brooke's eldest son and heir apparent—M.P. Warwick—family interest).

Hanmer, Sir Thomas (Duke of Grafton's stepfather, M.P. Thetford—on the Grafton interest).

Herbert, James (Earl of Pembroke's first cousin, Duke of Leeds's son-in-law, M.P. Aylesbury—Sir John Pakington's interest).

Holland, Sir John (Earl of Yarmouth's son-in-law—no political significance, Lord Yarmouth was a Jacobite—M.P. Norfolk—local interest).

Howard, Philip (Earl of Carlisle's first cousin, M.P. Carlisle—Lord Carlisle's interest).

(Hyde), Henry, Lord Hyde (Earl of Rochester's eldest son and heir apparent, M.P. Launceston—Lord Rochester's interest).

(Ingram), Arthur, Viscount Irwin (Earl of Manchester's nephew, M.P. Yorkshire—Lord Carlisle and Lord Wharton's interest).

Isham, Sir Justinian (Lord Leigh's nephew—no political significance—M.P. Northamptonshire—own interest).

Jekyll, Sir Joseph (Lord Somers's brother-in-law, M.P. Eye—Lord Cornwallis's interest).

(Jones), Richard, Earl of Ranelagh (Earl of Rochester's first cousin by marriage, M.P. West Looe—Bishop Trelawny's interest).

Lake, Warwick (Earl of Nottingham's cousin by marriage, M.P. Middlesex—local interest).

Leveson-Gower, Sir John (Earl of Bath's first cousin, M.P. Newcastle (Staffs.)—Leveson-Gower family interest).

Lowther, James (Viscount Lonsdale's second cousin, also his guardian, M.P. Carlisle—Lowther family interest).

(Manners), John, Lord Roos (Earl of Rutland's eldest son and heir apparent, M.P. Leicestershire—Lord Rutland's interest).

Mitchell, Robert (Earl of Halifax's brother-in-law, M.P. Petersfield—outsider there).

Montagu, Charles (Lord Crewe, Bishop of Durham's nephew, M.P. Durham—Bishop of Durham's interest).

Montagu, Christopher (Earl of Halifax's brother, M.P. Northampton—Lord Halifax's interest).

Montagu, Francis Wortley (Earl of Sandwich's first cousin, M.P. Huntingdon—his father Sidney Wortley Montagu's interest).

Montagu, Sidney Wortley (Earl of Sandwich's uncle and guardian, M.P. Peterborough—on his own interest).

Mordaunt, Harry (Earl of Peterborough's brother, Lord Wharton's second cousin, M.P. Brackley—Lord Wharton's interest).

(Mordaunt), John, Lord Mordaunt (Earl of Peterborough's eldest son and heir apparent, Wharton's second cousin, M.P. Chippenham—Lord Wharton's interest).

Neville, Richard (Lord Grey of Wark's brother-in-law—no political significance—M.P. Berkshire—on his own interest).

Nicholas, Edward (Earl of Northampton's first cousin, M.P. Shaftesbury—his own interest).

Norreys, Sir Edward (Earl of Abingdon's first cousin, M.P. Oxfordshire—Lord Abingdon's interest).

Norreys, Francis (son of Sir Edward and first cousin (one remove) of Lord Abingdon, M.P. Oxford City—Lord Abingdon's interest).

North, Charles (Earl of Guilford's brother, M.P. Banbury—North family interest).

Oxenden, Sir James (Lord Rockingham's brother-in-law, M.P. Sandwich—own interest plus Lord Rockingham's help).

Paget, Henry (Lord Paget's eldest son and heir apparent, M.P. Staffordshire—Paget family interest).

Pelham, Thomas (Duke of Newcastle's brother-in-law, Viscount Townsend's brother-in-law, M.P. Lewes—Pelham family interest).

Pierrepoint, Gervase (uncle of the Earl of Kingston and the Earl of Thanet, M.P. Appleby—Lord Thanet's interest).

Popham, Alexander (Lord Poulett's nephew, M.P. Bath—his own interest plus Lord Poulett's).

Powlett, Lord William (Duke of Bolton's brother, M.P. Winchester —Duke of Bolton's interest).

Robartes, Francis (Earl of Radnor's uncle, M.P. Tregoney—Lord Radnor's interest).

Robartes, Russell (Earl of Radnor's brother, M.P. Bodmin—Lord Radnor's interest).

Rolle, Robert (Earl of Ailesbury's nephew—no political significance —M.P. Callington—family interest).

Rooke, Sir George (Earl of Nottingham's first cousin by marriage, M.P. Portsmouth—gov't interest).

Russell, Lord Edward (Duke of Bedford's uncle, M.P. Bedfordshire —Russell family interest).

Russell, Lord James (Duke of Bedford's uncle, M.P. Tavistock—Russell family interest).

Russell, Lord Robert (Duke of Bedford's uncle, M.P. Tavistock also).

Sharp, John (Archbishop of York's son, M.P. Ripon—Archbishop Sharp's interest).

Sherrard, Bennet (Earl of Rutland's son-in-law, M.P. Leicestershire —Lord Rutland's interest).

Shuckburgh, Sir Charles (Lord Willoughby de Broke's son-in-law—no political significance—M.P. Warwickshire—own interest).

(Spencer), Charles, Lord Spencer (Earl of Sunderland's eldest son and heir apparent, M.P. Tiverton—on his own interest; the Junto peer).

Stanhope, James (Earl of Chesterfield's first cousin—no political significance—M.P. Newport, I. of Wight—gov't interest).

Stanley, James (Earl of Derby's next younger brother and heir presumptive, M.P. Lancashire—Stanley family interest).

Stapylton, Sir Bryan (Earl of Holderness's first cousin, M.P. Boroughbridge—own interest).

Sydenham, Sir Philip (Lord Poulett's first cousin, M.P. Somerset—Lord Poulett's interest plus his own).

Thompson, Maurice (Lord Haversham's eldest son and heir apparent, M.P. Gatton—family interest).

Thynne, Henry (Viscount Weymouth's eldest son and heir apparent, M.P. Tamworth—Lord Weymouth's interest).

Townshend, Roger (Viscount Townshend's brother, M.P. Norfolk—Townshend family interest).

Vane Lionel (Lord Barnard's first cousin—no political significance —M.P. Durham county—own interest).

Warton, Sir Michael (Lord Poulett's first cousin, M.P. Beverley—own interest).

Wharton, Goodwin (Lord Wharton's brother, M.P. Buckinghamshire —Lord Wharton's interest).

Williams, Sir John (Earl of Pembroke's brother-in-law, M.P. Pembrokeshire—his own interest plus that of Lord Pembroke).

Wodehouse, Sir John (Lord Poulett's nephew, M.P. Thetford—on his own interest).

APPENDIX II

Representation of Government Boroughs

Note. In the following list there are included those constituencies discussed in the text as 'government boroughs'. They are listed in the order in which they were discussed in Chapter IV, together with the Members for each constituency during the first decade or so of the century. For each Member the office or offices which he held is listed, but no attempt is made here to distinguish the 'pure government Member' from an office-holder who belonged rather to one of the party groups. That distinction will be made in Appendix III.

1. QUEENBOROUGH

First Seat:

1696–8: Thomas King (colonel in the army; Lieut.-Governor Sheerness, 1690–1722).
1698–1705: Robert Crawford (colonel in the army; Governor Sheerness, 1690–1706; M.P. for this, 2nd seat, 1689–98).
1705–8: Sir John Jennings (rear-admiral, 1705; admiral, 1709; C. in C. Thames and Medway, 1708; M.P., 2nd seat, 1708–10).
1708–10: Henry Withers (lieut.-gen.; Governor Sheerness, 1706–12).
1710–22: Colonel Thomas King (again).

Second Seat:

1689–98: Robert Crawford (see above).
1698–1708: Thomas King (see above).
1708–10: Sir John Jennings (see above).
1710–13: James Herbert, Jr. (no office, but a gov't nominee).
1713–15: Charles Fotherby (local landowner).
1715–22: Philip Jennings (nephew of Admiral Sir John Jennings).

2. PORTSMOUTH

First Seat:

1698–1701 (elected also for Wareham, 1701): Thomas Erle (brig.-gen., '93; Governor of Portsmouth, 1694–1712, and elected for same 1702, 1708, but preferred to sit for his own borough of Wareham; Lieut.-Gen. and Gen. of the Ordnance, 1703–12; C. in C. in Ireland, '02–'06; 2nd in command in Spain, 1707–9; Governor of Portsmouth and Lieut.-Gen. Ordnance (again), '14–'18).

1701–2: John Gibson (M.P., 2nd seat, '96–'98; col. of foot; Lieut.-Governor of Portsmouth, 1689–1717).

1702–8: Sir George Rooke (M.P., 2nd seat, '98–'02; admiral, '95; Lord Comm'r of the Admiralty, '94–'02; Prince's Council for the Admiralty, '02–'08; a Privy Councillor, '02).

1708–10: George Churchill (Admiral of the Blue; Marlborough's brother).

1710 (until unseated, 1711): Sir Charles Wager (rear-admiral, '07; Comptroller of the Navy, '15–'18; 1st Lord of the Admiralty, '33–'41, &c.; M.P. Portsmouth, 1715–34).

1711–15: Sir James Wishart (admiral, '08; Lord Comm'r of the Admiralty, '10–'14; C. in C. in Mediterr., '13).

1715–22: Sir Edward Ernle (son-in-law of General Erle, Governor of Portsmouth).

Second Seat:

1698–1702: Sir George Rooke (M.P., 1st seat, '02–'08; see above).

1702–8: William Gifford (Navy Comm'r Resident at Portsmouth).

1708: Gen. Erle (see above; preferred to sit for Wareham).

1708–10: Sir Thomas Littleton (Treasurer of the Navy, '99–'10—died).

1710: Sir Charles Wager (vice Littleton, deceased; see above).

1710 (until unseated, '11): Sir John Jennings (see Queenborough, 1st seat, '05).

1711–13: Sir William Gifford (again).

1713–15: Sir Thomas Mackworth (Rutland baronet, nominee of the Governor of Portsmouth ('12–'14), Lord North and Grey).

1715–34: Sir Charles Wager (again).

3. PLYMOUTH

First Seat:

1698–1713: Charles Trelawny (maj.-gen., '92; Governor of Plymouth, '93–'12).

1713–22: Sir John Rogers (Recorder of Plymouth).

Second Seat:

1701–2: Henry Trelawny (col. of foot; brig.-gen., '96; brother of the Governor).

1702–5: John Woollcombe (no office; nominee of Governor Trelawny).

1705–21: Sir George Byng (vice-admiral, '05; admiral, '08; C. in C. in Mediterr., '09; Lord Comm'r of the Admiralty, '09–'14).

4. ROCHESTER

First Seat:

1701–2: Francis Barrell (local barrister; perhaps returned on the Bishop of Rochester's interest).

1702–5: Edward Knatchbull (Sub-Comm'r Prizes, '02–'04; brother-in-law of Admiral Rooke; cousin of Secretary Nottingham; and a gov't nominee).
1705–8: Sir Cloudesley Shovell (rear-admiral, '90; admiral, '96; M.P., 2nd seat, '98–'01; Comptroller of the Victualling, '99–'04; C. in C. in Mediterr., '05–'07; drowned, '07).
1708–10: Sir Stafford Fairborne (vice-admiral, '03; C. in C. in the Channel, '05–'06; Prince's Council for the Admiralty, '07–'08).
1710–15: Sir John Leake (vice-admiral, '03; C. in C. in Channel, '07; admiral, '08, and C. in C. in Mediterr.; Lord Comm'r of the Admiralty, '09–'15; Vice-Admiral of England, '10).
1715–23: Sir Thomas Palmer (local landowner; perhaps a gov't nominee).

Second Seat:

1698–1701: Sir Cloudesley Shovell (M.P., 1st seat, '05–'08; see above).
1701–2: William Bokenham (capt. in the navy; Chatham Dockyard official).
1702–5: William Cage (local squire; nominee of Secretary Nottingham).
1705–8: Sir Stafford Fairborne (M.P., 1st seat, '08–'10; see above).
1708–10: Sir John Leake (M.P., 1st seat, '10–'15; see above).
1710–15: William Cage (again).
1715–22: Sir John Jennings (see Queenborough, 1st seat, 1705–8).

5. ISLE OF WIGHT—NEWPORT

First Seat:

1701–2: James Stanhope (col. of foot; brig.-gen., '05; C. in C. in Spain, '08–'10; lieut.-gen., '09; P.C. and Secretary of State, '14–'18; created Earl Stanhope, 1717; M.P. Cockermouth, '02–'13; Wendover, '13–'15).
1702–7: John, Lord Cutts (elected also, '95, '98, '01 (twice), but preferred to sit for Cambridgeshire) (Governor of the I. of Wight, '93–'07; maj.-gen., '96; lieut.-gen. and colonel of Dragoons regt., '03; C. in C. and a Lord Justice in Ireland, '05–'07; died, '07).
1707–10: Sir Tristram Dillington (captain of horse, '07; lieut.-col. Coldstream Guards, '09; nominee of the Governor of the I. of Wight ('07–'10), the Duke of Bolton).
1710–13: William Seymour (lieut.-gen., '07; nominee of the Governor of the I. of Wight ('10–'15), General Webb—next below).
1713–15: John Richmond Webb (elected also, 1710; but preferred to sit for Ludgershall) (lieut.-gen., '09; Governor of the I. of Wight, '10–'15).
1715–17: James Stanhope (again).
1717–21: Sir Tristram Dillington (again).

Second Seat:

1701–2: Edward Richards (local squire—probably backed by Lord Cutts).

1702–22: William Stephens (local squire; son of the former Lieut.-Governor of the I. of Wight; gave his interest to Lord Cutts).

6. ISLE OF WIGHT—NEWTOWN

First Seat:

1695–1701: James Worsley (head of local family with strong electoral interest, often placed at the disposal of the gov't).

1701–5: Thomas Hopson (vice-admiral, '94; Knt. and Comm'r of the Navy, '04–'08; M.P., 2nd seat, 1698–1701).

1705–22 (also 1727–42): James Worsley (again).

Second Seat:

1698–1701: Thomas Hopson (M.P., 1st seat, '01–'05; see above).

1701–2: Joseph Dudley (well-known Massachusetts figure; Lieut.-Governor of the I. of Wight, '94–'02; client and nominee of Lord Cutts).

1702–5: John Leigh (local man; probably nominee of Lord Cutts).

1705–15: Henry Worsley (lieut.-col. Foot Guards, '00–'08; Envoy to King of Spain, '08; Envoy to Hanover, '11; cousin of James Worsley).

1715–22: Sir Robert Worsley (nephew of Henry Worsley).

7. ISLE OF WIGHT—YARMOUTH

First Seat:

1695–1717 (unseated): Henry Holmes (major of foot, '92–'00; Governor of Hurst Castle, '93–'95, '02–'04; Lieut.-Governor of the I. of Wight, '02–'06, '10–'14).

Second Seat:

1695–1710: Anthony Morgan (major in Horse Guards, '94–'02; Lieut.-Governor of the I. of Wight, '06–'10, '15–'29; elected also for Newport, '15; M.P. Lymington, '27–'29; nominee of the Duke of Bolton; rival of Holmes).

1710–15: Sir Gilbert Dolben (Tory politician; Irish judge; nominee of Governor Webb and Major Holmes).

1715–17 (unseated): Sir Robert Raymond (Solicitor.-Gen., '10–'14; set up by General Webb and Major Holmes, but unseated).

1717–22: Sir Theodore Janssen (London banker and gov't contractor).

8. CINQUE PORTS—DOVER

First Seat:

1701–13: Matthew Aylmer (vice-admiral, '94; Lord Comm'r of the Admiralty, '94–'99; Navy Comm'r, '99–'02; Lord Comm'r of the Admiralty (again), '09–'10, '17–'18; Rear-Admiral of England and an Irish peer, '18; elected for Portsmouth, '95, but unseated; M.P., 2nd seat, '97–'01).

1713–15: Sir William Hardres (local squire).

1715–20: Admiral Aylmer (again).

Second Seat:

1697–1701: Matthew Aylmer (M.P., 1st seat, '01–'13, '15–'20; see above).

1701–20: Philip Papillon (London businessman with local connexions; Cashier of the Victualling Office, '93–'98; client of Lord Orford).

9. CINQUE PORTS—HASTINGS

First Seat:

1695–1705: John Pulteney (Secretary to the Lord Warden of the Cinque Ports ('94–'02), the Earl of Romney; Clerk of the Council in Ireland; Lord Comm'r of Trade and Plantations, '07–'11; M.P., 2nd seat, '05–'08).

1705–8: William Ashburnham (son and heir apparent of Lord Ashburnham; held no office; nominee in 1702 of Secretary Nottingham and his cousin Winchilsea, then Dep. Lord Warden of the Cinque Ports).

1708–10: John Pulteney (again).

1710 (for five months, until called to Lords): John Ashburnham (younger brother and successor of William, second Lord Ashburnham—above).

1710–13: Sir William Ashburnham (kinsman of other Ashburnhams; connexion and probably nominee of the Pelhams; Chamberlain of the Exchequer, '10–'55; M.P. Seaford, '15–'17; Hastings (again), '22–'41).

1713–22: Archibald Hutcheson (London barrister; Hanoverian Tory; and made Comm'r of Trade and Plantations, '14).

Second Seat:

1701–2: John Mounsher (Portsmouth Dockyard official).

1702–5: William Ashburnham (M.P., 1st seat, 1705–8; see above).

1705–8: John Pulteney (M.P., 1st seat, '95–'05; see above).

1708–10: William Ashburnham (again).

1710–15: Sir Joseph Martin (Turkey merchant; E. India Co. Director; consul in Muscovy, '02–'05; Comm'r for Concluding Commercial Treaty with France, '13; gov't nominee).

1715–22: Henry Pelham, Jr. (of Stanmer; cousin of Lord Pelham; given various offices under George I).

10. CINQUE PORTS—HYTHE

First Seat:

1690–1708: Sir Philip Boteler (patron of one seat at Hythe; no office).

1708–11 (unseated): John Fane (younger brother of the Dep. Lord Warden of the Cinque Ports ('07–'08), Lord Westmorland; captain of horse, '09; lieut.-col., '10; colonel, '15; Lieutenant of Dover Castle, '07–'10).

1711–13: John Boteler (brother of Sir Philip; cornet of horse, '92–'02; Lieut.-Governor of Gravesend and Tilbury Forts; M.P., 2nd seat, '01–'10).

1713–22: Jacob Des Bouverie (Sir Philip Boteler's brother-in-law).

Second Seat:

1695–1701: Jacob Des Bouverie (M.P., 1st seat, '13–'22; see above).

1701–10: John Boteler (M.P., 1st seat, '11–'13; see above).

1710–11 (unseated): Lord Shannon (colonel of a marine regt., '02; brig.-gen., '04; maj.-gen., '07; lieut.-gen., '09; Comm'r for Inspecting Army Clothing; cousin of the Lord Warden of the Cinque Ports ('08–'12), the Earl of Dorset).

1711–13: William Berners (Hertfordshire friend of the Botelers).

1713–15: John Boteler (again).

1715–27: Sir Samuel Lennard (lieut.-col. 2nd Horse Guards).

11. CINQUE PORTS—NEW ROMNEY

First Seat:

1689–1710: John Brewer (Auditor of the Excise, '92–'96; Recorder of Deal; Registrar of the Cinque Ports, '02; Treasurer of the Prize Office and Receiver-Gen. of Prize Money, '02–'07).

1710–13: Walter Whitfield (Paymaster of the Marines, '04–'11; M.P., 2nd seat, '04–'10).

1713—22: Edward Watson, Lord Sondes (son and heir apparent of Lord Rockingham, Lord Lieutenant of Kent).

Second Seat:

1701–2: Edward Goulston (local lawyer).

1702–4 (died): Sir Benjamin Bathurst (Treasurer of the Household to Prince George and of the Board of Green Cloth, '02–'04; old courtier).

1704–10: Walter Whitfield (M.P., 1st seat, '10–'13; see above).

1710–27: Robert (later Sir Robert) Furnese (son of Marlborough's favourite banker, the M.P. for Sandwich, '01–'02, &c.—see below).

12. CINQUE PORTS—RYE

First Seat:

1701–2: Joseph Offley (London lawyer; M.P., 2nd seat, '98–'01).

1702–8: Edward Southwell (Clerk of the Privy Council, '93; Comm'r of the Great Seal, '01–'02; Secretary of State for Ireland, '02–'08; cousin and nominee of Lord Nottingham, Secretary of State, '02–'04).

1708–10: Phillips Gibbon (Comm'r of the Revenue in Ireland, '15– ; a Lord of the Treasury after Walpole's fall, '42; M.P. for Rye to '62).

1710–22: Sir John Norris (rear-admiral, '07; vice-admiral, '08; admiral, '09; C. in C. in Mediterr., '10; Lord Comm'r of the Admiralty, '18–'30; M.P. Portsmouth, '22–'34; M.P. Rye (again), '34–'49).

Second Seat:

1698–1701: Joseph Offley (M.P., 1st seat, '01–'02; see above).

1701–5: Thomas Fagg (local squire).

1705–7 (accepted an office of profit and not re-elected): Philip Herbert (Comm'r of the Sick and Wounded, '02–'07; Governor of Sandgate Castle, '02–'07; connexion and nominee of the Lord Warden ('02–'07), Lord Winchilsea).

1707–8: Phillips Gibbon (M.P., 1st seat, '08–'10; see above).

1708–10: Sir John Norris (M.P., 1st seat, '10–'22; see above).

1710–22: Phillips Gibbon (again) (see above).

13. CINQUE PORTS—SANDWICH

First Seat:

1679–81 (3 parliaments), 1689–90, 1695–8, 1701: Sir James Oxenden (head of local family with electoral influence; brother-in-law of Lord Rockingham, sometime Lord Lieutenant of Kent).

1701–2: Sir Henry Furnese (Marlborough's favourite London banker; Trustee for Circulating Exchequer Bills; Director E. India Co. and the Bank; Sheriff of London, '01) (elected also, '00, but expelled).

1702–5: John Michel (local man, supported by Secretary Nottingham; M.P., 2nd seat, '95–'98, '01).

1705–13: Sir Henry Furnese (again).

1713–15: John Michel (again).

1715–20: Sir Henry Oxenden (nephew of Sir James; M.P., 2nd seat, '13–'15).

1720–54: Sir George Oxenden (son of Sir Henry).

Second Seat:

1695–8, 1701: John Michel (M.P., 1st seat, '02–'05, '13–'15; see above).

1701–2: Sir James Oxenden (M.P., 1st seat, '79–'81, &c.; see above).

1702–5: Sir Henry Furnese (M.P., 1st seat, '01–'02, '05–'13; see above).

1705–13: Josiah Burchett (Joint Secretary to the Admiralty, '94–'98; Sole Secretary to Admiralty, '98–'42; M.P. (again), '22–'41).

1713–15: Sir Henry Oxenden (M.P., 1st seat, '15–'20; see above).

1715–22: Thomas D'Aeth (son of a London merchant who bought property near Sandwich).

1722–41: Josiah Burchett (again).

14. CINQUE PORTS—SEAFORD

First Seat:

1661–85 (5 parliaments), 1698–1701: Sir William Thomas (head of family with strong interest at Seaford; willing to oblige the gov't). (Elected also 1701 but preferred Sussex).

1701–2: Thomas Chowne (neighbour and nominee of Thomas and the Pelhams).

1702–6 (died): Sir William Thomas (again).

1706–8: George Naylor (son-in-law and nominee of Thomas Pelham).

1708–15: William Lowndes (M.P., 2nd seat, '95–'08; Secretary of the Treasury; nicknamed 'Ways and Means' Lowndes; M.P. St. Mawes, '15–'22; East Looe, '23–'24).

1715–22: George Naylor (again).

Second Seat:

1695–1708: William Lowndes (M.P., 1st seat, '08–'15; see above).

1708–10: George Naylor (M.P., 1st seat, '06–'08, '15–'22; see above).

1710–13: Thomas Chowne (M.P., 1st seat, '01–'02).

1713–15: George Naylor (again).

1715–17 (accepted an office of profit): Sir William Ashburnham (connexion and nominee of the Pelhams; see under Hastings, 2nd seat, '10–'13).

1717–22: Henry Pelham of Halland (second son of Lord Pelham; future 1st Lord of the Treasury; younger brother of the Duke of Newcastle).

15. CINQUE PORTS—WINCHELSEA

First Seat:

1698–1700: John Hayes (London businessman and army clothing contractor).

1700–1: Thomas Newport (of Lord Bradford's family; Comm'r Customs).

1701–2: Robert Austen (lieutenant in the army; nominee of Secretary Nottingham).

1702–5: George Clarke (Secretary to the Prince's Council for the Admiralty, '02–'05; Secretary to the Lord Warden of the Cinque Ports; Lord Comm'r of the Admiralty, '10–'14).

1705–8: George Dodington (Secretary to the Treasurer of the Navy under Wm. III; Secretary to the Comm'rs for a Union with Scotland, '07–'08; Lord Comm'r of the Admiralty, '08–'10; elected also, '08, but preferred Bridgwater).

1708–13: Sir Francis Dashwood (son-in-law of the Lord Warden of the Cinque Ports ('07–'08), Lord Westmorland).

1713–15: George Dodington (again).

1715–38 (died): Robert Bristow (Clerk Comptroller of the Board of Green Cloth; Comm'r for Stating Debts due to the Army; M.P., 2nd seat, '08–'15).

Second Seat:

1698–1701: Robert Bristow (London merchant; Director of the Bank; father of the Member, 1715–38).

1701–2: John Hayes (M.P., 1st seat, '98–'00; see above).

1702–8: James Hayes (nephew of John Hayes; also a London merchant).

1708–15: Robert Bristow (M.P., 1st seat, '15–'38; see above).

1715–22: George Bubb (later Dodington) (nephew and heir of George Dodington; Envoy to Spain, '15–'17; Lord Comm'r of the Treasury, '24; later created Lord Melcombe—the notorious place-hunter and diarist).

16. PRESTON

First Seat:

1698–1700: Henry Ashurst (Town Clerk of London, '95; Atty.-Gen. of the Duchy of Lancaster, '98–'02; M.P., 2nd seat, '00–'02).

1700–1: Edward Rigby (captain in a marine regt.; steward to Lord Rivers, who had an interest at Preston; M.P. again, '05–'06).

1701–2: Thomas Molyneux (Turkey merchant; Joint Comptroller of the Mint; probably a Duchy of Lancaster nominee).

1702–5: Charles Stanley (younger brother of the Earl of Derby, Lord Lieutenant of Lancashire and head of the most important county family).

1705–6 (died): Edward Rigby (again).

1706–8: Arthur Manwaring (Secretary to the Duchess of Marlborough; Comm'r of Customs, '00–'05; Comm'r of Appeals in the Excise, '06–'12; nominee of the Chancellor of the Duchy).

1708–13: Henry Fleetwood (local landowner; client of the Duke of Hamilton, who had electoral interests in Lancashire).

1713–15: Edward Southwell (gov't nominee; M.P. Rye, 1st seat, '02–'08; see above).

1715–22: Sir Henry Hoghten (Comm'r of Forfeited Irish Estates, '16; Advocate-Gen. of the Land Forces, '20; M.P., 2nd seat, '10–'13; 1st seat (again), '27–'41; head of a local family).

Second Seat:

1695–1700: Thomas Molyneux (M.P., 1st seat, '01–'02; see above).

1700–2: Henry Ashurst (M.P., 1st seat, '98–'00; see above).

1702–5: Sir Cyril Wyche (Gentleman Usher of the Privy Chamber; great uncle and nominee of the Chancellor of the Duchy ('02–'06), Lord Gower).

1705–8: Arthur Annesley (friend and nominee of Lord Gower).

1708–10: Arthur Manwaring (M.P., 1st seat, '06–'08; see above).

1710–13: Sir Henry Hoghten (M.P., 1st seat, '15–'22, '27–'41; see above).

1713–22: Henry Fleetwood (M.P., 1st seat, '08–'13; see above).

17. WINDSOR

First Seat:

1695–1710: Viscount Fitzharding (colonel of a Dragoons regt., '85–'12; Teller of the Exchequer, '00 (for life); Treasurer of the Chamber, '02–'12; first cousin of Lord Godolphin and a well-known courtier).

1710–13: Richard Topham (contractor for royal fee-farm rents; Keeper of the Records in the Tower, '07– ; M.P., 2nd seat, '98–'10).

1713–15 (unseated): Christopher Wren, Jr. (Surveyor of the Works; son of the great architect; Court nominee).

1715–22: Sir Henry Ashurst (head of family of London merchants; first cousin of the Member for Preston, Henry Ashurst).

Second Seat:

1698–1710: Richard Topham (M.P., 1st seat, '10–'13; see above).

1710–11 (died): William Paul (place-seeker; owned local property; presumably had backing of the Constable of the Castle).

1711–12 (called to Upper House): Samuel Masham (husband of the queen's favourite, Abigail Hill; married, '07; colonel, regt. of horse, '07–'11; brig.-gen., '10; Cofferer of the Household, '11–'14; one of the twelve Tory peers, '12).

1712–15: Charles Aldworth (hot-headed young Jacobite, recommended by the Constable of the Castle, the Duke of Northumberland).

1715–22: Samuel Travers (Surveyor-Gen. of the Land Revenue; M.P. for two Cornish boroughs (Bossiney and Lostwithiel), '90–'01, '08–'10).

18. HARWICH

First Seat:

1695–1708: Sir Thomas Davall (Recorder of Harwich; London banker; contractor for remitting Exchequer payments).
1708 (elected, but preferred Rochester): Sir John Leake (see Rochester).
1708–9 (unseated): Sir Thomas Davall (again).
1709–13: Kenrick Edisbury (agent at Harwich for the Post-Office packet-boats; Comm'r of the Victualling Office, '04–'14).
1713–14 (died): Sir Thomas Davall (the Younger; son of the M.P., '95–'08).
1714–15: Benedict Leonard Calvert (son and heir apparent of Lord Baltimore; nominee of Secretary Bolingbroke, who succeeded Davall as Recorder of Harwich).
1715–34: Sir Philip Parker (brother-in-law of Viscount Perceval, later Earl of Egmont, an influential politician).

Second Seat:

1701–2: Dennis Lydell (Comm'r of the Navy, '00–'05).
1702–8: John Ellis (Under-Secretary of State, '95–'05; Comptroller of the Mint, '02–'11).
1708–13. Thomas Frankland (son of the Joint Postmaster-Gen.; M.P. later ('13–'47) for the family borough of Thirsk).
1713–15: Carew Mildmay (nominee of the Recorder ('10–'14), Bolingbroke).
1715–22: Thomas Heath (London E. Indies merchant; returned also in '14, but unseated).

19. WEYMOUTH
20. MELCOMBE REGIS

Note: These two Dorsetshire constituencies returned four Members jointly, the two at the head of the poll being named Members for Weymouth, the next two, Members for Melcombe Regis.

First Seat (Weymouth):

1700–1: Henry Thynne (eldest son and heir apparent of Viscount Weymouth, who was usually complimented with one seat at Weymouth).
1701–2: Charles Churchill (colonel of foot, '88; maj.-gen., '94; lieut.-gen., '02; Gent. of the Bedchamber to Prince George, '02–'08; Lieut.-Governor of the Tower, '02–'06; Governor of Guernsey, '06; Colonel 2nd Regt. of Foot Guards and General of Forces in England, '07; Marlborough's brother). (M.P., 2nd seat, '00–'10, '05–'10; 3rd seat, '02–'05.)

1702–9 (died): Henry Thynne (again).
1709–10: Edward Clavell (London E. Indies merchant).
1710–13: Maurice Ashley (brother of the Earl of Shaftesbury; one of the Carolina proprietors; M.P., 1st seat, '95–'98; 3rd seat, '00, '01, '05–'10).
1713–14 (unseated): Daniel Harvey (Colonel of Dragoon Guards, '99–'12; maj.-gen., '04; lieut.-gen., '07; general, '09; Lieut.-Governor of Guernsey, '14).
1714–15: Sir Thomas Hardy (rear-admiral, '11; C. in C. Thames and Medway, '11–'12, and in North Sea, '12–'14; M.P., 2nd seat, '11–'13).
1715–22: General Daniel Harvey (again).

Second Seat (Weymouth):
1700–1: Charles Churchill (M.P., 1st seat, '01–'02; see above).
1701–2: George St. Loe (captain in the navy; Comm'r of the Prize Office, '93; navy comm'r, '93–'04; M.P., 4th seat (Melcombe), '02–'05).
1702–5: Anthony Henley (*litterateur* and man-about-town; had a £2,000 pension from the gov't; M.P., 4th seat (Melcombe), '05–'10).
1705–10: Charles Churchill (again).
1710–11 (died): Anthony Henley (again).
1711–13: Reginald Marriott (Auditor of London; Deputy to one of the Tellers of the Exchequer; gov't man).
1713–14 (unseated): John Baker (rear-admiral, '08; vice-admiral, '09; M.P. also 1715–17 (died)).
1714–15: William Harvey (Tory squire who was always contesting elections; first cousin but political foe of Daniel Harvey; M.P., 4th seat, '11–'13).
1715–17 (died): Admiral Baker (again).

Third Seat (Melcombe Regis):
1700–1 (elected also, '01, but preferred Wiltshire): Maurice Ashley (M.P., 1st seat (Weymouth), '10–'13; see above).
1701–2: Anthony Henley (M.P., 2nd seat (Weymouth), '02–'05; see above).
1702–5: Charles Churchill (M.P., 1st seat, '01–'02; see above).
1705–10: Maurice Ashley (again).
1710–11 (unseated): James Littleton (commodore in the navy; great nephew and protégé of Sir Thomas Littleton, Treasurer of the Navy).
1711–13: Sir Thomas Hardy (M.P., 1st seat, '13–'14; see above).
1713–15: James Littleton (again).
1715–22: Thomas Littleton (another kinsman of the Navy Treasurer).

Fourth Seat (Melcombe Regis):
1701–2: Sir Christopher Wren (the noted architect; Surveyor-Gen. of His Majesty's Works).

1702–5: George St. Loe (M.P., 2nd seat, '01–'02; see above).
1705–10: Anthony Henley (M.P., 2nd seat, '02–'05; see above).
1710–11 (unseated): William Betts (London businessman).
1711–13: William Harvey (M.P., 2nd seat, '14–'15; see above).
1713–14 (again unseated): William Betts (again).
1714–15: Reginald Marriott (M.P., 2nd seat, '11–'13; see above).
1715–22: William Betts (again).

21. SOUTHAMPTON

First Seat:

1701–2: Adam de Cardonnell, Jr. (Chief Clerk in the War Office, '90; Secretary to the Comm'rs for the Sick and Wounded, '93; chief Secretary to the Commander-in-Chief (Marlborough), '02–'08; Joint Secretary at War, '08–'12).

1702–5: Frederick Tylney (wealthy Hampshire landowner who made a hobby of expensive election contests in Hampshire constituencies).

1705–8: Viscount Woodstock (son and heir apparent of William III's friend, Henry (Bentinck), Earl of Portland) (elected, '08, but preferred to sit for the county).

1708–10: Sir Simeon Stewart (no office until '12, when he became a Chamberlain of the Exchequer; local family).

1710–12 (expelled): Adam de Cardonnell (again) (M.P., 2nd seat, '02–'10).

1712–13: Roger Harris (local Tory squire).

1713–15: Richard Fleming (another local landowner).

1715–22: Thomas Lewis (like Tylney a wealthy landowner; related to the Duke of Somerset and the Earl of Dorset; made a hobby of fighting elections; M.P. for 5 other Hants constituencies, including the county).

Second Seat:

1701–2: Mitford Crow (London merchant; Governor of Barbados, '02; Envoy to Leghorn, '05–'06; Paymaster of the Army Accounts, '06).

1702–10: Adam de Cardonnell (M.P., 1st seat, '01–'02, '10–'12; see above).

1710–13: Richard Fleming (M.P., 1st seat, '13–'15; see above).

1713—15: Roger Harris (M.P., 1st seat, '12–'13; see above).

1715–22: Richard Fleming (again).

22. SHOREHAM

First Seat:

1700–1: Nathaniel Gould (London merchant; Director of the Bank; Director E. India Co.; contractor for naval stores; created a baronet; M.P., 2nd seat, '01–'05, '10–'13).

1701–2: Charles Sergison (Comm'r of the Navy, '99–'05).
1702–5: John Pery (London merchant; Secretary of the Royal African Co.; and a farmer of the Hearth Tax).
1705–8: Nathaniel Gould (again).
1708 (until disabled): Anthony Hammond (Comm'r of the Navy, '02–'08).
1708–13: Gregory Page (London brewer).
1713–29 (died): Nathaniel Gould (again).

Second Seat:

1700–1: Charles Sergison (M.P., 1st seat, '01–'02).
1701–5: Nathaniel Gould (M.P., 1st seat, '00–'01, '05–'08, '13–'20; see above).
1705–8: John Wicker (local landowner).
1708–10: Richard Lloyd (London W. Indies merchant).
1710–13: Nathaniel Gould (again).
1713–15: Francis Chamberlayne (Barbados merchant).
1715–20 (died): Gregory Page (M.P., 1st seat, '08–'13).
1720–29 (died): Francis Chamberlayne (again).

23. ARUNDEL

First Seat:

1698–1702: John Cooke (local squire).
1702–5: Edmund Dummer (Master Shipwright; Comm'r for Inspecting Plymouth Dock, '93; Surveyor of the Navy; M.P., 2nd seat, '95–'98, '00–'01).
1705–8: James Butler (Sussex landowner with Court connexions).
1708 (but preferred to sit for Sussex): Sir Harry Peachey (friend and follower of the Pelhams).
1708–10: Lord Lumley (son and heir apparent of the Earl of Scarbrough; colonel of a regt.).
1710–15: Lord Lumley (younger brother and successor of next above).
1715–22: Henry Lumley (uncle of the Lords Lumley; lieut.-gen., '03).

Second Seat:

1695–8, 1700–1: Edmund Dummer (M.P., 1st seat, '02–'05; see above).
1701–5: Carew Weekes (local squire).
1705–8: Edmund Dummer (again).
1708–10: Lord Shannon (M.P. Hythe, 2nd seat, '10–'11; see above).
1710–15: Earl of Thomond (step-son of the Earl of Bindon, of the Howard family, a former Member, and Muster-Master-General).
1715–18: Thomas Micklethwait (nominee of Lord Wharton, who got him an Irish place).

24. WESTMINSTER

First Seat:

1700–2: James Vernon (Under-Secretary of State, '90–'97; Comm'r of the Prize Office, '93–'05; Secretary of State, '97–'02; a Teller of the Exchequer, '02–'10; political follower of the Duke of Shrewsbury; M.P., 2nd seat, '98–'00).

1702–5: Sir Walter Clarges (local candidate of the Hyde–Seymour–Granville group; his aunt married General Monck, Duke of Albemarle).

1705–10: Henry Boyle (Lord Comm'r of the Treasury, '99–'00; Chancellor of the Exchequer, '01–'08; Lord Treasurer in Ireland, '04–'10; Secretary of State, '08–'10).

1710–13: Thomas Medlicott (Steward of the Court of Westminster, '05–'14; Comm'r of the Revenue in Ireland, '13–'14; client of Ormonde).

1713–15: Sir Thomas Crosse (Westminster brewer).

1715–22: Edward Wortley Montagu (cousin of the Earls of Sandwich; follower of the Junto; husband of the well-known Lady Mary).

Second Seat:

1698–1700: James Vernon (M.P., 1st seat, '00–'02; see above).

1700–1: Thomas Crosse (M.P., 1st seat, '13–'15; see above).

1701–2: Sir Henry Dutton Colt (busybody politician; had the Court interest in Westminster elections, '01–'08).

1702–5: Thomas Crosse (again).

1705–8: Sir Henry Dutton Colt (again).

1708–10: Thomas Medlicott (M.P., 1st seat, '10–'13; see above).

1710–13: Thomas Crosse (again).

1713–22: Thomas Medlicott (again).

APPENDIX III

Party Groups in the 1701 Parliament

PART I. THE GOVERNMENT INTEREST

VIRTUALLY all the Members listed here will be found also in Appendix I, Part IV ('Officeholders in the Commons'), and again, listed by constituency, in Appendix II ('Representation of Government Boroughs'). On the other hand, only a fraction of those listed there can be classified as 'pure government Members'—men owing their seat primarily to government influence and acting and voting as administration Members rather than as members of one of the organized party groups.

Such Members as held office and sat for a government borough but did *not* vote as administration Members but rather as members of a party group will be found listed below under the group to which they belonged.

Summary:

1.	Army Members: officers returned through the influence of the governor of a garrison (Plymouth, Portsmouth, &c.)	11
2.	Admiralty Members: men connected with the Admiralty and returned for a dockyard or maritime constituency	5
3.	Treasury Members: men with Treasury connexions, returned for boroughs where that department had influence	3
4.	Cinque Port Members: men, other than those listed in categories 2 and 3, returned for a Cinque Port because of their position as Cinque Port officials	2
5.	Others: official Members returned for other than government boroughs, usually on their own interest	17
	Total of the Government Interest	38

List of government Members:

Blathwayt, William (Bath) (Secretary at War; elected on his own interest).

Bokenham, William (Rochester) (Chatham Dockyard Official; Admiralty M.P.).

Brewer, John (New Romney) (Registrar of the Cinque Ports; Cinque Port M.P.).

Bridges, William (Liskeard) (Secretary to the Comm'rs for the Salt Duties; elected on his own interest).

Colt, Sir Henry Dutton (Westminster) (Court candidate for Westminster).

Crawford, Robert (Queenborough) (Governor of Sheerness; army Member).

Crawley, Richard (Wendover) (Registrar of the Admiralty; own interest).

Crow, Mitford (Southampton) (Governor of Barbados; own interest).

(Cutts), John, Lord Cutts (Newport, I. of Wight, and Cambridgeshire—preferred latter) (maj.-gen.; Governor of the I. of Wight; army M.P.).

Davall, Sir Thomas (Harwich) (gov't banker; own interest plus Treasury).

Dodson, Thomas (Liskeard) (Captain of Bermuda Castle; own interest).

Dudley, Joseph (Newtown, I. of Wight) (Lieut.-Governor of the I. of Wight; army M.P.).

Erle, Thomas (Portsmouth and Wareham—elected latter) (Governor of Portsmouth; army Member).

Fox, Sir Stephen (Cricklade) (Lord Comm'r of the Treasury; own interest).

Frankland, Sir Thomas (Thirsk) (Joint Postmaster-Gen.; own interest).

Furnese, Sir Henry (Sandwich) (gov't banker; own interest plus the Treasury).

Gibson, John (Portsmouth) (Lieut.-Governor of Portsmouth; army Member).

Goodricke, Sir Henry (Boroughbridge) (Lieutenant of the Ordnance and a Privy Councillor; own interest plus the Duke of Leeds).

Gould, Nathaniel (Shoreham) (contractor for the Admiralty; own interest plus that of the Admiralty).

Gwynne, Sir Rowland (Brecknockshire) (Clerk of the Board of Green Cloth and Chairman of the Commons' Committee of Privilege and Elections in the gov't interest; returned on his own interest).

Henley, Anthony (Melcombe Regis) (pensioner; own interest, plus gov't).

Lowndes, William (Seaford) (Secretary of the Treasury; Treasury M.P.).

Lydell, Dennis (Harwich) (Comm'r of the Navy; Admiralty Member).

Markes, Richard (Petersfield) (Portsmouth Dockyard official; own interest).

Methuen, John (Devizes) (Lord Chancellor in Ireland; own interest).

Mounsher, John (Hastings) (Portsmouth Dockyard official; Admiralty M.P.).

Pulteney, John (Hastings) (Secretary to the Lord Warden of the Cinque Ports; Secretary to Master-Gen. of the Ordnance; Cinque Port M.P.).

Richards, Edward (Newport, I. of Wight) (nominee of Lord Cutts; army M.P.).

St. Loe, George (Weymouth) (Comm'r of the Navy; Admiralty Member).

Sayer, George (Canterbury) (courtier and placeman; own interest).

Sergison, Charles (Shoreham) (Clerk of the Acts in the Navy Office; Admiralty Member).

Stanhope, James (Newport, I. of Wight) (lieut.-col. of Foot Guards; nominee of the Governor of the I. of Wight, Lord Cutts; army Member).

Topham, Richard (Windsor) (grantee of royal fee-farm rents; own interest plus that of the Court).

Trelawny, Charles (Plymouth) (maj.-gen.; Governor of Plymouth; army M.P.).

Vernon, James (Westminster) (Secretary of State and other offices; gov't candidate for Westminster).

Vincent, Henry (Truro) (Comm'r of the Victualling Office; own interest, with, probably, some help from the gov't).

Woollcombe, John (Plymouth) (nominee of the Governor of Plymouth; army M.P.).

Wren, Sir Christopher (Weymouth) (Surveyor-Gen. of His Majesty's Works; gov't interest plus his own).

PART II. THE JUNTO CONNEXION

Summary:

1. Nominees and followers of Lord Wharton	25
2. Nominees and followers of Lord Somers	6
3. Nominees and followers of Lord Halifax	7
4. Nominees and followers of Lord Orford and Lord Spencer	17[1]
5. Nominees and followers of the Duke of Bolton . .	9
Total membership of the Junto connexion	64

1. *Nominees and followers of Lord Wharton:*

Bertie, Peregrine (Boston) (Wharton's nephew; returned on Bertie's brother, the Earl of Lindsey's interest).

[1] The figure would be eighteen if Lord Hartington (who is listed under Orford's group) were included; but he is included under Walpole's total (below), since he owed his seat at Castle Rising to Walpole.

Blaake, Henry (Calne) (one of Wharton's 'Wiltshire gang').

Chase, James (Marlow) (London apothecary; client and nominee of Wharton for one of the Buckinghamshire boroughs where he had an electoral interest).

Denton, Sir Edmund (Buckingham) (neighbour and follower, whose younger brother, Alexander, served Wharton as Recorder of Buckingham, Secretary to Wharton as Lord Lieutenant of Ireland; and was later made a judge through Wharton's influence).

Dormer, Fleetwood (Wycombe) (client and nominee, and served Wharton as Recorder of Wycombe after '95, managing the Wharton interest there).

Dormer, Robert (Buckinghamshire) (elected also for Northallerton) (elder brother of next above; made Serjeant at Law, and later a judge, through Wharton's influence).

Dunch, Edmund (Cricklade) (married Marlborough's niece; but preferred to follow his kinsman Wharton; cousin of Wharton Dunch, below).

Dunch, Wharton (Appleby) (nephew and nominee of Wharton).

Godfrey, Charles (Wycombe) (married Marlborough's sister; but followed rather his friend and kinsman Wharton; Master of the Jewel Office since '98).

Hampden, Richard (Wendover) (great grandson of the 'Patriot'; neighbour and kinsman of Wharton and used the family interest at Wendover and in Buckinghamshire in co-operation with Wharton).

Hustler, Sir William (Northallerton) (follower and nominee of Wharton).

Hutton, John (Richmond) (native of Scotland; royal physician and Physician-Gen. of the Army; Wharton's nominee at Richmond).

Lamplugh, Thomas (Cockermouth) (Wharton's nominee at Cockermouth, set up in opposition to the Duke of Somerset's interest there).

Lascelles, Daniel (Northallerton) (son of a Cromwellian colonel; first cousin of St. Quintin (below); Wharton's nominee at this borough).

Lee, Sir Thomas (Ayesbury) (Wharton's nominee, set up against Sir John Pakington's interest).

Littleton, Sir Thomas (Woodstock) (veteran politician, particularly attached to Halifax, but owed this seat to Wharton).

Maister, William (Hull) (a friend and follower of Wharton, but won the seat at Hull on his own interest).

Mordaunt, Harry (Brackley) (colonel of Foot and Treasurer of the Ordnance; cousin and nominee of Wharton; uncle of Lord Mordaunt (below)).

(Mordaunt), John, Lord Mordaunt (Chippenham) (son and heir apparent of Lord Peterborough, but a follower and nominee of his cousin Wharton; nephew of Harry Mordaunt (next above)).

Palmes, William (Malton) (friend and follower of Wharton; controlled borough of Malton, giving second seat to his son-in-law Sir William Strickland (below)).

St. Quintin, Sir William (Hull) (another Yorkshire follower of Wharton, connected by blood or marriage with four others: Hustler, Maister, Palmes, and Strickland; Hull seat on his own interest).

Strickland, Sir William (Malton) (another friend of Wharton; owed his seat to his father-in-law Palmes (above)).

Temple, Sir Richard (Buckingham) (the future Lord Cobham; cousin of the Dentons (above); co-operated with Wharton in Buckingham elections and those for the county).

Wharton, Goodwin (Buckinghamshire) (Wharton's only brother; Member in other parliaments ('89–'98) for Malmesbury, Cockermouth, and Westmorland; colonel in the army and sometime ('97–'99) Lord Comm'r of the Admiralty; died, '04).

White, Walter (Chippenham) (one of Wharton's Wiltshire agents, and his nominee at this Wiltshire constituency).

2. *Nominees and followers of Lord Somers:*

Clarke, Edward (Taunton) (in order to 'mortify Ned Clark, as a friend of my Lord Chancellor's' (Somers), Comm'rs of the Excise, of whom Clarke was one, were disabled from sitting in the Commons, 1699; Clarke was also a close friend of John Locke).

Cocks, Charles (Droitwich) (Somers's brother-in-law, made Clerk of the Patents, '99, through Somers's influence).

Dowdeswell, Richard (Tewkesbury) (another Gloucester–Worcester friend of Somers; his father-in-law was Somers's first patron).

Harvey, Stephen (Reigate) (Middle Temple lawyer and a *litterateur*; Somers's nominee at Reigate, a royal manor granted him by Wm. III).

Jekyll, Sir Joseph (Eye) (another Middle Temple lawyer; Somers's brother-in-law and follower and made Chief Justice of Chester, '97, at Somers's request; owed his seat to Lord Cornwallis).

Wylde, Thomas (Worcester) (still another Middle Temple lawyer and friend of Somers; sat for Somers's native city, partly on Somers's interest).

3. *Nominees and followers of Lord Halifax:*

(Ingram), Arthur, Viscount Irwin (Yorkshire) (Halifax's first cousin; in the 1702 and 1705 elections stood with Lord Hartington (below) on the Junto interest; Scottish peer, Lord Lieutenant of the North Riding, and Governor of Scarborough).

Mitchell, Robert (Petersfield) (a brother-in-law of Halifax; gov't contractor and Director of the E. India Co.; won seat on his own).

Montagu, Charles (Durham) (younger brother of Sidney Wortley Montagu (below); nephew of Lord Crewe, Bishop of Durham, who made him Constable of Durham Castle and recommended him as Member for Durham).

Montagu, Christopher (Northampton) (Halifax's younger brother; an Excise Comm'r until forced to resign (like Ned Clarke—above) to avoid being disabled from sitting in the Commons).

Montagu, Francis Wortley (Huntingdon) (son of Sidney Wortley Montagu (below), and his nominee for Huntingdon).

Montagu, Sidney Wortley (Peterborough) (uncle and guardian of young Lord Sandwich; second cousin of Halifax; an able and influential Junto lieutenant; married a Yorkshire heiress named Wortley and added that name to Montagu; Lady Mary Wortley Montagu, the well-known letter-writer, was his daughter-in-law).

Newton, Sir Isaac (Cambridge University) (the great Sir Isaac owed his position at the Mint and his seat for the University to the patronage of Halifax).

4. *Nominees and followers of Lord Orford and Lord Spencer:*

Aylmer, Matthew (Dover) (client and follower of Lord Orford; vice-admiral, '94; Lord Comm'r of the Admiralty, '94–'98, but then demoted to Comm'r of the Navy, '99–'02; originally an Admiralty nominee at Dover, he kept the seat after losing his place in the Admiralty).

Bere, Thomas (Tiverton) (Lord Spencer's choice as colleague at Tiverton).

Cavendish, Lord James (Derby) (younger brother of Lord Hartington —next below; the Duke of Devonshire's son and nominee for a family borough).

(Cavendish), William, Marquis of Hartington (Castle Rising) (son and heir apparent of the Duke of Devonshire; a nephew of Orford, he usually sat for Derbyshire or Yorkshire, with Junto support; but in this parliament owed his seat to his friend Walpole of the Newcastle–Pelham–Townshend–Walpole connexion).

Cullen, Sir Rushout (Cambridgeshire) (Orford's nominee, and succeeded Russell as knight of the shire, when the latter went to the Lords).

Ellys, Richard (Grantham) (son and heir apparent of Sir William Ellys; see under Sir William—next below).

Ellys, Sir William (Grantham) (head of a family which usually controlled both seats at Grantham; the Ellys family was connected with Orford and later ('05–'10) made one seat available for Orford's nephew, Lord Roos (later Marquis of Granby)).

(Fairfax), Thomas, Lord Fairfax (Yorkshire) (Scottish peer, descended from the Lord General of the Civil War; joined in Yorkshire elections with Lord Irwin or some other Junto candidate, on the Junto interest, headed by Wharton; brig.-gen., '01).

Farrer, William (Bedford) (Deputy-Recorder of Bedford, for the Russell family; Russell nominee for Bedford; King's Council).

Gostwick, Sir William (Bedfordshire) (another Bedfordshire client and nominee of the Russells; connected with Orford and with Farrer (above) and William Spencer below)).

Hopkins, Edward (Coventry) (friend of Lord Spencer and a Junto follower; sat later for Lord Cornwallis's borough of Eye; Sunderland later chose his uncle Thomas Hopkins as Under-Secretary of State).

(Manners), John, Lord Roos (styled Marquis of Granby after 1703) (Leicestershire) (son and heir apparent of the Earl (later Duke) of Rutland; nephew of Orford, and a follower of the Junto).

Papillon, Philip (Dover) (client and follower of Orford, who had him made Cashier of the Victualling Office ('93–'98); colleague of Admiral Aylmer (above)).

Russell, Lord Edward (Bedfordshire) (elected also for Tavistock, but return controverted, so no by-election there) (first cousin and also brother-in-law of Orford; cousin of Spencer (later Lord Sunderland); Treasurer of the Chamber to 1702; represented Bedfordshire in thirteen parliaments; brother of Lord Robert).

Russell, Lord Robert (Tavistock) (see under Lord Edward; Clerk of the Pipe, '89–'03 (died)).

(Sherrard), Bennet, Lord Sherrard (Leicestershire) (brother-in-law of Lord Roos (above), the other Leicestershire Member; an Irish peer).

(Spencer), Charles, Lord Spencer (Tiverton) (son and heir apparent of the Earl of Sunderland, whom he succeeded in 1702; this is the Junto Lord Sunderland).

Spencer, William (Bedford) (Russell nominee; connected with Orford and the other Russell clients in Bedfordshire; one of the Band of Gentleman Pensioners).

5. *Nominees and followers of the Duke of Bolton:*

Bridges, George Rodney (Winchester) (friend and neighbour of Bolton; had the Bolton interest at Winchester, where he joined with Lord William Powlett (below)).

Burrard, Paul (Lymington) (co-patron of Lymington with the duke).
Chandler, Richard (Hampshire) (Bolton's candidate for the county; sat later for the duke's boroughs of Lymington and St. Ives).
Dore, Thomas (Lymington) (cousin of Paul Burrard (above) and the Burrard–Bolton nominee there; a lieut.-col. in the army).
Hawles, Sir John (St. Ives) (at this time ('95–'02) Solicitor-Gen. and given this seat by Bolton as a favour to the gov't).
Jervoise, Thomas (Hampshire) (kinsman and follower of Bolton and his other nominee for the county).
Morgan, Anthony (Yarmouth, I. of Wight) (client of Bolton; one of his honorary burgesses at Lymington; served under him as Lieut.-Governor of the I. of Wight ('06–'10) (also '94–'02); major in the Horse Guards).
Powlett, Lord William (Winchester) (younger brother of Bolton; close friend of the Junto lords and one of their most prominent lieutenants in the Commons).
Shrimpton, John (Whitchurch) (client and follower of Bolton, and of Wharton, who made him an honorary freeman at Wycombe; major in the Foot Guards).

PART III. THE NEWCASTLE–PELHAM–TOWNSHEND–WALPOLE CONNEXION

Summary:

1. Nominees and followers of the Duke of Newcastle . . .	5
2. Nominees and followers of Thomas, later first Lord Pelham	5
3. Nominees and followers of Viscount Townshend and Robert Walpole	6
Total membership of the Newcastle–Pelham–Townshend–Walpole Group	16

1. *Nominees and followers of the Duke of Newcastle:*

Molyneux, Sir Francis (Nottinghamshire) (Newcastle's candidate for his home county).
Monckton, Robert (Aldborough (Yorks.)) (client and nominee of the duke; later made a Comm'r of Trade and Plantations).
Oxenden, Sir James (Sandwich) (brother-in-law of Lord Rockingham, a first cousin and ally of Newcastle).

Pierrepoint, William (Nottingham) (Newcastle's second cousin and had the Duke's interest at Nottingham).

Thornhagh, John (Retford) (client and nominee of Newcastle at this Nottinghamshire constituency).

2. *Nominees and followers of Thomas Pelham:*

Chowne, Thomas (Seaford) (neighbour, friend, and nominee of Pelham).

Peachey, Sir Henry (Sussex) (Pelham candidate for the county).

Pelham, Henry (Lewes) (younger brother of Thomas Pelham; Clerk of the Pells).

Pelham, Thomas (Lewes) (succeeded to the baronetcy, '03; made a peer, '06; married Newcastle's sister and co-heiress; Townshend married his sister).

Thomas, Sir William (Sussex) (co-operated in elections for Seaford and for Sussex with Pelham).

3. *Nominees and followers of Townshend and Walpole:*

(Cavendish), William, Marquis of Hartington (Castle Rising) (see under Part II, 4 (the Junto Connexion: Orford's group); in this parliament Lord Hartington owed his seat to his friend Walpole).

Holland, Sir John (Norfolk) (friend and follower of Townshend and Walpole and had their backing in his election).

Townshend, Roger (Norfolk) (Lord Townshend's younger brother).

Turner, Sir Charles (Lynn) (married Walpole's sister; the Turners, leading merchants, had a good interest at Lynn).

Turner, Sir John (Lynn) (uncle of Sir Charles Turner).

Walpole, Robert (Castle Rising) (the future first Minister).

PART IV. MISCELLANEOUS: NOMINEES OF FIVE COURT MAGNATES (DUKE OF SOMERSET, EARLS OF CARLISLE, RADNOR, PEMBROKE, AND STAMFORD)

These five peers do not constitute the leadership of a single party group. Carlisle and Stamford were Court Whigs (fairly close to the Junto); Radnor and Somerset were plain Court; and Pembroke, Court Tory. They all had in common: electoral interests in at least three constituencies; an active interest in the Court and in politics; and a record of consistent office-holding. For these reasons they are discussed in this section together, as they were in the text.

Summary:

1. Nominees of the Duke of Somerset	2[1]
2. Nominees of the Earl of Carlisle	6
3. Nominees of the Earl of Radnor	5[2]
4. Nominees of the Earl of Pembroke	3
5. Nominees of the Earl of Stamford	6
Total number of Members returned by these five Court peers	22

1. *Nominees of the Duke of Somerset:*

Seymour, William (Cockermouth) (distant cousin and nominee of Somerset; younger brother of Sir Edward Seymour (and listed also with Sir Edward's following); colonel of foot).

Yard, Robert (Marlborough) (Somerset's nominee for Marlborough; Under-Secretary of State and Secretary to the Comm'rs of the Great Seal).

2. *Nominees of the Earl of Carlisle:*

Delaval, Sir John (Morpeth) (connexion and nominee of Carlisle for his pocket borough of Morpeth).

Fletcher, George (Cumberland) (political associate of Carlisle and had his interest, plus Wharton's, in the election for Cumberland).

Hassell, Sir Edward (Cumberland) (the other Carlisle candidate for the county of Cumberland).

Howard, Philip (Carlisle) (first cousin and nominee of Carlisle at the city from which he took his title; lieut.-col. of marines; had a £400 pension).

Howe, Emanuel (Morpeth) (Carlisle's other nominee for his pocket borough; brig.-gen.; Groom of the Bedchamber).

Sandford, Sir Richard (Westmorland) (Carlisle's and Wharton's candidate for this county; in other parliaments sat for Morpeth on Lord Carlisle's interest, and for Appleby, on Lord Wharton's).

3. *Nominees of the Earl of Radnor:*

Booth, George (Lostwithiel) (brother-in-law and nominee of Radnor; uncle of Lord Delamere; had a £600 pension).

Molesworth, Sir John (Bossiney; elected also for Lostwithiel, but return controverted) (second cousin of Radnor and shared an electoral interest at Bossiney and Lostwithiel inherited from their common great grandfather).

[1] Including Seymour, who voted with the Hyde–Seymour connexion.

[2] This figure includes Molesworth twice, as Member for Bossiney, and also for Lostwithiel—though his return for the latter was controverted.

Robartes, Francis (Tregoney) (uncle and nominee of Lord Radnor).

Robartes, Russell (Bodmin) (younger brother and nominee of Radnor).

4. *Nominees of the Earl of Pembroke:*

Ashurst, Sir Henry (Wilton) (London merchant; had Pembroke's recommendation at his borough of Wilton).

Gauntlett, John (Wilton) (Pembroke's other nominee at Wilton; Clerk of the Signet).

Williams, Sir John (Monmouthshire) (Pembroke's brother-in-law; had Pembroke's interest in Wales).

5. *Nominees of the Earl of Stamford:*

Ashurst, Henry (Preston) (Atty.-Gen. of the Duchy of Lancaster, under Stamford—at this time Chancellor; Duchy candidate; nephew of Sir Henry Ashurst, the Member for Wilton).

Carter, Lawrence (Leicester) (client and nominee of Stamford; his deputy as Steward of the Honour of Leicester; Receiver-Gen. of the Duchy of Lancaster; and later ('10–'22) Stamford's nominee as Member for Beeralston).

Cowper, William (Beeralston) (accepted this seat from Stamford, though a 'Country Whig'; King's Council; later Lord Chancellor).

King, Peter (Beeralston) (another Country Whig owing his seat at Beeralston to Stamford).

Molyneux, Thomas (Preston) (Stamford's Duchy candidate at Preston; Joint Comptroller of the Mint).

Rigby, Sir Alexander (Wigan) (Stamford's candidate on the Duchy interest; Clerk of the Crown for the Duchy of Lancaster).

PART V. THE MARLBOROUGH–GODOLPHIN CONNEXION

Summary:

1. Nominees and followers of the Marlboroughs	3
2. Nominees and followers of Godolphin	9
Total membership of the Marlborough–Godolphin connexion	12

1. *Followers of the Marlboroughs:*

Cardonnell, Adam de (Southampton) (Chief Clerk in the War Office; Secretary to Marlborough as Commander-in-Chief, '02–'12).

Churchill, Charles (Weymouth) (Marlborough's brother; general in army).

Churchill, George (St. Albans) (seat to Lady Marlborough's interest; Admiral, &c., and later sat for Portsmouth).

2. *Followers and nominees of Godolphin:*

(Berkeley), John, Viscount Fitzharding (Windsor) (Godolphin's first cousin; colonel in the army; his wife was a close friend of Anne).

Cotton, Sir Robert (Truro) (connexion and client of Godolphin; Joint Postmaster-Gen.; father-in-law of Samuel Trefusis (below)).

Felton, Sir Thomas (Bury) (father-in-law of Godolphin's kinsman, John Hervey (below); connected with the Suffolk Howards and close to the Princess Anne).

Fortescue, Hugh (Tregoney) (connexion of Godolphin, through the Boscawens, and a follower).

Godolphin, Francis (Helston) (Godolphin's eldest son and heir apparent).

Godolphin, Sidney (Helston) (Godolphin's second cousin, namesake, and nominee for the family borough).

Hervey, John (Bury) (cousin of Lady Godolphin and a follower of Godolphin; patron of Bury; made a peer in 1703).

Powys, Sir Thomas (Ludlow) (connexion and follower of Godolphin, who nominated him for one of his Cornish seats in the next election).

Trefusis, Samuel (Penryn) (connexion and follower of Godolphin).

PART VI. THE NOTTINGHAM-FINCH CONNEXION

Summary:

1.	Followers and nominees of Nottingham	20
2.	Followers and nominees of Nottingham's chief allies and kinsmen (Lords Guilford, Brooke, Exeter, Thanet, and Abingdon)	11
	Total membership of the Nottingham-Finch connexion	31

1. *Followers and nominees of Nottingham:*

Austen, Robert (Winchelsea) (Finch nominee at Winchelsea in 1702).

Barrington, Sir Charles (Essex) (nephew of Nottingham's first wife).

Bliss, Thomas (Maidstone) (Finch nominee; backed by Winchilsea).

Brereton, Edward (Denbigh) (connexion and follower of Nottingham; uncle of Warwick Lake (below)).

(Bulkeley), Richard, Viscount Bulkeley (Anglesey) (first cousin and follower of Nottingham; vice-admiral, North Wales, '02–'04).

Bulkeley, Robert (Beaumaris) (younger brother of Viscount Bulkeley).

Bulkeley, Thomas (Carnarvonshire) (uncle of Viscount Bulkeley).

Bunbury, Sir Henry (Chester) (follower of Nottingham; colleague of Peter Shakerly; brother-in-law of Sir T. Hanmer (below)).

Chivers, Henry (Calne) (Sir Charles Hedges's choice for a colleague as Member for Calne; for Hedges, see below).

Finch, Heneage (Oxford University) (Nottingham's younger brother; made a peer in 1703; next most influential man to Nottingham in this group).

Hanmer, Sir Thomas (Thetford) (follower of Nottingham; first cousin of Sir Roger Mostyn (below); Thetford seat on his wife's interest).

Harvey, William (Old Sarum) (second cousin and follower of Nottingham).

Hedges, Sir Charles (Malmesbury) (client and follower of Nottingham, who had him made Secretary with him in 1702; won the borough against Lord Wharton).

Lake, Warwick (Middlesex) (first cousin of Nottingham's first wife; follower of Nottingham; nephew of Edward Brereton (above)).

Lee, Henry (Canterbury) (connexion and follower of Nottingham; had the support of the Finch interest in this Kentish constituency).

Mostyn, Sir Roger (Flintshire) (Nottingham's prospective son-in-law and a disciple; cousin of Sir Thomas Hanmer (above)).

Pauncefort, Edward (Malmesbury) (Hedges's choice as a colleague on the anti-Wharton interest at Malmesbury; had a place in the Jewel Office and another place in the Pay Office).

Rooke, Sir George (Portsmouth) (connexion and disciple of Nottingham).

Shakerly, Peter (Chester) (follower of Nottingham; colleague and friend of Sir Henry Bunbury (above)).

Thynne, Henry (Tamworth, elected also for Milborne Port) (son and heir apparent of Lord Weymouth; nephew of Lord Winchilsea).

2. *Followers and nominees of Nottingham's allies: Abingdon, Brooke, Exeter, Guilford, and Thanet (all related to Lady Nottingham):*

Bertie, Charles (Stamford) (uncle of Abingdon; cousin of Lady Nottingham; Treasurer and Paymaster of the Ordnance; Nottingham follower).

Bertie, Henry (Westbury) (brother of Charles Bertie—next above).

Bertie, James (Woodstock) (younger brother of Lord Abingdon).

Bertie, Robert (Westbury) (another brother of Lord Abingdon).

Cecil, William (Stamford) (younger brother of Lord Exeter; cousin of Lady Nottingham; colleague of Charles Bertie (above)).

Greville, Algernon (Warwick) (younger son of Lord Brooke; connexion and follower of Lord Nottingham).

Greville, Francis (Warwick) (son and heir apparent of Lord Brooke; brother of Algernon Greville—next above).

Norreys, Sir Edward (Oxfordshire) (cousin and nominee of Lord Abingdon).

Norreys, Francis (Oxford) (son of Sir Edward Norreys—next above).

North, Charles (Banbury) (younger brother of Lord Guilford; cousin of Lady Nottingham; follower of Lord Nottingham).

Pierrepoint, Gervase (Appleby) (uncle and nominee of Lord Thanet).

PART VII. THE HYDE–GRANVILLE–GOWER–SEYMOUR CONNEXION

Summary:

1. Followers and nominees of the Earl of Rochester 12
2. Followers and nominees of the Granvilles and Gowers . . 9
3. Followers and nominees of Sir Edward Seymour . . . 26[1]

Total membership of the Hyde–Granville–Gower–Seymour connexion 47

1. *Nominees and followers of Laurence Hyde, Earl of Rochester:*

Bankes, John (Corfe Castle) (married Rochester's cousin; Hyde follower).

Boyle, Charles (Huntingdon) (first cousin of Lady Rochester and of Lady Sandwich; Huntingdon seat from latter; Rochester disciple).

Cary, William (Launceston) (connexion, colleague, and follower of Lord Hyde—below).

Ettrick, William (Christchurch) (Rochester's nominee for this pocket borough; kinsman, also, of Seymour; later ('01–'03) had a place in the Customs).

Gwyn, Francis (Christchurch) (Rochester's other nominee for this borough; another kinsman of Seymour; Seymour's Recorder for Totnes; had an Irish and a Welsh place; 'Lord Rotchester's Gwine').

Herbert, James (Aylesbury) (son-in-law of the Duke of Leeds (Danby); owed this seat to Rochester's cousin, Sir John Pakington (below)).

[1] This figure does *not* include William Seymour, who is counted under Somerset's group, in Part IV, above.

(Hyde), Henry, Lord Hyde (Launceston) (Rochester's son and heir apparent; married Sir John Leveson-Gower's sister; his sister married Seymour's son).

Jenkinson, Sir Robert (Oxfordshire) (close friend and follower of the Hydes; first cousin of John Bankes—above).

(Jones), Richard, Earl of Ranelagh (West Looe) (Irish peer; Paymaster-Gen.; first cousin of Lady Rochester; W. Looe seat from Bishop Trelawny).

Kendall, James (West Looe) (another Trelawny nominee; client of Rochester and his son-in-law Ormonde; his place as Comm'r of the Treasury in Ireland due to Rochester's influence).

Pakington, Sir John (Worcestershire) (married Rochester's cousin; had an electoral interest at Aylesbury which he put at the disposal of other members of the Hyde–Seymour connexion).

Parker, Hugh (Evesham) (Rochester's cousin; brother-in-law of Pakington (above) and of John Bankes (above)).

2. *Nominees of the Granville and Leveson-Gower families:*

Cotton, Rowland (Newcastle (Staffs.)) (nominee of the Gowers for their family borough; Steward of the borough in the Gower interest).

Drake, Sir William (Honiton) (married a first cousin of John Granville (below); follower of Rochester and Granville; held office, '10–'14).

Granville, John (Cornwall) (head of the Granvilles during minority of his nephew, the last Earl of Bath; uncle of Sir John Leveson-Gower (below) and of Lady Hyde).

Hickes, John (Fowey) (client and nominee of the Granvilles).

Leveson-Gower, Sir John (Newcastle (Staffs.)) (nephew of Granville; patron of Newcastle; made a peer in 1703).

Manley, John (Bossiney) (client and nominee of Granville).

Pendarves, Alexander (Penryn) (friend and follower of Granville; patron of one seat at Penryn).

Praed, James (St. Ives) (follower of Granville; connexion of Pendarves).

Vyvyan, Sir Richard (Michael) (friend and follower of Granville, whom he succeeded as knight of the shire, '03; patron of one seat at Michael).

3. *Followers and nominees of Sir Edward Seymour:*

Anderton, James (Ilchester) (client of Seymour and married Seymour's cousin; an attorney for the E. India Company).

Bankes, Sir Jacob (Minehead) (connexion and follower of Seymour; controlled Minehead during the minority of his nephew, head of the Luttrells of Dunster; married Alexander Luttrell's sister-in-law).

Coulson, Thomas (Totnes) (client of Seymour and his nominee for his borough of Totnes; an E. India Co. merchant).

Courtenay, George (East Looe) (Seymour's first cousin; first cousin of Bishop Trelawny, who gave him the seat at East Looe).

Courtenay, Sir William (Devonshire) (nephew of George (next above); first cousin of Seymour; head of the Devonshire Courtenays).

Coward, William (Wells) (married Seymour's first cousin; Recorder of Wells, which he and Seymour's brother, Henry Seymour Portman (below), represented in parliament).

Fownes, Richard (Corfe Castle) (connexion, through the Napiers (below), of Seymour; voted with the Seymour connexion).

Graham, Henry (Westmorland) (political associate of Seymour's friend Musgrave (below); co-operated with the Seymour group in parliament).

Lear, Sir Thomas (Ashburton) (connexion and follower of Seymour; married a Courtenay).

Luttrell, Alexander (Minehead) (heir presumptive to Dunster Castle and its electoral interest at Minehead; cousin and follower of Seymour; Sir Jacob Bankes (above) married his sister-in-law).

Musgrave, Sir Christopher (Totnes) (Seymour's northern ally and his nominee in this parliament and the next for his borough of Totnes).

Napier, Sir Nathaniel (Dorchester) (second cousin and follower of Seymour).

Napier, Nathaniel (Dorchester) (eldest son of Sir Nathaniel—next above).

Nicholas, Edward (Shaftesbury) (married Seymour's cousin; political friend and follower of Seymour).

Palmer, Nathaniel (Somerset) (married Seymour's cousin and connected with the Gowers; political follower of Seymour).

Popham, Alexander (Bath) (Sir Edward Seymour's nephew and a follower).

Scobell, Francis (Grampound) (married daughter of Sir Joseph Tredenham (below), patron of St. Mawes; his wife was Seymour's niece).

Seymour, Sir Edward (Exeter) (the head of the Seymours).

Seymour, Sir Henry (East Looe) (first cousin and nominee of Sir Edward Seymour and of Bishop Trelawny, who got him the seat at East Looe).

Seymour, William (Cockermouth) (younger son of Sir Edward, but since he owed his seat to the Duke of Somerset, he is counted *sub* 'Somerset').

Seymour-Conway, Francis (Bramber) (younger son of Sir Edward).

Seymour-Portman, Henry (Wells) (Sir Edward's younger brother).

Snell, John (Exeter) (nominee and follower of Seymour; his choice as colleague; an Exeter merchant).

Tredenham, John (St. Mawes) (son of Sir Joseph—next below).

Tredenham, Sir Joseph (St. Mawes) (married Seymour's sister; father-in-law of Scobell; political follower of Seymour).

Warre, Sir Francis (Taunton) (second cousin and follower of Seymour; Recorder of Taunton in the Seymour interest).

Wroth, Sir Thomas (Bridgwater) (connexion and follower of Seymour; nephew of Nathaniel Palmer (above)).

PART VIII. THE HARLEY CONNEXION

Total membership of the Harley–Foley connexion 20

Brydges, James (Hereford) (a political friend and follower of Harley; son and heir apparent of Lord Chandos).

Coke, Thomas (Derbyshire) (political friend and follower of Harley).

Foley, Edward (Leominster) (brother-in-law of Robert and Edward Harley).

Foley, Thomas, of Stoke Edith (Hereford) (first cousin of Edward Foley and Thomas Foley, of Witley).

Foley, Thomas, of Witley (Stafford) (brother of Edward Foley (above); brother-in-law of Robert and Edward Harley).

Harcourt, Simon (Abingdon) (schoolfellow, friend, and follower of Harley).

Harley, Edward (Leominster) (younger brother of Robert Harley).

Harley, Robert (Radnor) (head of the Harley–Foley connexion).

Harley, Thomas (Radnorshire) (first cousin and follower of Robert Harley).

Mansell, Thomas (Glamorganshire) (friend and follower of Harley).

Mansell, Thomas (Cardiff) (cousin and henchman of Thomas Mansell—next above).

Paget, Henry (Staffordshire) (cousin of Harcourt; connexion of the Foleys; follower of Harley; son and heir apparent of Lord Paget).

Price, Robert (Weobley) (friend, neighbour, and follower of Harley).

St. John, Henry (Wootton Bassett) (friend and disciple of Harley).

Sydenham, Sir Philip (Somerset) (first cousin of Harley's kinsman and follower, Lord Poulett).

Warton, Sir Michael (Beverley) (political follower of Harley).

Webb, Edmund (Ludgershall) (cousin and follower of St. John).

Webb, John Richmond (Ludgershall) (son of Edmund—next above; general in the army; cousin and follower of St. John).

Willoughby, Sir Thomas (Nottinghamshire) (first cousin of James Brydges (above); connexion of the Foleys; follower of Harley).

Winnington, Salway (Bewdley) (brother-in-law of Edward and Thomas Foley; follower of Harley).

Summary:

The Government interest	38
The Junto connexion	64
The Newcastle–Pelham–Townshend–Walpole connexion .	16
The Court Peers: Somerset, Carlisle, Radnor, Pembroke, and Stamford	22
The Marlborough–Godolphin connexion	12
The Nottingham–Finch connexion	31
The Hyde–Granville–Gower–Seymour connexion	47
The Harley–Foley connexion	20
Total membership of the organized parliamentary groups	250

APPENDIX IV

The General Election of 1702

INTRODUCTION

THIS appendix, taken together with the preceding one ('Party Groups in the 1701 Parliament'), serves as documentation for Chapter VI of the text, 'The Election of 1702'.

In that chapter the gains and losses registered in the 1702 election by the government interest and the seven principal party groups were summarized, since to present them in detail would impossibly encumber the account of the election.

Below will be found the breakdowns of these summaries, beginning with the losses suffered by the government interest and following with detailed data for each of the party groups, taken in the order in which they are discussed in Chapter VI of the text.

PART I. THE GOVERNMENT INTEREST

Summary:

	1701	*1702*
1. Re-elected	23	23
2. Succeeded	4	4
3. Newly elected		1
4. Failed of re-election	11	
Total in the old and in the new parliament	38	28

1. *Re-elected*: information about these Members has already been given in Appendix III, Part I, above; and will not be repeated here. Instead, the names of government Members re-elected will simply be listed in alphabetical order, with the name of the constituency.

Blathwayt, William (Bath)
Brewer, John (New Romney)
Bridges, William (Liskeard)
Crawford, Robert (Queenborough)
Cutts, Lord (Cambridgeshire)
Davall, Sir Thomas (Harwich)
Dodson, Thomas (Liskeard)
Erle, Thomas (Wareham)
Frankland, Sir Thomas (Thirsk)
Furnese, Sir Henry (Sandwich)
Goodricke, Sir Henry (Boroughbridge)

Gould, Nathaniel (Shoreham)
Henley, Anthony (Melcombe Regis)
Lowndes, William (Seaford)
Markes, Richard (Petersfield)
Methuen, John (Devizes)
Pulteney, John (Hastings)
St. Loe, George (Weymouth)
Sayer, George (Canterbury)
Topham, Richard (Windsor)
Trelawny, Charles (Plymouth)
Vincent, Henry (Truro)
Woollcombe, John (Plymouth)

2. *Succeeded* (i.e. replaced another government nominee):

Cutts, Lord (succeeded James Stanhope as M.P. for Newport, I. of Wight) (Cutts was also re-elected for Cambridgeshire—see above).

Erle, Thomas (succeeded John Gibson as M.P. for Portsmouth) (Erle was also re-elected for Wareham; in his case and Lord Cutts's it was presumed that the safe government seat would be handed over to another government Member if Erle and Cutts won their elections elsewhere).

Leigh, John (Newtown, I. of Wight, succeeding Joseph Dudley) (local man, nominee of the Governor, Lord Cutts).

Stephens, William (succeeded Edward Richards as gov't nominee for Yarmouth, I. of Wight) (for Stephens, cf. Appendix II, 5—above).

3. *Newly elected:*

Dummer, Edmund (Arundel, defeating John Cooke, Country Member) (master shipwright; Comm'r for Inspecting Plymouth Dock, '93; Surveyor of the Navy).

4. *Failed of Re-election*: information on these men has also been given already in Appendix III, Part I, above, and will not be repeated here.

Bokenham, William (Rochester, defeated by Nottingham's nominee, William Cage).

Colt, Sir Henry Dutton (Westminster, defeated by Rochester's nominee, Thomas Crosse).

Crawley, Richard (Wendover, defeated by Wharton's nominee, Sir Roger Hill).

Crow, Mitford (Southampton, defeated by the High Churchman, Frederick Tylney).

Fox, Sir Stephen (Cricklade, defeated by a Country Tory, Scorie Barker).

Gwynne, Sir Rowland (Brecknockshire, defeated by John Jeffries, independent merchant).

Lydell, Dennis (Harwich, defeated by the Finch candidate, John Ellis).

Mounsher, John (Hastings, defeated by another Finch nominee, William Ashburnham).

Sergison, Charles (Shoreham, defeated by John Pery, another independent merchant).

Vernon, James (Westminster, defeated by the Rochester candidate, Sir Walter Clarges).

Wren, Sir Christopher (Melcombe Regis, displaced by the Nottingham follower, Henry Thynne).

PART II. THE MARLBOROUGH–GODOLPHIN CONNEXION

Summary:

	1701	*1702*
1. Re-elected	11	11
2. Succeeded	1	1
3. Newly elected		6
4. Failed of re-election	none	
Total in the old and in the new parliament	12	18

1. *Re-elected*: information on these men has been given above, in Appendix II, Part V, and will not be repeated here. The initial 'M' against a Member's name indicates he is a follower primarily of Marlborough; the initial 'G', of Godolphin.

G (Berkeley), Lord Fitzharding (Windsor)
M Cardonnell, Adam (Southampton)
M Churchill, Charles (Weymouth)
M Churchill, George (St. Albans)
G Felton, Sir Thomas (Bury)
G Fortescue, Hugh (Tregoney)
G Godolphin, Francis (Helston)
G Godolphin, Sidney (Helston)
G Hervey, John (Bury)
G Powys, Sir Thomas (Ludlow)
G Trefusis, Samuel (Penryn)

2. *Succeeded:*

G Powys, Sir Thomas (succeeded Sir Robert Cotton as Godolphin nominee at Truro) (Powys was also re-elected for Ludlow, see above).

3. *Newly elected:*

M Bathurst, Sir Benjamin (New Romney, defeating Edward Goulston, Country Whig) (Treasurer of the Household to the Prince; acted as Marlborough's proxy at the latter's installation with the Garter; his wife was an intimate friend of Lady Marlborough).

G Boscawen, Hugh (Tregoney, displacing Radnor's uncle and nominee, Francis Robartes) (Marlborough's and Godolphin's nephew; Captain of St. Mawe's Castle, '96–'10; Groom of the Bedchamber to the Prince; Recorder of Penryn and Truro; later ('14–'20) Comptroller of the Household and created Viscount Falmouth).

M Craggs, James (Grampound, ousting a gov't Whig merchant, Sir William Scawen) (sometime secretary to Lady Marlborough; an army clothier; later ('15–'20) Joint Postmaster-Gen. and implicated in the South Sea Company scandal, 1720).

G Cullum, Sir Dudley (Suffolk, defeating Sir Samuel Barnardiston, Country Whig) (connexion and client of Godolphin and John Hervey).

G Godolphin, Sidney (West Looe, displacing James Kendall, Hyde–Seymour follower) (the same Sidney Godolphin who was re-elected for Helston—see above; this was a second seat for him).

G Guy, Henry (Hedon, defeating Sir Robert Hildyard, Country Member) (close follower of Godolphin at this time; old-line politician, formerly associated with Danby; Secretary to the Treasury, '90–'95).

PART III. THE NOTTINGHAM–FINCH CONNEXION

Summary:

	1701	*1702*
1. Re-elected	25	25
2. Succeeded	3	3
3. Newly elected		17
4. Failed of re-election	3	—
Total in the old and in the new parliament	31	45

1. *Re-elected*: information on these men has been given above, Appendix III, Part VI, and will not be repeated here. The initial 'N' opposite a Member's name indicates he is a follower primarily of Nottingham; 'A', of Lord Abingdon; 'B', Lord Brooke; 'E', Lord Exeter; 'G', Guilford; and 'T', Thanet.

N Barrington, Sir Charles (Essex)
A Bertie, Charles (Stamford)
A Bertie, James (Woodstock)
N Brereton, Edward (Denbigh)
N Bulkeley, Robert (Beaumaris)
N Bulkeley, Thomas (Carnarvonshire)
N Bulkeley, Viscount (Anglesey)

N Bunbury, Sir Henry (Chester)
E Cecil, William (Stamford)
N Chivers, Henry (Calne)
N Finch, Heneage (Oxford University)
B Greville, Algernon (Warwick)
B Greville, Francis (Warwick)
N Harvey, William (Old Sarum)
N Hedges, Sir Charles (Malmesbury)
N Lake, Warwick (Middlesex)
N Lee, Henry (Canterbury)
A Norreys, Sir Edw. (Oxfordshire)
A Norreys, Francis (Oxford)
G North, Charles (Banbury)
N Pauncefort, Edward (Malmesbury)
T Pierrepoint, Gervase (Appleby)
N Rooke, Sir George (Portsmouth)
N Shakerly, Peter (Chester)
N Thynne, Henry (Tamworth)

2. *Succeeded:*

N Benson, Robert (Thetford, succeeding Sir Thomas Hanmer, moved to seat for Flintshire) (follower of the Finch connexion; prospective son-in-law of Heneage Finch).

N Clarke, George (Winchelsea, successful Finch nominee, displacing another Finch nominee, Robert Austen, who was defeated) (Judge Advocate of the Fleet, Joint Secretary of the Admiralty, and Secretary to Prince George, '02–'05).

N Hanmer, Sir Thomas (Flintshire, replacing Sir Roger Mostyn, who won a seat for Cheshire) (for Hanmer, cf. Appendix III, Part VI, above).

3. *Newly elected:*

N Annesley, Arthur (Cambridge University, defeating Halifax's friend, Sir Isaac Newton) (cousin and follower of Nottingham; younger brother of Lord Anglesey; successful Finch candidate for High Steward of the University, '02; held office in the gov't, '02–'10).

N Ashburnham, William (Hastings, ousting the sitting Admiralty Member, James Mounsher) (Finch candidate for this Cinque Port).

N Blofield, Thomas (Norwich, defeating a Country Whig, Edward Clarke) (Finch candidate, supported by Nottingham's friend, Humphrey Prideaux, Dean of Norwich).

N Bruce, James (Bedwin, defeating a Country Whig, Michael Mitford) (kinsman and follower of Nottingham; younger brother of the Jacobite Earl of Ailesbury and brother of Robert Bruce —next below).

N Bruce, Robert (Marlborough, displacing Somerset's nominee, Under-Secretary Yard) (brother of James Bruce—next above).

N Cage, William (Rochester, defeating the sitting Admiralty Member, James Bokenham) (local candidate, elected on the Finch interest).

N Ellis, John (Harwich, displacing the sitting gov't Member, Dennis Lydell, Comm'r of the Navy) (client and nominee of Nottingham; Under-Secretary in Sir Charles Hedges's office).

A Glyn, Sir William (Woodstock, defeating the Junto Member, Sir Thomas Littleton, who took refuge in Walpole's borough of Castle Rising) (client and nominee of Lord Abingdon).

N Hedges, Sir Charles (Calne, defeating Wharton's man, Henry Blaake) (this was a second seat for Hedges, re-elected for Malmesbury).

N Howe, Sir James (Hindon, defeating a Country Tory, Reynolds Calthorpe) (connexion and follower of Nottingham; related also to Sir George Rooke and Henry Lee, other members of the Finch group).

N Howe, Richard Grubham (Wiltshire, defeating a Court Whig, Maurice Ashley) (brother-in-law of Nottingham's kinsman and friend, Lord Weymouth; second cousin of Sir James Howe—next above).

N Knatchbull, Edward (Rochester, defeating a Country Tory, Francis Barrell) (Nottingham's first cousin and nominee; Sir George Rooke married his sister).

N Michell, John (Sandwich, displacing a Newcastle–Pelham Member, Sir James Oxenden) (Finch nominee at this Cinque Port).

N Mostyn, Sir Roger (Cheshire, defeating a Country Whig, Sir John Manwaring) (Mostyn sat for Flintshire in the old parliament).

N —, — (Flint, defeating a Country Tory, Sir John Conway (another seat won in this election by Nottingham's future son-in-law).

N Southwell, Edward (Rye, election controverted, and Southwell seated on petition, ousting the sitting Member, Joseph Offley, a Country Whig) (Finch nominee at this Cinque Port; for Southwell, see Appendix II, 12, above).

N Thynne, Henry (Weymouth, displacing the gov't nominee, Sir Christopher Wren) (Thynne was also re-elected for Tamworth).

4. *Failed of re-election:*

A Bertie, Henry (Westbury, defeated by a Country Whig, Wm. Trenchard).

A Bertie, Robert (Westbury, defeated by another Country Whig, Thomas Phipps).

N Bliss, Thomas (Maidstone, defeated by a Country Whig, Sir Thomas Roberts).

PART IV. THE HYDE–GRANVILLE–GOWER–SEYMOUR CONNEXION

Summary:

	1701	*1702*
1. Re-elected	44	44
2. Succeeded	1	1
3. Newly elected		21
4. Failed of re-election	2	
Total in the old and in the new parliament	47	66

1. *Re-elected*: information on these Members has been given above, Appendix III, Part VII, and will not be repeated here. The initial 'R' opposite a Member's name indicates he was a follower primarily of Lord Rochester; 'G', of Colonel Granville; 'LG' of Sir John Leveson-Gower; and 'S', of Sir Edward Seymour.

S Anderton, James (Ilchester)
S Bankes, Sir Jacob (Minehead)
R Bankes, John (Corfe Castle)
R Boyle, Charles (Huntingdon)
R Cary, William (Launceston)
LG Cotton, Rowland (Newcastle (Staffs.))
S Coulson, Thomas (Totnes)
S Courtenay, Sir William (Devon)
S Coward, William (Wells)
G Drake, Sir William (Honiton)
R Ettrick, William (Christchurch)
S Fownes, Richard (Corfe Castle)
S Graham, Henry (Westmorland)
G Granville, John (Cornwall)
R Gwyn, Francis (Christchurch)
R Herbert, James (Aylesbury)
G Hickes, John (Fowey)
R (Hyde), Lord Hyde (Launceston)
R Jenkinson, Sir Robert (Oxfordshire)
R (Jones), Lord Ranelagh (West Looe)
S Lear, Sir Thomas (Ashburton)
LG Leveson-Gower, Sir John (Newcastle (Staffs.))
S Luttrell, Alexander (Minehead)
G Manley, John (Bossiney)
S Musgrave, Sir Christopher (Totnes)
S Napier, Sir Nathaniel (Dorchester)
S Napier, Nathaniel (Dorchester)
S Nicholas, Edward (Shaftesbury)
R Pakington, Sir John (Worcestershire)
S Palmer, Nathaniel (Somerset)
R Parker, Hugh (Evesham)
G Pendarves, Alexander (Penryn)
S Popham, Alexander (Bath)
G Praed, James (St. Ives)
S Scobell, Francis (Grampound)
S Seymour, Sir Edward (Exeter)

S Seymour, Sir Henry (East Looe)
S Seymour-Conway, Francis (Bramber)
S Seymour-Portman, Henry (Wells)
S Snell, John (Exeter)
S Tredenham, John (St. Mawes)
S Tredenham, Sir Joseph (St. Mawes)
S Warre, Sir Francis (Taunton)
S Wroth, Sir Thomas (Bridgwater)

2. *Succeeded:*

G Bellott, Renatus (Michael, succeeding Sir Richard Vyvyan) (Hyde–Granville nominee, through Vyvyan, who contested Cornwall unsuccessfully; nephew of Alexander Pendarves, above).

3. *Newly elected:*

G Anstis, John (St. Germans, defeating a Country Whig, Richard Edgecombe) (client and nominee of Granville; a barrister; drew the impeachments of the Junto lords, '00; given office, '03).

G Bassett, Francis (Michael, defeating a Country Tory, William Courtenay, no kin of Seymour's Courtenay cousins) (client, connexion, and nominee of Granville; related to Granville, Vyvyan, and Pendarves).

LG Bridgeman, Orlando (Wigan, supplanting Sir Alexander Rigby, nominee of the former Chancellor of the Duchy, Lord Stamford) (nominee of the new Chancellor, Leveson-Gower; barrister, owning property near Wigan).

R Clarges, Sir Walter (Westminster, defeating the sitting gov't Member, James Vernon) (Rochester–Ormonde nominee; kinsman and client of Granville).

R Crosse, Thomas (Westminster, defeating the other Court Member, Sir Henry Dutton Colt) (Rochester–Ormonde candidate; local brewer).

S Graham, James (Appleby, defeating Wharton's nominee and nephew, Wharton Dunch) (father of Musgrave's friend, Henry Graham).

G Granville, George (Fowey, supplanting a Country Member, John Williams) ('Granville the Polite'; cousin and later heir of John Granville; intimate of St. John and Harley, and made Lord Lansdowne by them).

R Hammond, Anthony (Huntingdon, supplanting Halifax's cousin, Francis Wortley Montagu) (nominee of Rochester's kinswoman, Lady Sandwich; active Hyde–Seymour partisan; Comm'r of the Navy, '02–'08).

R Howe, John Grubham (Gloucestershire, defeating a Country Whig, Sir Richard Cocks) (the notorious Jack Howe, virulent Hyde–Seymour partisan, helped to no less than four seats in this election).

R —, —— (Gloucester, supplanting a Court Whig, Lord Durseley).

R —, —— (Newton, Lancashire, replacing a High Churchman, Thomas Legh of Ridge, as nominee of the patron, Thos. Legh of Lyme).

G —, —— (Bodmin, supplanting Lord Radnor's brother and nominee, Russell Robartes) (this seat was due to Granville's assistance).

S Hungerford, John (Scarborough, defeating a Court Whig, Sir Charles Hotham) (client of Seymour; London lawyer; did legal work for Seymour and for his friends of the Old E. India Company).

R Hyde, Robert (Wiltshire, defeating a Court Whig, William Ashe) (second cousin and client of Rochester; uncle of Hugh Parker).

G Leech, Sir Simon (Okehampton, defeating a Country Member, William Harris) (first cousin and client of Granville).

S Mackworth, Sir Humphrey (Cardiganshire, replacing a Country Tory, Lewis Price) (political crony of Seymour and Musgrave; sat for Seymour's borough of Totnes in the next parliament; Welsh coal owner and Deputy Governor of the Mine Adventurers).

S Musgrave, Sir Christopher (Westmorland, defeating the Junto–Carlisle candidate, Sir Richard Sandford) (re-elected also for Seymour's borough of Totnes—see above).

S Musgrave, Christopher (Carlisle, defeating Lord Carlisle's cousin and nominee, Philip Howard) (son of Sir Christopher Musgrave).

R Pakington, Sir John (Aylesbury, defeating Wharton's candidate, Sir Thomas Lee) (re-elected also for Worcestershire—see above).

LG Stanley, Charles (Preston, defeating the candidate of the former Chancellor (Stamford), namely Thomas Molyneux) (nominee of the new Chancellor, Leveson-Gower; younger brother of Lord Derby).

LG Wyche, Sir Cyril (Preston, defeating Stamford's other nominee, Henry Ashurst) (Leveson-Gower's other nominee; great-uncle of Leveson-Gower; uncle of Granville; Gentleman Usher of the Privy Chamber).

4. *Failed of re-election:*

S Courtenay, George (East Looe, supplanted by a Court Tory, Sir John Pole, presumably on Bishop Trelawny's recommendation).

R Kendall, James (West Looe, supplanted by Godolphin's cousin, namesake, and nominee, Sidney Godolphin, also standing, presumably, on the Trelawny interest).

PART V. THE HARLEY–FOLEY CONNEXION

Summary:

	1701	*1702*
1. Re-elected	17	17
2. Succeeded	1	1
3. Newly elected		2
4. Failed of re-election	2	
	—	—
Total in the old and in the new parliament	20	20

1. *Re-elected*: for information on these Members see Appendix III, Part VIII.

Brydges, James (Hereford)
Coke, Thomas (Derbyshire)
Foley, Edward (Leominster)
Foley, Thomas (Hereford)
Foley, Thomas (Stafford)
Harcourt, Simon (Abingdon)
Harley, Edward (Leominster)
Harley, Robert (Radnor)
Harley, Thomas (Radnorshire)
Mansell, Thomas (Cardiff)
Mansell, Thomas (Glamorganshire)
Paget, Henry (Staffordshire)
St. John, Henry (Wootton Bassett)
Sydenham, Sir Philip (Somerset)
Webb, Edmund (Ludgershall)
Webb, John Richmond (Ludgershall)
Winnington, Salway (Bewdley)

2. *Succeeded:*

Price, Thomas (Weobley, succeeded his father, Robert Price).

3. *Newly elected:*

Pinnell, Henry (Wootton Bassett, supplanting the Country Whig, Thomas Jacob) (client and nominee of St. John; thrown over by St. John, 1705, and had to take refuge in one of Granville's boroughs, henceforth counting as one of the Hyde–Granville connexion).

Webb, Thomas (Cricklade, defeating Wharton's friend, Edmund

Dunch) (son of Edmund Webb, and brother of John Richmond Webb—above).

4. *Failed of re-election:*

Warton, Sir Michael (Beverley, defeated by a Court Whig, Sir Charles Hotham).

Willoughby, Sir Thomas (Nottinghamshire, defeated by a Country Tory, Gervase Eyre).

PART VI. NOMINEES OF THE FIVE COURT PEERS

Though not constituting a single group, the nominees of Lords Carlisle, Stamford, Radnor, Somerset, and Pembroke are treated together, both here and in the text as a matter of convenience. In the list of Members the initial 'C' opposite a man's name indicates he was a nominee of Carlisle; 'P', of Pembroke; 'R', of Radnor; 'So', of Somerset; and 'St', of Stamford.

Summary:

	Re-elected	*Succeeded*	*Newly elected*	*Failed of re-election*	*Total: 1701*	*Total: 1702*
Carlisle	2	0	0	4	6	2
Stamford	2	0	0	4	6	2
Radnor	1	1	0	3	5	2
Somerset	0	1	1	1	2	2
Pembroke	1	1	0	1	3	2
Totals	6	3	1	13	22	10

1. *Re-elected*: for information on these men, see Appendix III, Part IV, above.

St Cowper, William (Beeralston)
C Delaval, Sir John (Morpeth)
C Howe, Emmanuel (Morpeth)
St King, Peter (Beeralston)
R Molesworth, Sir John (Bossiney)
P Williams, Sir John (Monmouthshire)

2. *Succeeded:*

P Hawles, Sir John (Wilton, succeeded Sir Henry Ashurst as Pembroke's nominee for his pocket borough) (sat for Bolton's borough of St. Ives, '98–'00, '01–'02; see Appendix III, Part II).

R Robartes, Russell (Lostwithiel, succeeded Radnor's brother-in-law, George Booth) (Radnor's brother, sat for Bodmin, '01–'02).

So Stanhope, James (Cockermouth, succeeded another general, William Seymour, as Somerset's nominee) (Stanhope sat for Newport, I. of Wight, on the gov't interest, '01–'02; see Appendix II, 5, above).

3. *Newly elected:*

So Lumley, Henry (Sussex, defeating the Pelham candidate, Sir William Thomas) (Somerset's candidate for knight of the shire; colonel of horse; younger brother of the Earl of Scarborough; M.P. Arundel, '15–'22; see above, Appendix II, 23).

4. *Failed of re-election*: see Appendix III, Part IV, for these men.

St Ashurst, Henry (Preston, ousted by Leveson-Gower's nominee, Sir Cyril Wyche).

St Carter, Laurence (Leicester, defeated by a High Churchman, Sir George Beaumont).

C Fletcher, George (Cumberland, defeated by a Country Tory, Richard Musgrave—not a close relative or follower of Sir Christopher).

P Gauntlett, John (Wilton, defeated by an independent merchant, George Boddington).

C Hassell, Sir Edward (Cumberland, defeated by an independent Tory, Gilfred Lawson).

C Howard, Philip (Carlisle, defeated by Sir Christopher Musgrave's son).

R Molesworth, Sir John (Lostwithiel) (defeated by an independent merchant, William Hooker) (Molesworth, however, was re-elected for Bossiney—see above).

St Molyneux, Thomas (Preston, defeated by Leveson-Gower's candidate, Charles Stanley).

St Rigby, Sir Alexander (Wigan, defeated by Leveson-Gower's candidate, Orlando Bridgeman).

R Robartes, Francis (Tregoney, supplanted by Godolphin's nephew, Hugh Boscawen).

R Robartes, Russell (Bodmin, defeated by the Hyde–Seymour nominee, Jack Howe) (Robartes succeeded his brother-in-law George Booth at Lostwithiel).

C Sandford, Sir Richard (Westmorland, defeated by Sir Christopher Musgrave, leader of the Hyde–Seymour connexion).

So Yard, Robert (Marlborough, defeated by Nottingham's kinsman and follower, Robert Bruce).

PART VII. THE NEWCASTLE–PELHAM–TOWNSHEND–WALPOLE CONNEXION

Summary:

	1701	*1702*
1. Re-elected	7	7
2. Succeeded	6	6
3. Newly elected		3
4. Failed of re-election	3	
	—	—
Total in the old and in the new parliament	16	16

1. *Re-elected*: information on these men has already been given in Appendix III, Part III, and will not be repeated here. The initial 'N' opposite a man's name indicates he was a nominee or follower primarily of Newcastle; 'P', of Pelham; 'T', of Townshend; and 'W', of Walpole.

T Holland, Sir John (Norfolk)
N Molyneux, Sir Francis (Nottinghamshire)
N Monckton, Robert (Aldborough (Yorks.))
P Pelham, Thomas (Lewes)
N Pierrepoint, William (Nottingham)
N Thornhagh, John (Retford)
W Turner, Sir Charles (Lynn)

2. *Succeeded:*

W Littleton, Sir Thomas (Castle Rising, succeeded another Junto follower, Lord Hartington, who won a seat for Yorkshire).
P Payne, Richard (Lewes, succeeded Henry Pelham, as Pelham nominee here).
P Pelham, Thomas (Sussex, succeeded Sir Henry Peachey as Pelham candidate for knight of the shire).
P Thomas, Sir William (Seaford, succeeded Pelham nominee, Thomas Chowne).
W Walpole, Robert (Lynn, succeeded Sir John Turner, who retired).
W Walpole, Horatio (Castle Rising, succeeded his nephew Robert Walpole, who moved to the larger constituency of Lynn—see next above).

3. *Newly elected:*

N Gregory, George (Nottingham, defeating a Country Tory, Robert Sacheverell) (local candidate set up by Newcastle; M.P., '27–'46, for Newcastle's Yorkshire borough, Boroughbridge; Comm'r of Forfeited Estates, '15–'17; Storekeeper of the Ordnance, '27–'46).

N Jessop, William (Aldborough (Yorks.), defeating Cyril Arthington, Country Tory) (client, nominee, and legal agent for Newcastle; latter had him made a Welsh judge, '07, and later a Comm'r of the Alienation Office, and Chief Justice of Chester; Recorder of Retford, Newcastle being High Steward; first cousin of his colleague, Robert Monckton).

N White, Thomas (Retford, defeating a High Churchman, Sir Willoughby Hickman, who petitioned against White's return and won back the seat) (Newcastle's candidate; M.P., '08–'10, '15–'33; elected also, '01, '02, '10, but petitioned against and unseated on all three occasions).

4. *Failed of re-election:* see Appendix III, Part III, for these men.

N Oxenden, Sir James (Sandwich, lost his seat to a nominee of Nottingham, John Michell).

P Thomas, Sir William (Sussex, defeated by Somerset's candidate, Henry Lumley; took refuge at Seaford—see above).

T Townshend, Roger (Norfolk, lost this seat to a Country Tory, Sir Jacob Astley).

PART VIII. THE JUNTO CONNEXION

Summary:

	Re-elected	*Succeeded*	*Newly elected*	*Failed of re-election*	*Total in 1701*	*Total in 1702*
Wharton	14	1	3	10	25	18
Orford and Spencer	11	2	1	4	17	14
Halifax	2	1	0	4	7	3
Somers	6	0	0	0	6	6
Bolton	6	1	1	2	9	8
Totals	39	5	5	20	64	49

1. *Re-elected*: information on these Members has been given above, Appendix III, Part II, and will not be repeated here. The letter 'B' opposite a man's name indicates he was a nominee or follower primarily of the Duke of Bolton; 'H', of Halifax; 'O', of Orford; 'So', of Somers; 'Sp', of Spencer; and 'W', of Wharton.

O Aylmer, Matthew (Dover)
Sp Bere, Thomas (Tiverton)
W Bertie, Peregrine (Boston)
B Bridges, George Rodney (Winchester)
B Burrard, Paul (Lymington)
W Chase, James (Marlow)
So Clarke, Edward (Taunton)
So Cocks, Charles (Droitwich)
O Cullen, Sir Rushout (Cambridgeshire)
W Denton, Sir Edmund (Bucks)

B Dore, Thomas (Lymington)
W Dormer, Fleetwood (Wycombe)
So Dowdeswell, Richard (Tewkesbury)
O Ellys, Richard (Grantham)
O Ellys, Sir William (Grantham)
W Godfrey, Charles (Wycombe)
O Gostwick, Sir William (Bedfordshire)
W Hampden, Richard (Wendover)
So Harvey, Stephen (Reigate)
W Hustler, Sir William (Northallerton)
So Jekyll, Sir Joseph (Eye)
W Lamplugh, Thomas (Cockermouth)
W Maister, William (Hull)
H Mitchell, Robert (Petersfield)
H Montagu, Sidney Wortley (Peterborough)
W (Mordaunt), Lord Mordaunt (Chippenham)
B Morgan, Anthony (Yarmouth, I. of Wight)
W Palmes, William (Malton)
O Papillon, Philip (Dover)
B Powlett, Lord William (Winchester)
O Russell, Lord Edward (Bedfordshire)
O Russell, Lord Robert (Tavistock)
W St. Quintin, Sir William (Hull)
B Shrimpton, John (Whitchurch)
Sp (Spencer), Lord Spencer (Tiverton)
O Spencer, William (Bedford)
W Strickland, Sir William (Malton)
W Wharton, Goodwin (Buckinghamshire)
So Wylde, Thomas (Worcester)

2. *Succeeded:*

O Carteret, Edward (Bedford, succeeded William Farrer) (Russell nominee; cousin of Halifax; uncle of Lord Carteret; M.P., Huntingdon, on the Montagu interest, '97–'98; M.P., Beeralston, on Lord Stamford's interest, '17–'21; Joint Postmaster-Gen., '21).

O (Cavendish), Lord Hartington (Yorkshire, succeeding Lord Fairfax) (for Lord Hartington, see Appendix III, Part II, above).

B Chandler, Richard (St. Ives, succeeding Sir John Hawles) (M.P. for Hampshire, '00–'02, but defeated for county and took refuge at St. Ives).

H Dudley, Sir Matthew (Northampton, succeeding Christopher Montagu) (client of Halifax; Comm'r of the Customs (and ineligible to sit in Commons), '06–'12; M.P. Huntingdonshire, on the Montagu interest, '13–'15).

H Littleton,[1] Sir Thomas (Castle Rising, succeeding Lord Hartington, who won his election for Yorkshire) (Littleton and Hartington are the only two Members who at various times were returned to parliament both on the Junto and on the Newcastle–Pelham–Walpole interest).

[1] Littleton is not included in the total of the Junto connexion, since he is already included under the Nottingham–Pelham–Townshend–Walpole group.

W Montagu, James (Chippenham, succeeding Wharton's previous candidate, Walter White) (Wharton nominee; second cousin of Halifax).

3. *Newly elected:*

W Hill, Sir Roger (Wendover, defeating a gov't Member, Richard Crawley) (nominee and friend of Wharton and Hampden; Inner Temple barrister; lost the seat when Crawley successfully petitioned).

W Hustler, Sir William (Ripon, defeating a gov't Tory, John Aislabie) (Hustler was also re-elected for Northallerton—see above).

B Jervoise, Thomas (Plympton, defeating a Country Tory, Richard Hele) (Bolton's other defeated candidate for Hampshire in this election; won this seat at Plympton, but lost it to Hele on petition).

O Russell, Lord James (Tavistock, in place of a vacant second seat for his brother Lord Edward; there was no by-election because Lord Edward's return for Tavistock was controverted) (brother of Lord Robert and Lord Edward Russell).

W Walsh, William (Worcestershire, defeating a Country Tory, William Bromley—*not* the well-known High Churchman) (client of Somers and Wharton; poet and beau; Gentleman to the Master of the Horse, '02–'08; M.P. for Richmond, '05–'08, on Wharton's recommendation).

4. *Failed of re-election:*

W Blaake, Henry (Calne, defeated by Nottingham's friend and colleague, Sir Charles Hedges).

O Cavendish, Lord James (Derby, defeated by a Country Tory, Thomas Stanhope).

B Chandler, Richard (Hampshire, defeated by a Country Tory, Richard Norton).

W Dormer, Robert (Bucks, defeated by a Court Tory, Lord Newhaven).

W Dunch, Edmund (Cricklade, defeated by a kinsman of St. John, Thomas Webb).

W Dunch, Wharton (Appleby, defeated by Musgrave's friend, James Graham).

Sp Hopkins, Edward (Coventry, defeated by a High Churchman, Thomas Gery).

W Hutton, John (Richmond, defeated by a High Churchman, James Darcy).

H (Ingram), Lord Irwin (Yorkshire, defeated by a Country Tory, Sir John Kaye).

B Jervoise, Thomas (Hampshire, defeated by a Country Tory, George Pitt).

W Lascelles, Daniel (Northallerton, defeated by a Court Tory, J. Aislabie).

W Lee, Sir Thomas (Aylesbury, defeated by Rochester's cousin, Sir John Pakington, lord of the manor of Aylesbury).

W Littleton, Sir Thomas (Woodstock, defeated by Abingdon's nominee, Sir William Glyn—this was a loss for the Junto; given a seat by Walpole at Castle Rising—a case of succession for the Walpole connexion).

O (Manners), Lord Roos (Leicestershire, defeated by a Country Tory, John Verney).

H Montagu, Charles (Durham, replaced by a Court Tory, Thomas Conyers).

H Montagu, Francis Wortley (Huntingdon, defeated by a Hyde–Seymour follower, supported by Lady Sandwich, Anthony Hammond).

W Mordaunt, Harry (Brackley, defeated by a High Churchman, John James).

H Newton, Sir Isaac (Cambridge University, defeated by Nottingham's candidate, Arthur Annesley).

O (Sherrard), Lord Sherrard (Leicestershire, defeated by a Country Tory, John Wilkins).

W Temple, Sir Richard (Buckingham, defeated by a Country Tory, Roger Price).

SUMMARY OF THE CHANGES IN PARTY-GROUP STRENGTH EFFECTED BY THE 1702 ELECTION

Party group	*Re-elected*	*Succeeded*	*Newly elected*	*Not re-elected*	*Total in 1701*	*Total in 1702*
1. Government Interest	23	4	1	11	38	28
2. Marlborough–Godolphin	11	1	6	0	12	18
3. Nottingham–Finch	25	3	17	3	31	45
4. Hyde–Seymour	44	1	21	2	47	66
5. Harley–Foley	17	1	2	2	20	20
6. Court Peers	6	3	1	13	22	10
7. Newcastle–Pelham–Walpole	7	6	3	3	16	16
8. Junto	39	5	5	20	64	49
Totals	172	24	56	54	250	252

APPENDIX V

Scottish Members in the First Parliament of Great Britain (1707–8)

Summary:

1. The Scottish Court Party:

(*a*) Followers and nominees of Lord Queensberry	15
(*b*) Followers of Lord Seafield	5
(*c*) Followers of the Duke of Argyll	4
(*d*) Followers of Lord Justice-General Cromarty	2
(*e*) Followers of Lord Stair	2
Total of Scottish Court Party	28
2. The *Squadrone*	13
3. Independent Members	4
Total of Scottish Members	45

1. *The Scottish Court Party*: The initial 'Q' designates a follower of Queensberry; 'Se', Seafield; 'St', Stair; 'A', Argyll; and 'C', Cromarty.

Se Abercrombie, Alexander (Banff-shire) (lieutenant of Lord Mar's regt.; made Comm'r of the Equivalent and paid £300; nominee of Seafield).

Se Allardyce, George (Kintore Burgh) (of Allardyce; brother-in-law and client of Seafield).

Q Burnet, Sir Thomas (Kincardine-shire) (of Leys; made Comm'r of Equivalent by Queensberry; kinsman of Seton).

A Campbell, Daniel (Inverary Burgh) (of Ardentenny; Comm'r for the Union; an Argyle-shire Campbell and client of Argyll).

A Campbell, James (Argyle-shire) (of Ardinglass; lieutenant in Lord Argyll's Guards regt. and a follower of Argyll).

A Campbell, Sir James (Argyle-shire) (of Auchinbrek; major in the army; client of Argyll).

A Campbell, John (Argyle-shire) (of Mamore; Groom of the Bedchamber and Surveyor of the Works in Scotland; uncle and nominee of Argyll).

Q Clark, John (Whithorn Burgh) (of Pennycuik; Comm'r of the

Union; Comm'r of the Equivalent; made an Exchequer Baron, '07; client of Queensberry).

St Dalrymple, Sir David (Culross Burgh) (younger brother of Lord Stair; a gov't lawyer).

St Dalrymple, William (Ayr-shire) (younger son of Lord Stair; colonel in the army).

Q Douglas, Sir Alexander (Orkney and Zetland) (of Egilshay; received a pension of £200; a nominee of Queensberry).

Q Douglas, Archibald (Roxburgh-shire) (of Cavers; Receiver-Gen. of the Land Tax; client of Queensberry).

Q Erskine, John (Stirling) (of Carnock; Governor and Provost of Stirling; Governor of Dumbarton; colonel in the army; client of Queensberry).

Se Grant, Alexander (Inverness-shire) (of Grant; colonel in Lord Mar's regt.; a client of Seafield).

Q Johnstone, Sir John (Dumfries Burgh) (of Westerhall; lieut.-col. in the army; nominee of Queensberry).

Q Johnstone, Sir Patrick (Edinburgh) (Lord Provost of Edinburgh; a Comm'r of the Union; Comm'r of the Excise).

C Mackenzie, Sir Kenneth (Cromarty Burgh) (younger son of Lord Cromarty).

Q Maitland, Alexander (Bervie Burgh) (of Pitrichie; henchman of Queensberry, who had him made an Exchequer Baron, '07).

Se Montgomerie, Francis (Ayr-shire) (of Giffen; Comm'r of the Union; a Lord of the Treasury in Scotland; uncle and client of Seafield).

Q Murray, John (Peeble-shire) (of Bowhill; a Lord of Session, '07; younger brother of the Lord Advocate; henchman of Queensberry).

Se Ogilvie, Patrick (Cullen Burgh) (of Lonmay; an officer in the army; younger brother of Lord Seafield).

Q Pollock, Sir Robert (Renfrew-shire) (of Pollock; Governor of Fort William; follower of Queensberry).

Q Pringle, John (Selkirk-shire) (of Hayning; Keeper of the Signet; Comm'r of the Equivalent; gov't lawyer and client of Queensberry).

C Rose, Hugh (Nairn-shire) (of Kilravock; follower of Cromarty and Queensberry).

Q Seton, William (Aberdeen-shire) (of Pitmedden; Comm'r of the Union; Comm'r of the Equivalent; a follower of Queensberry).

Q Smollett, Sir James (Dumbarton Burgh) (of Bonhill; Comm'r of the Union; a Writer of the Signet; Judge of Edinburgh Court; gov't lawyer).

Q Stewart, John (Wigtown-shire) (of Sorbie; lieut.-col. of the Scots Guards; first cousin and follower of Queensberry).

Q Swinton, Sir John (Berwick-shire) (of Swinton; Comm'r of the Equivalent; a follower of Queensberry).

2. *The* Squadrone:

Baillie, George (Lanark-shire) (of Jerviswood; brother-in-law of Marchmont; close friend of Roxburgh; and a leading *squadrone* member).

Bennet, William (Roxburgh-shire) (of Grulbet; nephew of Morison; first cousin of Nisbet; muster-master general).

Bruce, John (Kinross-shire) (of Kinross; stepfather of Montrose).

Cockburn, John (Haddington-shire) (of Ormiston; leading *squadrone* member).

Erskine, Sir John (Burntisland) (of Alva; father-in-law of Haldane; follower of Montrose).

Graham, Mungo (Perth-shire) (of Gorthie; kinsman and follower of Montrose).

Haldane, John (Perth-shire) (of Gleneagles; brother-in-law of Erskine; a comm'r of police).

Halkett, Sir Peter (Dunfermline Burgh) (of Pitfirline, *squadrone* member).

Halyburton, James (Forfar-shire) (of Pitcur; kinsman and client of Roxburgh).

Hume, Sir Andrew (Kirkcudbright) (younger son of Lord Marchmont; brother-in-law of Baillie; a *squadrone* leader).

Kerr, Sir William (Roxburgh-shire) (of Greenhead; kinsman and client of Roxburgh).

Morrison, William (Peeble-shire) (of Prestongrange; Comm'r of the Union; uncle of Bennet; great uncle of Nisbet; leading *squadrone* member).

Nisbet, William (Haddington-shire) (of Dirleton; great nephew of Morrison; and first cousin of Bennet; a *squadrone* follower).

3. *Independent Members:*

Moncrieff, Patrick (Kinghorn Burgh) (of Reidie; Country Member, but supported the Union).

Montgomery, Hugh (Glasgow) (of Busbie; Provost of Glasgow; voted against the Union).

Ramsay, Sir David (Kincardine-shire) (of Balmain; an opponent of the Union).

Scott, James (Montrose Burgh) (of Logie; independent Country Member).

BIBLIOGRAPHY

I. MANUSCRIPT SOURCES

A. *British Museum*

Letters of Dr. Charles Davenant to his son, 1703–1707. Lansdowne MSS. 775.

'State of Political Parties during Queen Anne's Reign', by Lord Coningsby. Lansdowne MSS. 885.

Correspondence of Lord Sunderland with the Duke of Newcastle, 1708. Lansdowne MSS. 1236.

Correspondence of the Duke of Shrewsbury with the Duchess of Marlborough. Egerton MSS. 1695.

Stepney Papers. Add. MSS. 7058–9, 7061–79.

Coxe Transcripts of the Blenheim MSS. Add. MSS. 9078–283.

Dutch Transcripts. Add. MSS. 16788, XX–FFF.

Wentworth Papers. Add. MSS. 22183–267.

Godolphin Papers. Add. MSS. 28052–70.

Ellis Papers. Add. MSS. 28875–956.

Hatton–Finch Papers. Add. MSS. 29588–9, 29594–5.

Mackintosh Papers. Add. MSS. 34487–526.

B. *Christ Church, Oxford*

Wake MSS.

II. PRINTED SOURCES

A. *Official Documents*

Acts of the Parliament of Scotland, 1593–1707, edited by T. Thomson and C. Innes. H.M. Stationery Office, 1814–75. Vols. xi–xii.

Calendar of State Papers, Colonial Series, America and West Indies, Preserved in the Public Record Office, edited by J. W. Fortescue and Cecil Headlam. H.M. Stationery Office, 1901–24. Vols. for 1689–1714.

Calendar of State Papers, Domestic Series, of the Reign of Anne, Preserved in the Public Record Office, edited by R. P. Mahaffy. 2 vols. H.M. Stationery Office, 1916–24.

Calendar of Treasury Books, Preserved in the Public Record Office, edited by W. A. Shaw. H.M. Stationery Office, 1931–54. Vols. viii–xxvi.

Calendar of Treasury Papers, Preserved in the Public Record Office, edited by J. Redington. H.M. Stationery Office, 1868–89. Vols. ii–v.

Journal of the Commissioners for Trade and Plantations, Preserved in the Public Record Office, edited by E. G. Atkinson. H.M. Stationery Office (in progress). Vols. i–ii (1704–15).

Journals of the House of Commons. Vols. vii–xviii.

Journals of the House of Lords. Vols. xvi–xix.

Statutes of the Realm. Printed by command of H.M. George III (folio edn.). London, 1810–28. Vols. vii–ix.

B. *Reports of the Historical Manuscripts Commission*

Report on the MSS. of the Marquis of Ailesbury. 15th Report, Appendix, Part VII. London, 1898.

Report on the MSS. of the Duke of Athole. 12th Report, Appendix, Part VIII. London, 1891.

Report on the MSS. of Capt. J. F. Bagot. 10th Report, Appendix, Part IV, pp. 331 et seq. London, 1885.

Report on the MSS. of the Marquis of Bath, at Longleat. London, 1904–8. Vols. i and iii.

Report on the MSS. of the Duke of Buccleuch, Montagu House, Whitehall. London, 1903. Vol. ii, part ii.

Report on the MSS. of the Corporation of Chester. 8th Report, Appendix, Part I, pp. 394 et seq. London, 1881.

Report on the MSS. of Earl Cowper, at Melbourne. 12th Report, Appendix, Part III. London, 1889. Vol. iii.

Report on the MSS. of the Earl of Dartmouth. 12th Report, Appendix, Part V. London, 1887. Vol. i.

Report on the MSS. of the Earl of Egmont. London, 1909. Vol. ii, part ii.

Report on the MSS. of J. B. Fortescue, Esq. 13th Report, Appendix, Part III. London, 1892. Vol. i.

Report on the MSS. of Mrs. Frankland-Russell-Astley. London, 1900.

Report on the MSS. of the House of Lords. New Series. 10 vols. London, 1900–.

Report on the MSS. of Lord Kenyon. 14th Report, Appendix, Part IV, pp. 187–238. London, 1894.

Report on the MSS. of F. W. Leyborne-Popham, Esq. London, 1899.

Report on the MSS. of the Earl of Lonsdale, at Lowther Castle. 13th Report, Appendix, Part VII. London, 1893.

Report on the MSS. of the Earl of Mar and Kellie. London, 1904.

Report on the MSS. of the Earl of Marchmont. 14th Report, Appendix, Part III. London, 1894.

Report on the MSS. of the Duke of Ormonde. New Series. London, 1920. Vol. viii.

Report on the MSS. of the Duke of Portland. 13th and later Reports. London, 1899–1931. Vols. ii–v, vii–x.

Report on the MSS. of the Duke of Rutland. 12th Report, Appendix, Part V. London, 1889. Vol. ii.

Report on the MSS. of the Countess Dowager of Seafield. 14th Report, Appendix, Part III, pp. 191 et seq. London, 1894.

Report on the MSS. of the Marquis of Townshend. 11th Report, Appendix, Part IV, pp. 48 et seq. London, 1887.

Report on the MSS. of the Earl of Westmorland. 10th Report, Appendix, Part IV, pp. 55 et seq. London, 1885.

C. *Other Original Correspondence and Diaries*

The Letters of Joseph Addison, edited by Walter Graham. Oxford, 1941.

Letters and Domestic Instructions of Queen Anne, edited by Beatrice Curtis Browne. London, 1935.

Correspondence of George Baillie of Jerviswood, 1702–1708, edited by the Earl of Minto for the Bannatyne Club. Edinburgh, 1842.

State Papers and Letters Addressed to William Carstares . . . during the Reign of King William and Queen Anne, edited by J. McCormick. Edinburgh, 1774.

Memoirs of the Life of Sir John Clerk of Pennicuik, edited by J. M. Gray for the Roxburghe Club. London, 1895.

The Private Diary of William Lord Cowper, edited by E. C. Hawtrey for the Roxburghe Club. London, 1833.

'Some Observations relating to Myselfe', by Sir James Etheredge, copied from the Etheredge Bible in the possession of P. C. S. Bruere, Esq., in *Miscellanea Genealogica et Heraldica,* New Series, i, pp. 211–15. London, 1874.

The Diary of John Evelyn, edited by H. B. Wheatley. London, 1879. Vol. iv.

Debates in the House of Commons, 1667–1694, collected by Hon. Anchitel Grey, Esq. London, 1763. Vols. ix–x.

The Correspondence of Sir Thomas Hanmer . . . , edited by Sir Henry Bunbury. London, 1838.

Remarks and Collections of Thomas Hearne, edited by C. E. Doble, D. W. Rannie, and H. E. Salter for the Oxford Historical Society. Oxford, 1885–1918. Vols. i–ii.

The Diary of John Hervey, First Earl of Bristol, with Extracts from His Book of Expenses, 1688–1742. (Suffolk Green Books, No. 2.) Wells, 1894.

The Letter Books of John Hervey, First Earl of Bristol. (Suffolk Green Books, No. 1.) Wells, 1894.

Correspondence of Colonel N. Hooke, Agent from the Court of France to the Scottish Jacobites in the Years 1703–1707, edited by W. D. Macray for the Roxburghe Club. 2 vols. London, 1870–71).

'Memoirs of Edward Hopkins, M.P. for Coventry' edited by M. D. Harris, in the *English Historical Review*, xxxiv (1919), pp. 495 et seq.

Correspondence of Henry Hyde, Earl of Clarendon, and of his Brother, Laurence Hyde, Earl of Rochester . . ., edited by S. W. Singer. London, 1828. Vol. ii.

A Brief Historical Relation of State Affairs . . ., by Narcissus Luttrell. 6 vols. Oxford, 1857.

A Selection from the Papers of the Earls of Marchmont in the Possession of the Rt. Hon. Sir George Henry Rose . . ., edited by G. H. Rose. London, 1831. Vol. iii.

Letters and Despatches of John Churchill, Duke of Marlborough, edited by Sir George Murray. 5 vols. London, 1845.

Private Correspondence of Sarah, Duchess of Marlborough (2nd edn.). 2 vols. London, 1838.

'Bishop Nicolson's Diaries', in *Transactions of the Cumberland and Westmorland Antiquarian and Archeological Society*, New Series, i–v, *passim.*

The Norris Papers, edited by T. Heywood for the Chetham Society. Chetham Society Publications, vol. ix (1846).

Letters of Humphrey Prideaux . . . to John Ellis, edited by E. M. Thompson. Publications of the Camden Society, New Series, xv. London, 1875.

Letters and Correspondence, Public and Private, of Henry St. John, Lord Viscount Bolingbroke . . ., edited by G. Parke. 2 vols. London, 1798.

Private and Original Correspondence of Charles Talbot, Duke of Shrewsbury, edited by W. Coxe. London, 1821.

The Correspondence of Jonathan Swift, edited by F. Elrington Ball. 6 vols. London, 1910–14.

Letters of Two Queens, edited by the Hon. Benjamin Bathurst. London, 1924.

Verney Letters . . . of the Eighteenth Century from the MSS. at Claydon House, edited by Margaret Maria, Lady Verney. London, 1930. Vol. i.

Letters Illustrative of the Reign of William III from 1696 to 1708 . . ., by James Vernon, Secretary of State, edited by G. P. R. James. London, 1841. Vol. iii.

The Wentworth Papers, 1705–1739 . . ., edited by J. J. Cartwright. London, 1883.

'Correspondence of Some Wiltshire Politicians *c.* 1700', edited by Lord Lansdowne, in *Wiltshire Archeological and Natural History Magazine*, vol. xlvi.

D. *Accounts and Memoirs Written by Contemporaries After the Event*

Thomas Bruce, Second Earl of Ailesbury—Memoirs, written by himself, edited by W. E. Buckley, for the Roxburghe Club. Westminster, 1890. Vol. ii.

Bolingbroke's Works. 8 vols. London, 1809.

Memoirs of the Life and Ministerial Conduct . . . of the Late Lord Viscount Bolingbroke (anonymous). London, 1752.

Bishop Burnet's History of His Own Time (with notes by Swift, Dartmouth, Onslow, and Hardwick). 6 vols. Oxford, 1833.

The History of the Union of Great Britain, by Daniel Defoe. Edinburgh, 1709.

Memoirs of the Family of Guise of Elmore, Gloucestershire, edited by G. Davies. Camden Society Publications, 1917.

The Lockhart Papers: containing Memoirs and Commentaries upon the Affairs of Scotland from 1702 to 1715, by George Lockhart, Esq. of Carnwarth, edited by A. Aufrere. London, 1817. Vol. i.

Memoirs of the Secret Service of John Macky during the Reigns of King William, Queen Anne, and King George I, edited for the Roxburghe Club. London, 1895.

The Conduct of the Duke of Marlborough during the Present War, with Original Papers, by Francis Hare. London, 1712.

The History of England during the Reigns of King William and Queen Mary, Queen Anne, King George I, by John Oldmixon. London, 1735.

Account of the Earl of Peterborough's Conduct in Spain . . . with Original Papers, by Dr. J. Freind. London, 1707.

The Prose Works of Jonathan Swift, edited by W. Temple Scott. 12 vols. London, 1897–1908.

Memoirs relating to Lord Torrington, edited by Sir John Knox Laughton. Camden Society Publications, 1889.

Memoirs of the Life of . . . Thomas, Late Marquess of Wharton . . . (anonymous). London, 1715.

E. *Compilations—chiefly of Original Documents and Other Original Papers*

An Account of the Proceedings of the House of Peers upon the Observations of the Commissioners for . . . Publick Accounts. London, 1702.

Angliae Notitia, or The Present State of England (Edward and John Chamberlayne. London: 19th to 22nd editions, 1700, '02, '04, '07. (Continued as *Magnae Britanniae Notitia*).

Cobbett's Complete Collection of State Trials . . . London, 1809–28. Vols. iii–vi.

Complete Collection of the Protests of the Lords, edited by James E. Thorold Rogers. Oxford, 1875. Vol. i.

Court and Society from Elizabeth to Anne, edited from the Papers at Kimbolton by the Duke of Manchester. London, 1864. Vol. ii.

English Army Lists and Commission Registers, 1661–1714, compiled by Charles Dalton. 6 vols. London, 1892–1904.

An Historical Account of the Rights of Elections . . . (election petitions and other proceedings in controverted elections, compiled from the *Commons Journals* and arranged by constituency, alphabetically, by T. Carew). 2 vols. London, 1755.

The History and Proceedings of the House of Commons from the Restoration to the Present Time (published by Chandler and commonly known as *Chandler's Debates*). London, 1742–4. Vols. i–iv.

The History and Proceedings of the House of Lords from the Restoration in 1660 to the Present Time (published by Timberland and commonly known as *Timberland's Debates*). London, 1742–3. Vols. i–iii.

The History of the Reign of Queen Anne digested into Annals, by Abel Boyer, Huguenot newswriter. 8 vols. London, 1702 and subsequent years (continued, 1711–40, as *The Political State of Great Britain*).

Letters relating to Scotland in the Reign of Queen Anne, edited by P. Hume Brown for the Scottish Historical Society. Edinburgh, 1915.

Magnae Britanniae Notitia, by Edward and John Chamberlayne. London, 1708 and following years (a continuation of *Angliae Notitia*).

Mémoires pour servir à l'histoire du XVIIIme siècle, contenant . . . documents authentiques, edited by G. de Lamberty, newswriter at The Hague employed by Lord Cutts. The Hague, 1724–40. Vol. xiii.

Miscellaneous State Papers from 1501 to 1726 from the Collection of the Earl of Hardwick, edited by Philip Yorke. London, 1778. Vol. ii.

Original Papers containing the Secret History of Great Britain, edited by J. Macpherson. London, 1775. Vol. ii.

The Political State of Great Britain, by Abel Boyer. London, annual editions, 1711– ; (a continuation of Boyer's *Annals*).

The Report of the Lords Committees . . . so far as relates to the Accompts of . . . Edward, Earl of Orford, late Treasurer of the Navy. London, 1704.

F. *Secondary Works containing Valuable Selections of Original Materials*

Clarke, T. E. S., and Foxcroft, H. C., *A Life of Gilbert Burnet, Bishop of Salisbury*. Cambridge, 1907.

Coxe, William, *Memoirs of John, Duke of Marlborough, with His Original Correspondence* (2nd edn.). 6 vols. London, 1820.

—— *Memoirs of the Life and Administration of Sir Robert Walpole*. 2 vols. London, 1798.

Dalrymple, Sir J., *Memoirs of Great Britain and Ireland*. London, 1790. Vol. iii.

Fraser, Sir William, *The Earls of Cromartie: Their Kindred, Country, and Correspondence*. 2 vols. Edinburgh, 1876.

—— *The Melvilles, Earls of Melville, and the Levens, Earls of Leven*. Edinburgh, 1890. Vol. ii.

—— *Memorials of the Earls of Haddington*. Edinburgh, 1889. Vol. ii.

—— *Memorials of the Family of Wemyss of Wemyss*. Edinburgh, 1888. Vol. iii.

Graham, J. M., *Annals and Correspondence of the Viscount and the First and Second Earls of Stair*. Edinburgh, 1875. Vol. i.

Klopp, Onno, *Der Fall des Hauses Stuart, und die Succession des Hauses Hannover*. Vienna, 1887–. Vols. ix–xiii (containing extracts from the dispatches of the Austrian envoy).

Lathbury, T., *History of the Convocation of the Church of England*. London, 1842.

More, Trenchard L., *Isaac Newton*. London, 1934. (Prints letters from Halifax to Newton concerning the Cambridge University election, 1705.)

Noorden, Carl Von, *Europaische Geschichte im Achtzehnten Jahrhundert: Erste Abtheilung, Der Spanische Erbfolgekrieg*. 3 vols. (no more published). Leipzig, 1883.

Papillon, A. F. W., *Memoirs of Thomas Papillon of London, Merchant (1632–1702)*. Reading, 1887.

Ralph, James, *The Other Side of the Question: or an Attempt to Rescue the Characters of the two Royal Sisters Q. Mary and Q. Anne. . . .* London, 1742.

Sharp, T., *The Life of John Sharp . . . Archbishop of York . . . collected from his Diary, Letters, &c.* 2 vols. London, 1825.

INDEX

Note. The abbreviation 'parl. consty.' after a name denotes a parliamentary constituency.